The

INN COOK BOOK

New England

IGOR and MARJORIE KROPOTKIN

LITTLE, BROWN AND COMPANY — BOSTON — TORONTO

FIRST EDITION

LIBRARY OF CONGRESS CATALOGING IN PUBLICATION DATA
Kropotkin, Igor.
The inn cookbook, New England.
1. Cookery, American — New England. 2. Hotels, taverns, etc. —
New England. I. Kropotkin, Marjorie. II. Title.
TX715.K899   1983   641.5   83–749
ISBN 0–316–50473–4
ISBN 0–316–50474–2 (pbk.)

BP

Designed by Susan Windheim

*Published simultaneously in Canada
by Little, Brown & Company (Canada) Limited*

PRINTED IN THE UNITED STATES OF AMERICA

The

INN COOK BOOK

For
Valerie,
Michael, and
Brian
           with love

Contents

RECIPES

VI Poultry 121

VII Eggs and Cheese 152

VIII Vegetables 162

INNS

By way of introduction . . .

Our book is not intended to be a complete and all-inclusive guide to inns — there are more than five hundred such establishments dotting the towns, villages, and countryside of New England — but rather a sampling of the wide range of food and accommodations that is available to travelers and vacationers.

As modes of travel and tastes changed over the years, many inns — some of which dated from the seventeenth century — fell into disfavor, giving way to a wave of large, modern structures offering fast food and frequently topped by neon signs proclaiming "motel." But in the past few years there has been a renaissance of the inn concept, and in an age of volatility it seems almost a happy contradiction to find this kind of return to a more gracious era.

For us, staying at an inn is much like spending a weekend in the country with a favorite aunt who happens to be a splendid cook and won't let you help with the dishes or even make your own bed. Of course, inns are not the perfect escape for all. Vacationers seeking thrills and excitement would do better to look elsewhere. The same is true for those traveling with young children. While a few resort inns do provide recreational facilities and special menus for children, most do not. So it was only a few years ago, after our own children were grown, that we became dedicated "inn people."

Certainly there are already a number of books serving as guides to inns throughout the country. Many of the ones we have used in our travels are excellent. They range from the very elaborately illustrated ones, with full-color photographs and extensive descriptive texts, to the compact, portable, purely utilitarian ones. We hope that this volume will be accepted as the inn book with a difference.

The first section of the book is a collection of prized recipes submitted by the innkeepers or their chefs. The second decribes each inn and the facilities it offers.

Many of the best chefs are not necessarily the best teachers. While they practice their art with their hearts, their heads, and their skilled hands, they cannot always commit to paper exact proportions and step-by-step instructions. Thus, while the recipes have been presented in the words of the innkeeper or chef were possible, some have been clarified and adapted for home use and all have been standardized.

In some instances this was no simple matter. Foreign gastronomic terms that are not familiar to all Americans were often used. Some recipes from European chefs used metric weights and measures; some mixed United States equivalents and metric units.

The distractions of a busy season for the innkeepers occasionally caused some amusing errors. In one case, we received instructions for a recipe that had not been reduced in size and would have served fifty people instead of four to eight. Another recipe omitted the prime ingredient necessary for flavor and for which the dish had been named.

You will note that in the left-hand margin opposite the description of an inn there appears the logo used by that inn or ascribed to it by us. Since the recipes are arranged by category, the source of each is identified by use of the inn's logo.

You will also see that there is a wide range of dishes — some purely regional, some traditional American, some European — and most, if not all, include inventive personal touches. All of the recipes have been served at the inns again and again over the years and have proved to be favorites with their guests.

Among the more elaborate recipes are many native offerings from other countries, particularly France, Germany, Holland, Italy, and Switzerland. One inn, for example, has first-generation innkeepers from Austria and a Portuguese chef. Here we found an exceptional menu that was part American, part Austrian, and part Portuguese — and all the dishes were extremely appetizing and well presented.

Prices are not quoted in the descriptive section since many factors influence charges, and we all know that "prices are subject to change without prior notice." We suggest that you check with the innkeeper when telephoning or writing.

No attempt has been made to rate the inns. Accommodations range from luxurious to simple, but all are comfortable.

We hope that this volume will work for you as a selection and driving guide, as a somewhat uncommon cook book, and as a preview of what to expect when you plan a visit to one or more of these New England inns.

Our sincere thanks to an old friend, Roger Donald, Senior Editor at Little, Brown, for his help and guidance, and to Sylvia Rosenthal, an excellent cook and author of several popular cook books, who acted as food consultant and recipe doctor as well as tester and taster, and added the cooking suggestions that follow some of the recipes.

RECIPES

I Appetizers and Hors d'Oeuvres

Aubergine

AVOCADO MOUSSELINE WITH TOMATO SAUCE

Serves 6 or more

1 tablespoon melted butter
2 medium-sized ripe avocados
1 cup heavy cream
4 eggs
2 egg yolks
3 tablespoons chopped fresh parsley
3 tablespoons chopped fresh basil or 2 teaspoons dried
Salt and freshly ground pepper
Fresh tomato sauce (below)

Preheat oven to 350°. Brush a 3- to 4-cup soufflé dish or ovenproof crock with melted butter and set aside.

Peel avocados, cut into chunks, and place in food processor, using steel blade. Process until smooth. Add the cream, eggs, egg yolks, chopped parsley, and basil, and continue to process until well blended. Season to taste with salt and pepper.

Spoon mixture into the prepared baking dish. Cover the top of the mousse with a sheet of buttered waxed paper or aluminum foil. Set dish in a larger baking pan and place in oven. Pour into the pan enough hot water to come halfway up the sides of the baking dish. Bake for 25 to 30 minutes, or until a knife inserted in the middle comes out clean. Remove from oven and discard paper from the top. Cool, then refrigerate to chill thoroughly.

To serve, dip the mold for a moment in hot water. Run a thin-bladed knife around the outside of the mousse. Place a serving dish over the mold and, holding it down tightly, invert and turn out the mousse. Serve chilled with fresh tomato sauce.

FRESH TOMATO SAUCE

2 pounds ripe tomatoes, peeled and seeded
2 large cloves garlic, chopped
¼ cup herb vinegar
Salt and freshly ground pepper
2 tablespoons fresh herbs, chopped (parsley, basil, chervil, etc.)

Place tomatoes, garlic, and vinegar in a food processor and process until smooth. Transfer to a saucepan and cook uncovered until the sauce is reduced by one-third. While still warm, add salt, pepper, and fresh herbs to taste. Chill thoroughly and use sparingly.

ANDOVER INN

BAKED STUFFED CLAMS
Serves 6 as appetizer; 3 to 4 as main dish

24 fresh clams in shells
½ cup water
3 tablespoons butter
1 cup finely chopped celery
1 medium onion, finely chopped
½ teaspoon dried thyme
Freshly ground pepper
1 cup crabmeat
¼ cup minced fresh parsley
1 tablespoon lemon juice
¼ cup dry white wine
½ cup (approximately) thick Béchamel sauce**
½ cup breadcrumbs
4 slices crisp bacon, finely crumbled
2 tablespoons butter

Scrub the clams well with a stiff brush under running water. Place them in a deep pot with ¼ cup water. Cover the pot tightly, bring to a boil, lower heat, and let steam for 6 to 10 minutes, or just until the shells open. Discard any that do not open. Lift the clams out of the pot with a slotted spoon. Let the cooking liquid settle so that the sand will fall to the bottom. Strain and reserve this broth. Open the clams over a bowl to save every bit of the juice. Detach the clams from the shells, reserving 24 half shells. Strain the juice through a very fine strainer and set aside.

Heat 3 tablespoons of butter in a skillet and sauté the chopped celery, onion, and thyme until soft, but not brown. Stir in the pepper, crabmeat, parsley, lemon juice, and white wine.

Chop the clams fine and add them with their juice to the mixture. Mix well and add enough Béchamel sauce to bind the mixture together. Pack 24 clam shells with the mixture, mounding it firmly. Sprinkle with breadcrumbs and crumbled bacon. Dot with butter and bake in a 375° oven for 10 to 12 minutes, or until heated through.

**Béchamel Sauce (supplied by the editors)*

3 tablespoons butter
3 tablespoons all-purpose flour
1/2 cup reserved clam broth
1/2 cup water

Heat the butter and blend in the flour, stirring for 2 or 3 minutes, until bubbly. Don't let it turn color. Remove from heat and stir in the reserved clam broth and water. Whisk to blend smoothly. Return to moderately high heat and stir and cook until the sauce is thickened and smooth, 4 or 5 minutes longer.

Mountain Top Inn

CLUB CHEESE "CHARLIE JONES"
Makes about 2 cups

1 12-ounce container Cheddar cheese spread at room
    temperature
3 ounces cream cheese at room temperature
2/3 cup large-curd cottage cheese
1 tablespoon finely minced onion
1 teaspoon Worcestershire sauce
1/4 teaspoon Tabasco sauce
1/2 teaspoon caraway seeds

continued

Place all ingredients in a good-sized bowl and, with electric mixer at low speed, blend until well mixed. Taste for seasoning — you may want to add another dash of Tabasco or Worcestershire sauce. Pack into a small serving bowl, cover with plastic wrap, and refrigerate for 24 hours before serving.

Serve with assorted crackers and small knives for spreading.

🏠 Sugar Hill Inn
CRAB SPREAD
Serves 6 or more

    8 ounces cream cheese at room temperature
    1 tablespoon milk
    2 tablespoons chopped onion
    1 6½-ounce can crabmeat, well drained (or fresh)
    ½ tablespoon horseradish
    Salt and pepper
    Paprika

Preheat oven to 375°. Grease a small ovenproof baking dish.

Mash the cream cheese and milk until creamy and blend in the chopped onion, crabmeat, and horseradish, mixing well. Season with salt and pepper. Sprinkle top with paprika. Bake for 15 to 20 minutes. Serve on crackers or party rye bread.

DÉLICES DE GRUYÈRE
Makes 24 to 30, depending on size

1¹/₂ cups milk
¹/₄ cup (¹/₂ stick) butter
Salt and pepper
Grating of fresh nutmeg
1 cup all-purpose flour
¹/₂ cup (2 ounces) grated Emmentaler cheese
¹/₂ cup (2 ounces) grated imported Gruyère cheese
3 egg yolks
Egg wash (2 or 3 eggs, beaten)
2 cups fine breadcrumbs
Oil for deep-fat frying *or*
4 tablespoons butter for sautéing (more if needed)

Heat the milk, butter, salt, pepper, and nutmeg in a heavy-bottomed pan just until bubbles form around the sides of the pan and steam escapes. Remove from the heat and immediately stir in the flour. Stir briskly to a mashed-potato consistency. Quickly add both cheeses and stir until melted and smooth. Cool slightly and add the egg yolks. Mix thoroughly until evenly blended.

Spread out in a shallow bowl and refrigerate for 4 hours. When ready to cook, roll into small finger-sized croquettes. Spread a portion of the breadcrumbs on a square of waxed paper. Dip the croquettes in egg-wash mixture and roll carefully in the breadcrumbs. (Spread the breadcrumbs a little at a time, since they are likely to get dampened by the egg wash on the croquettes as you roll them.)

Deep fry in oil or sauté in butter until crisp, golden brown, and warmed completely through to the centers. Don't crowd he pan if sautéing; you need room to turn them. Serve warm.

DUCKLING PÂTÉ
Serves 2 or 3

1/4 cup (1/2 stick) butter
2 duck livers, chopped
1 tablespoon minced onion
1 tablespoon minced scallion (green onion)
1 tart apple, peeled, cored, and diced
Pinch thyme
Grinding of fresh nutmeg
Salt and freshly ground pepper
2 tablespoons brandy or Grand Marnier
1 tablespoon orange marmalade

In a medium-sized skillet, heat the butter and sauté the livers gently with the minced onions. Add the chopped apple, thyme, nutmeg, and salt and pepper to taste. Cook, stirring, until the livers are no longer pink.

Transfer the liver mixture to a blender with the brandy or Grand Marnier and marmalade. Blend until smooth, adding more melted butter if needed. You may have to stop the blender from time to time and stir the mixture with a rubber spatula to blend thoroughly.

Scrape the mixture into a small crock or container. Cover the top with a thin layer of melted butter. Cool and chill until it becomes firm.

GRANE'S
FAIRHAVEN

EASY SPREAD FOR CRACKERS
Serves 12

2 1/2 cups (10 ounces) shredded extra-sharp Cheddar cheese at
    room temperature
1 large onion, minced
6 slices raw bacon, finely minced
Salt and pepper

Mash the Cheddar cheese and add onion, bacon, and salt and pepper to taste. Mix well. Preheat broiler to medium.

Mound on crisp crackers or party rye and place on large cookie sheet. Broil about 3 inches from heat source until browned and hot.

ESCARGOTS À LA BOURGUIGNONNE
Serves 6

1 can small snails (3 dozen)
Dry white wine
Pinch of thyme
¹/₂ bay leaf
Pinch of salt

BUTTER FOR SNAILS
1¹/₂ cups (3 sticks) butter at room temperature
4 tablespoons finely chopped shallots
4 large cloves garlic, finely chopped
1 tablespoon chopped fresh parsley
Salt and pepper

Drain the snails and place in a saucepan with enough dry white wine to just cover them. Add thyme, bay leaf, and salt. Bring to a boil and remove from heat. Allow the snails to cool in the liquid.

Preheat the oven to 450°. Drain the snails and set them in individual baking dishes or snail shells.

Mix the softened butter with shallot, garlic, and parsley. If you have used salted butter you may not need additional salt. Add a small amount of pepper and blend well.

Cover the snails with the butter. Bake for 5 to 7 minutes until snails are heated through and butter is melted and bubbling.

GOURMET FRIED CHEESE
Makes approximately 30 pieces

8 ounces Brie or Camembert cheese
$1/2$ cup all-purpose flour
1 egg
$1/2$ cup milk
1 cup fine breadcrumbs
Oil for deep frying

Cut the cheese into bite-sized pieces. Spread the flour on a square of waxed paper. Beat the egg with a fork and mix well with the milk in a shallow bowl. Spread the breadcrumbs on another square of waxed paper.

Heat oil in a deep-fat fryer or wok to 325°.

Dip the pieces of cheese in flour, shaking off excess. Dip in the egg-and-milk mixture and roll in breadcrumbs.

Deep fry for 10 to 15 seconds, or until golden brown. Serve immediately.

HERBED CREAM CHEESE DIP
Makes about 1 cup

8 ounces cream cheese at room temperature
$1/4$ cup grated Parmesan cheese
1 tablespoon garlic powder
1 teaspoon lemon juice
Dash Tabasco sauce
Dash Worcestershire sauce
1 tablespoon chopped onion
1 tablespoon whole caraway seeds
1 tablespoon whole celery seeds
$1/4$ cup chopped fresh chives
Salt and freshly ground pepper

Combine all ingredients in a bowl and mix with an electric mixer for about 2 minutes, or until well blended. Mound in a bowl, cover, and chill before serving. Serve with crisp crackers or as a dip with vegetables (cucumber, zucchini, yellow summer squash, etc.) cut in rounds.

MUSHROOMS MARSALA
Serves 4

1 pound mushrooms
2 tablespoons butter
Juice of ½ lemon
¼ cup dry Marsala
Salt and freshly ground pepper
1 tablespoon minced fresh parsley

Wipe mushrooms with a damp towel. If they are very dirty, wash them quickly in warm salted water and wipe dry with paper towels. (Mushrooms become waterlogged when soaked.) Cut off stems and save them for your next pot of soup. Leave the mushroom caps whole.

Heat butter in a skillet and sauté the mushrooms, gently stirring until lightly browned but still firm. Add lemon juice, Marsala, salt and pepper to taste, and minced parsley. Cook and stir 2 minutes longer and serve hot.

MUSHROOM PÂTÉ
Serves 10 to 12

1 pound mushrooms, chopped
$^1/_2$ cup chopped celery
$^1/_4$ cup chopped fresh parsley
$^1/_2$ cup chopped shallots or red onions
2 tablespoons butter
$^1/_4$ teaspoon rosemary
$^1/_4$ teaspoon basil
15 ounces ricotta cheese
2 eggs
1 cup fine breadcrumbs
1 cup chopped walnuts
Dash cayenne pepper
1 teaspoon salt
$^1/_4$ cup sweet vermouth

Sauté the chopped mushrooms, celery, parsley, and shallots or red onions in butter until tender, 7 or 8 minutes, stirring often. Mix in the rosemary and basil.

Place the ricotta cheese and eggs in the food processor and process until mixed. Add the breadcrumbs, walnuts, mushroom-vegetable mixture, and the remaining ingredients. Process until fairly fine, but with some texture left.

Preheat oven to 400°. Grease generously a 1$^1/_2$-quart pâté mold or 5 × 8-inch bread pan. Scrape the mixture into the prepared mold or pan and cover tightly with heavy aluminum foil. Bake for 1$^1/_2$ hours. Cool before unmolding.

The chef says: "This keeps well, refrigerated, for a week to ten days."

MUSHROOM TART
Serves 6 as appetizer; 4 as a main course

PASTRY
2 cups all-purpose flour, sifted
10 tablespoons butter, firmly chilled and cut into small pieces
2 egg yolks
1/2 teaspoon salt
3 1/2–4 tablespoons ice water
Egg glaze: beaten egg yolk

FILLING
2 tablespoons butter
1 onion, finely chopped
1/2 pound mushrooms, finely chopped
3 shallots, finely chopped
2 tablespoons all-purpose flour
1 1/2 cups light cream or 1 cup milk and 1/2 cup heavy cream
Salt and freshly ground pepper
Freshly grated nutmeg
3 egg yolks, lightly beaten
2 tablespoons minced fresh parsley

Place the flour in a mixing bowl and make a well in the center. Put the butter in the well. With your fingertips, quickly work the flour and butter together until the mixture forms small crumbs. Blend in the egg yolks, salt, and 3 1/2 tablespoons cold water.

Press the dough firmly together, gathering in any crumbs from the sides and bottom of the bowl. Place on a lightly floured board or counter top. The dough should feel moist but not sticky. If sticky, sprinkle with a couple teaspoons of flour and blend in; if dry, sprinkle with the remaining half tablespoon of water and knead in. Push the dough away from you with the heel of the hand, gather it together with a dough scraper or a spatula, and repeat until it is smooth and pliable. (This process is called the *fraisage*; its purpose is to completely blend the flour and butter.) Press the dough into a ball, wrap in foil, plastic wrap, or waxed paper, and refrigerate for 30 minutes or until the dough is firm. (It may also be stored in the refrigerator tightly wrapped for up to 3 days.)

continued

Filling: Melt the butter in a heavy-bottomed saucepan. Add the onion and cook over medium heat until soft but not brown. Stir in the mushrooms and cook over medium-high heat, stirring from time to time, until all the moisture has evaporated. Add the shallots and cook another minute or two. Reduce heat and stir in the flour. Mix well, and add the cream, salt, pepper, and nutmeg. Cook and stir until the mixture thickens, and simmer for 2 minutes. Remove from heat and cool slightly. Slowly beat in the egg yolks. Add the parsley, taste, and correct seasoning. Let mixture cool.

Preheat oven to 400°. Roll out two-thirds of the dough on a lightly floured surface and line a 9-inch pie plate or flan ring. Prick the crust all over with a fork and chill in the refrigerator.

When the filling is cool, spread it in the chilled pie shell. Roll out the remaining dough into an oblong ¼ inch thick and 10 inches long. Cut 9 strips of dough about ½ inch wide. Place 4 strips over the tart filling. Place the remaining 5 strips diagonally over the bottom 4 to fashion a lattice effect. Fold the edge of the bottom crust over the ends of the strips and press firmly. Flute or crimp the outside edge. Brush the lattice with egg glaze and bake for 25 to 35 minutes, or until the pastry is brown and the filling starts to bubble. Serve hot.

The chef says: "The pie can be baked a day ahead and reheated, or it can be prepared a day ahead to bake just before serving."

MUSSELS PRIMAVERA
6 to 8 servings as appetizer

2 cups celery in julienne strips
2 cups carrots in julienne strips
1 bunch broccoli cut into small flowerets and stems into julienne
    strips
2 large onions, sliced and cut into strips
2 cups thinly shredded red cabbage
1¹/₂ cups (3 sticks) butter at room temperature
10–12 cloves garlic, finely minced
1 cup dry white wine
1 cup water
¹/₂ teaspoon salt
1 bay leaf
30–40 mussels in shells, scrubbed and debearded
¹/₂ cup chopped fresh parsley
6–8 lemon slices

Cut up all the vegetables and set aside.

Add minced garlic to softened butter and blend well.

Place wine, water, salt, and bay leaf in a large kettle and bring to a boil. Add the vegetables, then the mussels on top. Steam for 10 minutes, or until the mussels open. Remove from heat and discard any mussels that do not open.

While the mussels are cooking, melt the garlic butter in a separate saucepan.

To serve, place mussels in individual soup bowls and top with vegetables and a little broth. Pour garlic butter over mussels and vegetables. Sprinkle with chopped parsley and garnish each serving with a lemon slice. Accompany with hot, crusty French bread.

The chef says: "This dish makes a great appetizer, or if you prefer to serve it as a main course, add a few more mussels to each serving."

ONION CANAPÉS
Makes 3 to 4 dozen canapés, depending on size

4 tablespoons grated Parmesan cheese
1/2 cup mayonnaise
Bread rounds, 1 1/2–2 inches in diameter (cut with cookie cutter)
Butter
Onion, very thinly sliced

Mix together 3 tablespoons of the grated cheese with the mayonnaise. Butter one side of bread rounds, place on ungreased baking sheet, and toast under broiler until lightly toasted.

Place a thin slice of onion the same size as the bread rounds on the untoasted side and top with mayonnaise mixture. Sprinkle tops lightly with the remaining Parmesan cheese. Just before serving, place under broiler until golden brown. Serve piping hot.

Palmer House

PALMER HOUSE PÂTÉ
Makes about 1 cup

2 turkey livers, or 7–8 chicken livers
2 eggs
2 ounces fatty tissue (approximately 1/3 to 1/2 cup) from fresh
   poultry
1 small onion, cut up
1 sprig parsley
Salt and freshly ground pepper

Trim livers of fat and bile sack. Place the livers, unshelled eggs, and fatty tissue in a saucepan and cover with salted water. Bring to a boil and boil gently for 15 to 20 minutes. Set the pan with entire contents in the refrigerator until cold and the fat congealed. Skim off the fat and set aside with the livers. Shell the eggs and cut into chunks. Place livers, fat, and eggs in blender. Add onion and parsley.

Blend at low speed so that the mixture is not liquefied — it should be a little coarse, with detectable particles of liver, egg white, onion, and parsley. Season with salt and pepper. Transfer to a small mold or bowl and refrigerate at once. It will firm up as it cools and can be sliced or spread on crackers or rye or pumpernickel bread.

GRANE'S
FAIRHAVEN

PITA BREAD SPREAD
Makes 96 pieces

1 cup sour cream
½ cup salad dressing, such as Miracle Whip
½ cup freshly grated Parmesan cheese
2 teaspoons oregano
1 teaspoon basil
1–2 cloves garlic, finely minced or squeezed through garlic press
Salt and pepper
4 large pita rounds

Combine all the ingredients except the pita bread and blend well.

Cut each pita into 4 quarters and, with a sharp-pointed knife, separate the upper and lower crusts. Cut each quarter into 3 triangles. (Each pita will yield 24 triangles). Cover the pita triangles with spread and broil until browned. Serve hot.

Note: This mixture will keep fresh in the refrigerator for up to 3 weeks, putting you on the ready for hot hors d'oeuvres at any time.

RUMAKI
Serves 12 (4 per person)

16 fresh chicken livers
12–16 slices bacon
12 water chestnuts, each sliced into 4 pieces
12 scallions (green onions), cut into quarters

MARINADE
3 tablespoons soy sauce
2 tablespoons oil
2 tablespoons lemon juice
3 tablespoons light brown sugar
$1/2$ teaspoon ground ginger
1 small clove garlic, squeezed through a garlic press

Cut each chicken liver into thirds. Roll individual pieces of liver in $1/4$ to $1/3$ slice of bacon (depending on length of slices), enclosing a slice of water chestnut and piece of scallion. Secure with a toothpick.

Combine marinade ingredients in a bowl and blend well. Marinate the rolls for 2 hours.

When ready to cook, heat broiler. Arrange the rolls on a rack in the broiler pan and broil for 5 minutes on the first side. Turn and broil 3 or 4 minutes on the second side. Watch carefully to make sure they don't scorch; the second side needs less time than the first.

SAVORY CHEESE BALL
Serves 12 or more

8 ounces cream cheese at room temperature
3 ounces blue cheese, crumbled
2 cups (8 ounces) shredded sharp Cheddar cheese at room
   temperature
1 tablespoon Worcestershire sauce
1/2 teaspoon onion powder
1/4 cup chopped fresh parsley
1/4 cup finely chopped walnuts

Beat cream cheese until fluffy. Mix in blue cheese and Cheddar cheese and blend well. Stir in Worcestershire sauce, onion powder, parsley, and walnuts, and blend well. Shape into a ball, wrap, and chill. If you wish, you can coat the outside lightly with more finely chopped nuts and parsley.

   Let it come to room temperature to serve. Serve with assorted crackers.

SEVICHE
Serves 4 or 5

1 pound tiny bay scallops, or sea scallops cut into cubes
2–3 green peppers, diced
2–3 fresh tomatoes, peeled, seeded, and diced
2 canned pimientos, diced
1–1 1/2 cups fresh lemon juice
Salt and freshly ground pepper

Arrange the scallops, peppers, tomatoes, and pimientos in a flat baking dish, and pour over the lemon juice. Cover dish and let marinate in the refrigerator overnight. The effect of the citrus juice is to "cook" the fish, turning it opaque and firm.

   Season with salt and freshly ground pepper. Serve cold, drained, on a scallop shell.

Aubergine

SMOKED TROUT PÂTÉ
Serves 8 to 10

1 pound fish fillets (trout, sole, flounder) cut into pieces
¹/₂ pound smoked trout, boned and skinned*
2 tablespoons chopped fresh parsley
3 egg whites
1 cup heavy cream
4 egg yolks
3 grinds black pepper
¹/₄ teaspoon salt
Few gratings fresh nutmeg
1 tablespoon butter at room temperature
Blender mayonnaise**

Place fish fillets, smoked fish, and parsley in the container of a food processor with the metal blade in place, and process until fine and smooth. Add the egg whites gradually through the feed tube until the mixture is fluffy, about 2 or 3 minutes. Scrape the puree into a bowl, place the bowl in a larger one containing cracked ice, and slowly stir in the cream, egg yolks, and seasonings. Taste and correct seasoning.

Preheat oven to 400°. Butter a 2-quart ring mold, soufflé dish, or terrine with the softened butter. Stir the fish mixture thoroughly and spoon into the mold. Cover the top with a sheet of buttered foil or waxed paper and set the dish into a larger baking pan in the lower third of the oven. Pour in enough hot water to come halfway up the sides of the mold and bake for about 30 minutes, or until a firm-bladed knife inserted in the center comes out clean.

Remove the dish from the oven and its water bath. Discard the waxed paper. The paté can be served from the terrine or unmolded on a serving platter. Let stand for 5 minutes before unmolding. It is good either hot or cold. If serving cold, accompany with fresh home-made mayonnaise laced with finely chopped herbs, such as basil, chervil, dill, thyme, parsley, etc.

*Smoked brook trout generally weigh between ¹/₂ and ³/₄ pound each. For ¹/₂ pound of boned and skinned trout, you will generally need the meat of 1¹/₂ trouts.

**Blender Mayonnaise *(supplied by the editors)*
Makes about 1¹/₄ cups

1 egg
1 teaspoon Dijon mustard
1¹/₂ teaspoons wine vinegar
¹/₃ teaspoon salt
1 cup oil
1–2 tablespoons lemon juice
1 tablespoon boiling water

Combine the egg, mustard, vinegar, salt, and ¹/₄ cup of the oil in the blender container. Blend on medium speed until frothy. Add the remainder of the oil in a thin, steady stream, adding it more quickly as the sauce emulsifies and thickens. Add lemon juice to taste and then the water. The water acts as a stabilizer. Blend only until thick and smooth. Refrigerate in a covered bowl or jar.

Avon
STUFFED ARTICHOKE BOTTOMS
Serves 2

2 whole cooked artichoke bottoms
4 large cooked shrimp, cut into thirds
1 tablespoon finely chopped celery
1 tablespoon finely chopped green pepper
1 tablespoon finely chopped carrots
1 tablespoon finely chopped onion
1 tablespoon finely chopped pimiento
Salt and pepper
¹/₄ teaspoon oregano
Juice of 2 lemons (about 6 tablespoons)
1 tablespoon oil
Dash of vinegar

Mix all ingredients in a glass or earthenware bowl or crock, cover, and marinate for 2 days in the refrigerator. To serve, place artichoke bottoms on a bed of lettuce and fill with mixture.

II Soups and Chowders

CHILLED SOUPS

Gateways Inn

COLD CRANBERRY SOUP

Makes approximately eight 7-ounce portions

2 oranges
1 tablespoon butter
1¼ cups sugar
1 cup sherry
1 pound fresh or frozen cranberries
1 cup dry Sauterne
1 cup light cream
1 cup sour cream
1 cup club soda
Garnish: pecan halves

Peel the rind from the oranges with a vegetable peeler or a stripper and cut into very fine julienne strips. Squeeze the oranges and reserve the juice.

Melt the butter in a saucepan. *Do not brown.* Sauté the orange rind in the butter. Add sugar, sherry, and orange juice. Boil for 2 minutes.

Add the cranberries and cover. Boil for 2 minutes. Uncover and boil for another 3 minutes. This mixture may be made a day in advance and chilled overnight.

After the mixture is chilled, put it in a blender and add the dry Sauterne. (Since the quantity may be too large to do in the blender at one time, the blending may have to be done in 2 or more batches.) Blend at moderate speed for 1 minute. Add the light cream and sour cream and blend at moderate speed for 1 minute more. Strain the orange rind and cranberry seeds from mixture.

Before serving, add the club soda and mix well. Chill well and serve on ice. Garnish with 2 pecan halves per cup.

Note: This is a hot-weather luncheon offering likely to make spirits soar.

COLD CUCUMBER SOUP
Serves 4

2 cups peeled and diced cucumber
$\frac{1}{2}$ cup water
1 slice onion
Pinch of salt and white pepper
2 tablespoons flour
1 cup chicken broth
$\frac{1}{2}$ bay leaf
6 tablespoons sour cream
2 tablespoons chopped fresh dill

In a medium-sized saucepan, combine cucumber, water, onion, salt, and pepper, and cook until very soft. Push through a fine sieve or a food mill. Return to pot. In a screw-top jar, shake together the flour and $\frac{1}{4}$ cup of cold chicken broth and add to pot with the balance of the broth. Add bay leaf. Cook and stir over medium heat until the mixture is slightly thickened and smooth. Simmer over low heat for 2 or 3 minutes more and cool. Discard bay leaf. When cool, cover and chill in the refrigerator.

Before serving, stir in sour cream and 2 tablespoons of dill. Taste for seasoning and correct. Serve very cold, sprinkled with additional dill.

GAZPACHO
Serves 4

3 large tomatoes, peeled and cut into chunks
2 stalks celery, cut up
1 green pepper, cut up
1 onion, cut up
1 cucumber, peeled and cut up
³/₄ cup tomato juice
2 eggs
4 tablespoons tomato puree
1 clove garlic, crushed
2 tablespoons cider vinegar
1 tablespoon olive oil
¹/₈ teaspoon Tabasco sauce
¹/₄ teaspoon thyme
Salt and freshly ground pepper
Garnish: 1 to 2 tablespoons each chopped tomato, celery, green
   pepper, onion, and cucumber

Place in blender tomatoes, celery, green pepper, onion, cucumber, and half the tomato juice. Blend until almost smooth. Add all the remaining ingredients except the salt and pepper and reblend until completely smooth. (Since the quantity may be too large to do in the blender at one time, the blending may have to be done in 2 or more batches.) Add salt and pepper to taste.

Refrigerate and serve very cold. Garnish each portion with a small amount of the chopped vegetables.

RUSSIAN VICHYSSOISE
Serves 8 to 10

2 tablespoons butter
3 tablespoons chopped onion
3 large russet potatoes, peeled and cubed
2 cups water
1 teaspoon salt
1 cup milk
1½ cups sour cream
Salt and white pepper
½ cup heavy cream
Garnish: 3 tablespoons chopped fresh chives
         3 tablespoons chopped fresh parsley

Heat the butter in a large saucepan. Add onion and sauté for 2 to 3 minutes. Add potatoes, water, and salt. Boil until tender. Cool. Puree mixture in food processor or blender.

Transfer to a bowl and stir in milk and sour cream. Add salt and pepper to taste. Chill for 2 hours or more.

To serve, stir in cream. Taste and add additional salt and pepper if needed. Sprinkle with mixed chives and parsley.

SUMMER SQUASH SOUP
Serves 4

3 summer squash (about 1½ pounds)
1 tablespoon butter
4 scallions (green onions), chopped (white part only)
1½ cups chicken broth
Salt and freshly ground pepper
Pinch of nutmeg
1 cup light cream
2 tablespoons chopped fresh parsley

continued

Scrub squashes well, leaving the skins. Slice or cut into chunks.

Melt butter in a large saucepan and sauté scallions until golden. Add squash and broth, cover pot, and cook until squash is tender, about 15 minutes. Puree mixture in blender. Transfer to a bowl. Season to taste with salt, pepper, and nutmeg. Stir in cream and chill well. Serve very cold, garnished with chopped parsley.

GRANE'S
FAIRHAVEN

BEST FISH CHOWDER DOWN EAST
Serves 6 to 8

2 pounds fish fillets (1 pound haddock, 1 pound cod or cusk)
1/4 teaspoon *fines herbes* (or mixture such as marjoram, thyme,
  and basil)
1/2 cup dry white wine
Water
4–5 medium potatoes, cut into 1/2-inch cubes
2-inch-square cube of salt pork, finely diced
2 slices bacon, finely chopped
3 tablespoons butter
2 large onions, coarsely chopped
4 tablespoons all-purpose flour
Salt and freshly ground pepper
3 cups milk
2 tablespoons chopped fresh parsley
1 cup light cream
2 tablespoons butter
Chopped chives

Wash the fish and cut into 2-inch pieces. Place the fish in a heavy 5-
quart pot or soup kettle, sprinkle with *fines herbes*, add the wine and
enough water to cover the fish by 1 inch. Bring to a boil, reduce heat,
and simmer, covered, for 4 to 5 minutes, just until fish loses its
translucency. Remove the fish with a slotted spoon. Set aside.

Add the potatoes to the same liquid, adding more water if needed.
Cook slowly, uncovered, until the potatoes are tender, 10 to 12 minutes. Return fish to the kettle without discarding any of the liquid.

In a large skillet, cook salt pork and bacon until crisp. Add salt pork
and bacon crisps to soup kettle, reserving the fat in the skillet.

In the same skillet (with the fat), heat the butter and sauté onions until wilted, about 8 minutes. Do not brown. Sprinkle with flour, salt, and pepper, and cook until bubbly. Remove from heat, add milk all at once, and whisk vigorously. Return to medium heat and cook and stir until smooth and thickened. Stir in parsley. Add to soup kettle with the cream and blend well.

Let stand in refrigerator at least one day. At serving time, heat gently, uncovered, until piping hot, but do not boil. Swirl in 2 tablespoons butter. Taste and correct seasoning. Serve each portion garnished with a sprinkle of chopped chives.

The Inn at Mt Ascutney

BRANDIED PUMPKIN SOUP
Serves 6 to 8

1/4 cup (1/2 stick) butter
1 medium onion, very finely chopped
1 15-ounce can plain pumpkin
4 cups chicken broth
1/2 teaspoon ground ginger
1/2 teaspoon nutmeg
3/4 cup milk
3 tablespoons brandy
Salt and freshly ground pepper

Heat the butter in a saucepan and add the onion. Cook gently until onion is tender and transparent. Stir in the pumpkin, broth, ginger, and nutmeg, and blend well. Bring to a boil.

Lower heat and add the milk and brandy. Do not allow to come to a boil but heat through. Add salt and pepper to taste. Serve with toasted croutons.

CECI ROMANO
Serves 8 to 10

2 cups cooked or canned chick peas
3 quarts chicken broth
1 teaspoon dried rosemary
3 cloves garlic, peeled
3 anchovy fillets
1/2 pound elbow macaroni
Salt and freshly ground pepper

In a large soup pot, combine chick peas and chicken broth. Tie the rosemary in a cheesecloth square or place in a metal tea ball and add to the pot. Mash together the garlic cloves and anchovies to make a paste and stir into the soup. Bring soup to a full boil. Turn off heat and let rest for the full flavor of the rosemary to infuse, overnight if possible. Cover the pot when cool and refrigerate.

When ready to serve, cook elbow macaroni in boiling salted water only until it loses its stiffness and becomes tender enough so that you can bite through without snapping it (known as *al dente*, or firm to the bite), 8 to 10 minutes. Drain immediately. Add to the soup. Heat through and remove the rosemary. Add salt and pepper to taste.

CLAM BISQUE
Serves 6

3 tablespoons butter
3/4 cup chopped celery (2 large ribs)
1/2 cup chopped onion
2 parsley sprigs, minced
1/3 cup flour
2–3 dashes paprika
10 ounces clams, fresh or canned, chopped, with liquid
1 cup clam juice
5 cups milk
Salt to taste
Freshly ground pepper

continued

Melt the butter in a large saucepan and add the celery, onion, and parsley sprigs. Sauté until the vegetables are soft and tender. Sprinkle with flour gradually, stirring well while adding. Mix in paprika.

In another saucepan, place the chopped clams and clam juice and heat gently over low heat. Add the milk and heat, but do not allow to come to a boil. Add the heated liquid and clams to the sautéed vegetables, a little at a time, stirring constantly so that the bisque remains smooth. Add salt and pepper to taste. Clam juice is generally salty, so taste as you go.

The chef says: "If the clam bisque becomes too thick, add more milk and reheat."

Gateways Inn
COCK-A-LEEKIE SOUP
Serves 5 to 6

2 tablespoons butter
1 cup onion in julienne strips
1 8-ounce leek, washed and cut into julienne strips
1–2 pinches white pepper
1 clove garlic, minced
2 pinches marjoram
4 scallions (green onions), minced
6 cups clear chicken broth
1 cup diced chicken
8 pitted prunes, minced
Salt and pepper

Heat the butter in a large saucepan and sauté the julienne of onions and leeks. Add the white pepper, garlic, marjoram, scallions, and chicken broth. Simmer for 10 minutes. Add the chicken meat and prunes and simmer over low heat for 5 more minutes. Add salt and pepper to taste.

The chef says: "Fine noodles or finely diced potatoes may be added with the chicken and prunes."

CRAB AND CHEDDAR SOUP
Serves 8

$^1/_2$ cup (1 stick) butter
1 pound fresh crabmeat, picked over
$^1/_2$ cup flour
6 cups milk, heated
1 cup heavy cream
1 pound Cheddar cheese, grated
2 tablespoons Worcestershire sauce
White pepper
Dash nutmeg
$^1/_4$ cup dry sherry

Melt the butter in a large saucepan. Add the crabmeat and sauté 5 minutes or so, until some of the color comes from the crabmeat into the butter. Sprinkle with flour and cook over low heat for another 5 minutes, stirring gently.

Add the heated milk slowly, stirring constantly, and cook for another 10 minutes, stirring. Add the cream and grated cheese and cook over very low heat for another 10 minutes, stirring, until the cheese is melted. The soup should be smooth and thick. Season with Worcestershire sauce, pepper, nutmeg, and sherry.

CREAM OF BROCCOLI SOUP
Serves 4

3 tablespoons butter
1/3 cup diced leeks
1/3 cup diced onion
1/3 cup diced celery
1 cup diced broccoli
3 tablespoons flour
3 cups chicken broth
Salt and freshly ground pepper
1/2 teaspoon dried thyme
1/3 cup dry white wine
1 cup light cream

Melt the butter in a saucepan and add leeks, onion, celery, and broccoli. Sauté about 5 minutes over low heat so that the butter won't brown.

Sprinkle the flour in, mixing well, and add the chicken broth slowly, stirring constantly. Cook until it comes to a boil. Season with salt and pepper to taste and mix in thyme and wine. Let simmer until vegetables are tender, about 20 minutes. Puree in a blender and return to low heat. Add cream just before serving and heat through, but do not boil.

The chef says: "Any vegetable may be substituted for the broccoli, such as zucchini, carrots, spinach, asparagus, mushrooms, Brussels sprouts, etc."

CREAM OF WINTER SQUASH SOUP
Serves 5 or 6

2 pounds butternut squash
3 tablespoons butter
1 tablespoon finely chopped onion
3 tablespoons flour
1 quart hot chicken broth
Salt and freshly ground pepper
Dash of nutmeg

Peel and seed the squash. Cut into small chunks and cook, covered, in boiling salted water until soft. Drain well and mash or puree until smooth. Set aside.

Using the same pot, melt butter and sauté onion until limp. Sprinkle with flour and cook and stir for 2 or 3 minutes. Slowly add the chicken broth and blend well, stirring constantly. Cook until thickened and smooth. Stir in the squash and blend well. Season with salt, pepper, and nutmeg. Serve hot.

CURRIED CREAM OF PEA SOUP
Serves 4 to 6

1 onion, coarsely chopped
1 medium potato, cut up
1 carrot, sliced
1 stalk celery, cut up
1 clove garlic, minced
1 cup peas (frozen, fresh, or leftover)
2 cups chicken broth
1 teaspoon curry powder
Salt to taste
1/2–1 cup milk or light cream

Place all the vegetables in a large saucepan with the chicken broth. Add curry powder and salt. Cook, covered, for 20 minutes or until the vegetables are tender. Transfer to blender and blend at high speed until smooth. (Since the quantity may be too large to do in the blender at one time, the blending may have to be done in 2 or more batches.) Return to pot and add milk or cream until the desired consistency is reached. Taste for seasoning and correct. Heat through but do not boil.

The innkeeper-chef says: "This has a tantalizing flavor and can be served with pride."

GRANE'S CORN CHOWDER
Serves 8

1 ounce salt pork, minced
2 medium onions, finely chopped
1¹/₂ cups water
2 large potatoes, cut in ¹/₂-inch cubes
2 cups canned cream-style corn
1 15-ounce can whole kernel corn or 2 cups fresh when available
   (about 4 ears)
1 quart milk
1 cup light cream
4 tablespoons butter
2 tablespoons chopped fresh parsley
2 tablespoons chopped fresh chives
Salt and freshly ground pepper

In a large, heavy pot, fry the salt pork. Add onions and sauté in the hot fat until wilted and soft. Do not brown. Add water and potatoes and cook until tender, about 5 minutes. Add the remaining ingredients and simmer gently for 1 hour, stirring from time to time.

When cool, cover and refrigerate for at least 1 day. The flavor improves on standing. At serving time, reheat slowly. Do not allow to boil.

*Lincoln
House*

MUSHROOM SOUP
Serves 8 generously

9 cups chicken broth
4 tablespoons soy sauce
2 bay leaves
$1/4$ cup vinegar
$1/4$ teaspoon thyme
5 parsley sprigs
6 tablespoons butter
4 medium onions, finely chopped
$1^1/2$ pounds mushrooms, sliced
$1/4$ cup all-purpose flour
Salt and freshly ground pepper
3 tablespoons uncooked rice
Garnish: chopped fresh chives

In a large pot or soup kettle combine chicken broth, soy sauce, bay leaves, vinegar, thyme, and parsley. Simmer slowly for 15 to 20 minutes. Strain into a bowl and set aside.

Using the same pot, heat the butter and sauté the onions until limp and transparent. Mix in the sliced mushrooms and sprinkle evenly with the flour, stirring well. Pour in the strained broth and stir and cook over medium heat until smooth and slightly thickened. Taste for seasoning and add salt and pepper if necessary. (A well-seasoned broth in combination with the soy sauce may not need further seasoning.) Bring to a boil, add uncooked rice, cover pot, and reduce heat. Simmer slowly for 25 minutes. Serve hot, garnished with chopped chives.

NEW ENGLAND CLAM CHOWDER
Serves 6

3-inch cube salt pork, diced
3 medium onions, sliced
3 cups raw potatoes, diced
Salt and pepper
1 quart shucked chowder clams, chopped, plus juice
2 cups water
3 cups milk
2 tablespoons butter

In a large heavy pot, cook the salt pork until crisp. Remove from pot and sauté the onions gently in the hot pork fat until limp. Add the potatoes, salt, and pepper, and cook and stir for 10 minutes. Add the chopped clams and juice and water, and cook for 20 minutes. Remove from heat and allow to "ripen" on the back of the stove for about 1 hour. Just before serving, add milk and heat gently. Top with butter.

OLD NEW ENGLAND CHEDDAR CHEESE SOUP
Serves 8 to 10

6 tablespoons butter
1 green pepper, seeded and diced
1 carrot, scraped and diced
1 stalk celery, diced
1 onion, diced
$^1/_2$ cup all-purpose flour
$2^1/_2$ quarts warm milk
$1^1/_4$ cups chicken broth
1 cup (4 ounces) shredded American cheese
$^3/_4$ cup (3 ounces) shredded Cheddar cheese
$^1/_4$ cup dark beer or ale

Heat 3 of the tablespoons of butter and sauté the green pepper, carrot, celery, and onion for about 10 minutes, or until tender. Remove from pot and set aside.

In the same pot, heat the remaining 3 tablespoons of butter. Whisk in the flour and cook, whisking until it foams and bubbles, 2 or 3 minutes. Remove from heat and add the warm milk and broth, whisking vigorously to blend well. Return to heat and cook, stirring, until smooth and thickened, about 10 minutes. Add the sautéed vegetables and heat through. Reduce heat to very low and add the shredded cheeses, stirring with a fork until melted. Stir in the beer or ale and heat through. Taste for seasoning; the cheeses may be salty enough not to require any further seasoning.

ONION SOUP
Serves 6 to 8

4 tablespoons butter
4 large onions, thinly sliced
8 cups beef broth
1 tablespoon sugar
$\frac{1}{4}$ teaspoon pepper
$\frac{1}{4}$ cup dry sherry
Dash cognac
Salt to taste
6–8 slices French bread, toasted
$\frac{1}{2}$ cup (2 ounces) grated Swiss cheese

Melt the butter in a heavy skillet, add the onions, and cook them very slowly over low heat, stirring often, for at least 30 minutes. The slow cooking will bring out their full flavor and give them a deep golden color without scorching.

While they are cooking, place the broth in a separate large saucepan and bring to a boil. When the onions are a deep gold, add them to the broth with the sugar and pepper. Add the sherry and cognac and simmer, partially covered, for 1 hour. Add salt to taste.

Place the soup in individual onion soup casseroles or in a larger casserole and place slices of the toasted French bread on top with a generous layer of grated Swiss cheese. Place in broiler under medium-high heat and broil until cheese is brown and bubbly.

Snowbill
OUR MUSHROOM SOUP
Serves 6

4 tablespoons butter
2 cups chopped onion
Salt
3/4 pound fresh mushrooms, sliced
1 tablespoon finely minced fresh dillweed, or 1 teaspoon dried
2 cups chicken broth
1 tablespoon tamari sauce*
1 tablespoon sweet Hungarian paprika
3 tablespoons all-purpose flour
1 cup milk
Freshly ground pepper
2 teaspoons fresh lemon juice
1/2 cup sour cream
1 tablespoon minced fresh dillweed (optional)
Garnish: 1/4 cup chopped fresh parsley

In a medium-sized saucepan, sauté the onions in 2 of the tablespoons of butter, stirring occasionally, until soft but not brown. Sprinkle lightly with salt. Add the mushrooms, dillweed, 1/2 cup of broth, tamari sauce, and paprika. Cover pot and simmer for 15 minutes.

Heat the remaining 2 tablespoons of butter in a large saucepan. Whisk in the flour and cook, stirring, until the mixture foams and bubbles. Remove from the heat, add the milk all at once, and whisk vigorously to blend well. Return to moderate heat and continue to whisk until the sauce is thickened and smooth, about 10 minutes.

Stir in the mushroom mixture and remaining broth. Cover pot and simmer for 10 to 15 minutes.

Just before serving, add salt and pepper to taste, lemon juice, sour cream, and extra dillweed, if desired. Blend well and heat through, but do not allow to boil. Serve garnished with parsley.

*Tamari sauce is a natural soy sauce.

**Combes
Family Inn**

PUREE OF GREEN PEA SOUP

Serves 8

5 tablespoons oil
1 large onion, coarsely chopped
5 tablespoons all-purpose flour
2 quarts hot chicken broth
2 10-ounce packages frozen green peas
Salt and freshly ground pepper

In a large pot, sauté onions in oil until soft and tender. Sprinkle with flour and blend well. Cook slowly for 3 or 4 minutes, stirring, but don't let it brown. Add half the chicken broth slowly, stirring constantly, until slightly thickened and smooth.

In another pot, cook peas in the remainder of the chicken broth until soft. Put peas and broth through a food mill, reserving about 1/3 of a cup of peas for garnish. Add the puree to the chicken broth and mix well. Taste for seasoning and add salt and pepper as needed. Serve hot with a few peas floating in each portion.

The innkeeper says: "This is popular with weight-watchers, since the soup does not require cream."

Palmer House

PUREE OF MUSHROOM SOUP

Serves 4

1 pound sliced fresh mushrooms
3 tablespoons butter
2 tablespoons all-purpose flour
4 cups chicken broth
1/4 cup dry sherry
Salt and freshly ground pepper

Place mushrooms in a large heavy-bottomed saucepan without water or oil. Cover and cook over very low heat for about 15 minutes until only a small amount of mushroom liquid remains. Add butter and stir until it melts. Sprinkle with flour and cook and stir for a few more minutes.

Slowly add chicken broth, stirring constantly until smooth. Then simmer for 10 minutes. With slotted spoon remove mushrooms to a blender or food processor. Add sherry and ¼ cup of soup liquid and process until smooth. Stir pureed mushrooms back into the liquid, stir well, and season with salt and pepper. Reheat and serve.

The chef says: "In the colder months we keep a soup stock pot simmering on the woodstoves making variations of chicken, vegetable, and split pea and lentil soups. In the really hot weather we serve cold soups or this easy and delectable fresh mushroom soup."

Jay Village

SEAFOOD CHOWDER
Serves 8

2 pounds fish fillets (any combination of white fish such as
    haddock, cod, cusk, halibut, etc.)
2 cups cold water
½ cup chopped salt pork
¼ cup finely chopped onion
½ cup chopped celery and leaves
¼ cup chopped carrots, cut into ¼-inch dice
2 cups boiling water
2 cups potatoes, cut into ½-inch cubes
1 bay leaf
½ teaspoon dried tarragon
Dash of paprika
Salt and freshly ground pepper
3 tablespoons all-purpose flour dissolved in ½ cup cold milk
3 cups milk, heated
½ pound scallops, coarsely chopped
¼ pound shrimp, coarsely chopped
¼ pound crabmeat
3 tablespoons butter
Chopped fresh parsley

Wash the fish and cut into 2-inch pieces. Place in a large heavy pot with 2 cups of cold water. Bring to a boil and simmer, covered, for 4 to 5 minutes. Remove the fish with a slotted spoon and set aside. Reserve the broth.

In the same pot, sauté the salt pork lightly. Add onions, celery, and carrots, and sauté in the pork fat until tender.

Add 2 cups of boiling water, potatoes, bay leaf, tarragon, paprika, and salt and pepper to taste. Cook until potatoes are tender, 8 to 10 minutes. In a small screw-top jar, shake together the flour and cold milk until blended, and stir in. Add the hot milk and cook and stir until the mixture is slightly thickened and smooth. Pour in the reserved stock and add the fish, scallops, shrimp, and crab. Mix well and reheat gently.

Swirl in the butter and sprinkle each portion with chopped parsley.

Snowbill
TOMATO SOUP WITH COGNAC
Serves 6

3 pounds fresh or canned peeled tomatoes
6 tablespoons butter
1 large onion, chopped
1/4 cup fresh basil leaves, chopped
2 cups heavy cream
1 teaspoon light brown sugar
4–5 tablespoons cognac
Salt and freshly ground pepper

If the tomatoes are fresh, dip them in boiling water for a minute to loosen the skins, and peel. Cut into chunks and chop in a food processor. Place in a bowl. Canned tomatoes may be roughly cut.

Sauté the chopped onion in melted butter in a medium-sized saucepan. When the onion turns a deep gold color, add the tomatoes and basil. Simmer for 30 minutes and put through the food processor again.

In a larger saucepan, heat the cream and sugar just to the boiling point, when small bubbles begin to form around the outside rim. Pour the tomato puree into the cream, stir, and add cognac. Season to taste with salt and pepper. Reheat gently, but do not allow it to come to a boil.

VERMONT-STYLE FISH SOUP
Serves 6

3–4 tablespoons butter
1 medium Spanish onion, diced
1 teaspoon dried thyme
$^{1}/_{2}$ teaspoon saffron
2 pounds scrod or haddock, coarsely chopped
1 cup dry white wine
1 cup fish stock (page 62)
2 cups light cream
$^{1}/_{3}$–$^{1}/_{2}$ cup brandy
Salt and freshly ground pepper

Melt the butter in a 2-quart saucepan. Add the onion and sauté until golden, adding the thyme and saffron a few minutes before the onion is cooked. Add the chopped fish and cook and stir gently for 2 minutes.

Add wine and fish stock and bring to a boil. Reduce heat and simmer for 5 minutes. Add the cream and brandy and over very low heat simmer for another few minutes until heated through. Do not allow to come to a boil. Taste for seasoning and add salt and pepper as needed.

III Salads and Salad Dressings

SALADS

ARABIAN PEACH MOLD
Serves 12

12 canned peach halves, drained (reserve juice)
$^1/_2$ cup vinegar
$^3/_4$ cup sugar
4 pieces cinnamon bark
1 tablespoon whole cloves
1 6-ounce package orange-flavored gelatin

In a medium-sized saucepan, combine peach syrup, vinegar, sugar, cinnamon bark and cloves (tied together in a cheesecloth bag), and enough water to make 1 quart. Bring to a boil. Reduce heat and simmer 10 minutes. Place the powdered gelatin in a bowl and strain the liquid directly over it. Stir until it dissolves and the liquid becomes clear.

Place peach halves in 12 individual molds or custard cups and pour in gelatin. Chill until set.

Unmold on crisp lettuce cups and serve with whipped cream, sour cream dressing, or salad oil and lemon juice.

AVOCADO SALAD
Serves 5 or 6

3 medium avocados, peeled and cut into large cubes
4 cloves garlic, crushed and minced
1 cup mayonnaise (below)
2–3 tablespoons lime juice
Salt and pepper
Crisp lettuce leaves
8 red radishes, sliced

continued

Place avocados, garlic, mayonnaise, and lime juice in the container of blender and blend until smooth. Add salt and pepper to taste. Put on crisp lettuce leaves and garnish with radishes. Serve immediately.

MAYONNAISE
Makes about 1¹/₄ cups

1 egg
¹/₈ medium onion, chopped
1 clove garlic, cut up
3 sprigs cilantro (leaves only, no stems), or ¹/₂ teaspoon dried
    coriander
3 tablespoons lime juice
1 cup oil
Salt and pepper

Put the egg, onion, garlic, cilantro or coriander, and lime juice in a blender and blend at high speed for 5 or 6 seconds. Remove the cover insert and, with the machine running, add the oil in a thin, slow, steady stream. When it begins to thicken, you can add the oil more quickly. Blend only until thick and smooth. Stir in salt and pepper to taste. If made in advance, refrigerate mayonnaise in a covered bowl.

CAESAR SALAD
Serves 2

2–3 anchovy fillets, chopped
1 egg, coddled 1 minute
2 tablespoons oil
1 tablespoon vinegar
2 teaspoons lemon juice
Salt and freshly ground pepper
1 teaspoon Dijon mustard
¹/₂ small bunch Romaine lettuce, washed, dried, and broken into
    large bite-sized pieces
¹/₂ cup croutons
¹/₄ cup freshly grated Parmesan cheese

In a large, dry salad bowl, mash anchovies against side of bowl with back of spoon. Add coddled egg and mash and mix together. Add oil, vinegar, lemon juice, salt, pepper, and mustard, mixing well.

Add lettuce, croutons, and Parmesan cheese. Toss thoroughly.

CATALINA SALAD
Serves 8

1/2 pound fresh spinach, washed, coarse stems removed, and
    crisped
1/2 bunch endive, washed and crisped
1 bunch leaf lettuce, washed and crisped
1/2 bunch romaine lettuce, washed and crisped
1 cup mandarin orange sections, drained
1 tomato, peeled, seeded, and cubed
3 tablespoons capers, drained
Dressing (below)

Tear the greens into bite-sized pieces. Place in a large salad bowl and chill in the refrigerator.

To serve, add mandarin orange sections, tomato, and capers to the greens and toss with dressing.

DRESSING
1/2 cup sugar (or to taste)
Salt
1 teaspoon dry mustard
1 teaspoon paprika
1 teaspoon celery salt
1 teaspoon grated onion
1 cup oil
1/4 cup wine vinegar

Combine all ingredients in a blender or food processor and blend until smooth and creamy.

CHINESE SALAD
Serves 2

10 snow pea pods
6 asparagus tips, cooked fresh or canned
¼ cup bamboo shoots, drained
6 water chestnuts, sliced
¾ cup shredded Chinese cabbage
4 fresh mushrooms, sliced
1½ tablespoons lemon juice
2 teaspoons soy sauce
½ teaspoon dry mustard
1 tablespoon chopped fresh parsley

Blanch the snow peas in boiling salted water for 1 minute, or until they turn bright green, and drain. Let cool. In a salad bowl, combine the pea pods, asparagus tips, bamboo shoots, water chestnuts, cabbage, and mushrooms.

Mix the lemon juice, soy sauce, and dry mustard in a covered jar and shake well. Pour over vegetables and toss. Sprinkle with parsley.

DILLED CUCUMBER SALAD WITH YOGURT
Serves 6

2 large cucumbers, pared and thinly sliced
1 teaspoon salt
1 cup plain yogurt
1 tablespoon finely chopped onion
½ teaspoon sugar
Dash of Tabasco sauce
1 tablespoon finely chopped fresh dill or 1 teaspoon dried
   dillweed
Lettuce leaves, washed and crisped
2 tomatoes, peeled and cut into wedges

Toss cucumbers with salt and place in colander for 1 hour. Rinse well and drain thoroughly.

Combine yogurt, onion, sugar, Tabasco sauce, and dill in a medium-sized bowl. Pat cucumbers dry with paper towels and add to yogurt dressing. Toss well.

Serve on lettuce leaves and garnish with tomato wedges.

FRUITED CABBAGE SLAW
Serves 6 to 8

1/2 pound green cabbage, shredded (about 3 cups)
1 cup shredded carrots
1 cup pineapple tidbits
1/2 cup raisins
1 red apple, cored and cubed
1 cup plain yogurt
1 teaspoon cider vinegar
1 teaspoon sugar
1 teaspoon salt
1/2 teaspoon celery seeds
1 banana, sliced

In a large bowl, combine cabbage, carrots, pineapple, raisins, and apple. Set aside.

Mix together yogurt, vinegar, sugar, salt, and celery seeds. Pour over cabbage mixture and toss until well mixed. Refrigerate 1 hour or more. Just before serving, add sliced banana and toss.

Gateways Inn
INSALATA DI FONTINA
(Pepper and Fontina Cheese Salad)
Serves 6

6 bell peppers (yellow or red, preferably)
1/4 pound Fontina cheese, diced
1/3 cup pitted green olives, sliced

DRESSING
1/2 cup olive oil
1 1/2 teaspoons Dijon mustard
Salt
6 crushed peppercorns
3 tablespoons light cream
1 tablespoon chopped fresh parsley
1 tablespoon finely chopped scallions (green onions)

Trim the stem ends of the peppers and cut the peppers in half vertically. Remove core and seeds. Place pepper halves on a foil-lined cookie sheet (to make cleaning up easier) and either bake in a 450° oven or broil under high heat (latter is better) until the skins blacken and blister. While still warm, scrape off the skin and cut the peppers into long even strips, about 3/8 inch wide. Place the strips in a bowl with the diced cheese and olives.

For the dressing, mix all ingredients in a screw-top jar and shake well. Add to the pepper mixture, stir well, and chill for 1 1/2 hours.

Serve drained pepper mixture on lettuce-lined salad plates.

🌲 Sugar Hill Inn
MARINATED CARROTS
Serves 6 to 8

8 large carrots
½ cup olive oil
¼ cup red wine vinegar
4 cloves garlic, sliced
1 teaspoon salt
½ teaspoon pepper
2 teaspoons dried oregano
1 4-ounce jar of sliced mushrooms, drained (optional)

Scrape the carrots and cut into ½-inch-thick diagonal slices. Cover with salted water and cook until just crisp-tender. Don't overcook.

Combine hot drained carrots in a bowl with the remaining ingredients. Cover and refrigerate overnight. Remove garlic cloves. Drain and serve on crisp lettuce leaves.

Gateways Inn
ORANGE SALAD
Serves 6

6 navel oranges
1 small Bermuda onion, sliced very thin
½ cup dry sherry
Juice of 1 lemon
3 tablespoons oil
3 tablespoons orange blossom honey
¼ teaspoon ground white pepper
2 tablespoons Pernod
1 bunch watercress, washed and dried

Peel the oranges carefully, removing every bit of the bitter white membrane.

Separate the onion slices into rings. Place in a colander and run cold water over them for 5 to 8 minutes. Place rings on paper towels to drain and pat dry. Put in a small bowl and pour the sherry over them. Marinate for 1½ hours.

In another bowl, combine the lemon juice, oil, honey, pepper, and Pernod. Add 3 tablespoons of the sherry marinade from the onions, and beat with a wire whisk until well blended.

Before serving, arrange the watercress on 6 glass salad plates. Slice the oranges very thinly and arrange slices — 1 orange per serving— over the watercress, overlapping the slices to form a circle. Drain the onion rings and scatter the rings over the orange slices. Beat the dressing again and pour over all.

PRINCESS SALAD
Serves 6 to 8

½ cup sesame seeds, toasted
¼ cup grated Parmesan cheese
10 ounces fresh young spinach, washed, coarse stems removed, and crisped
1 bunch leaf lettuce, washed and crisped

DRESSING
¼ cup mayonnaise
½ cup sour cream
1 tablespoon tarragon vinegar
1 tablespoon sugar (optional)
¼ cup minced green pepper
2 tablespoons minced onion
Salt
¼ teaspoon garlic powder

Combine the toasted sesame seeds and cheese and set aside.

Tear spinach and lettuce into bite-sized pieces and place in salad bowl.

Combine all the dressing ingredients and blend well. Toss greens with dressing and three-quarters of sesame seed mixture. Sprinkle salad with remaining sesame seed mixture.

Gateways Inn
SALAD ANDALUSIAN
Serves 6 to 8

3 hard-cooked egg yolks
4 tablespoons olive oil
1 clove garlic, minced
1 large sweet red onion, thinly sliced
1 cup green pepper, cut in strips
1 cup red pepper, cut in strips
2 cucumbers, peeled, seeded, and cut in strips
6 tomatoes, peeled, seeded, and cut in strips
Juice of 2 limes
Salt and freshly ground pepper
1 tablespoon chopped fresh parsley

In a large bowl, combine the egg yolks, olive oil, and garlic, and mash into a paste. Add the onions, pepper, cucumber, and tomatoes. Pour the lime juice over the vegetables and toss gently. Add salt and pepper to taste. Chill in the refrigerator for an hour. Sprinkle with parsley before serving.

SALADE PARISIENNE
Serves 2

8 slices tomato
8 slices peeled cucumber
1 hard-cooked egg, cut in 8 slices
4 olives
1 tablespoon finely minced fresh parsley
Vinaigrette dressing**

Arrange on 2 individual salad plates 4 slices each of tomato, cucumber, and hard-cooked egg. Garnish with olives and chopped parsley. Dribble vinaigrette dressing over all.

**Vinaigrette Dressing (supplied by the editors)

2 tablespoons wine vinegar or lemon juice
1 teaspoon finely minced shallots
1 tablespoon Dijon mustard
6 tablespoons oil
2 teaspoons chopped fresh parsley
Salt and freshly ground pepper

Combine the vinegar, minced shallots, and mustard in a small mixing bowl. Stir with a whisk, gradually adding the oil. Stir in fresh parsley, and add salt and pepper to taste.

THREE-GREEN SALAD
Serves 6 to 8

½ pound fresh young string beans
1 medium red onion, thinly sliced
1 cup Italian salad dressing (or homemade vinaigrette)
1 pound fresh young spinach
1 bunch watercress
Salt and freshly ground pepper

Snip end of beans, wash, and cook until just crisp-tender. Cool. Spread the onion slices over the cooled string beans. Pour salad dressing over and marinate overnight.

Wash and pick over spinach and watercress, discarding coarse stems from each. Spin dry.

When ready to serve, combine all, including the marinade. Add more dressing if necessary. Season to taste with salt and pepper.

SALAD DRESSINGS

BERNERHOF SWISS-STYLE SALAD DRESSING
Makes 3¹/₄ cups

1 cup milk
1 cup heavy cream
1 cup cider vinegar
¹/₄ cup Dijon mustard
¹/₂ teaspoon salt
¹/₄ teaspoon ground white pepper
1 tablespoon seasoning and browning sauce, such as Maggi,
   Gravy Master, or Kitchen Bouquet

Combine all ingredients in a large bowl and mix well. Cover tightly and refrigerate.

Note: This is the Bernerhof's house dressing, where it is served tossed with Bibb lettuce.

Edson Hill
MANOR

BLUE CHEESE DRESSING
Makes 2¹/₂ cups

2 cloves garlic, crushed
1 tablespoon finely chopped fresh dill
1 cup sour cream
1 cup mayonnaise
¹/₄ cup buttermilk
¹/₄ cup wine vinegar
1 teaspoon Worcestershire sauce
¹/₈ teaspoon Tabasco sauce
¹/₂ teaspoon salt
¹/₄ teaspoon white pepper
3 ounces blue cheese, crumbled

Combine all ingredients in a medium-sized bowl. Mix well with a wooden spoon or rubber spatula. Taste and correct seasonings.

The chef says: "This dressing is best made at least twenty-four hours in advance so that the garlic has a chance to permeate and the flavors to blend. It stores well for two weeks or more if refrigerated in a tightly covered plastic container."

CREAMY BLUE CHEESE SALAD DRESSING
Makes 1¹/₂ cups

²/₃ cup olive oil
¹/₃ cup combined white vinegar and lemon juice
¹/₄ teaspoon paprika
¹/₂ teaspoon dry mustard
¹/₂ teaspoon sugar
¹/₂ cup mayonnaise
¹/₄ pound blue cheese, coarsely crumbled

Place all ingredients in the blender and blend well until smooth. Chill in the refrigerator until ready to use.

GRANE'S
FAIRHAVEN

GRANE'S DRESSING FOR GREENS
Makes about 1 cup, serves 8 to 10

1 egg, coddled 1 minute
³/₄ cup oil
3 tablespoons fresh lemon juice
1 teaspoon garlic powder, or 1 large clove garlic, crushed
1 tablespoon Worcestershire sauce
½ teaspoon pepper
½ teaspoon salt
¼ cup grated Parmesan cheese

Place coddled egg in blender and blend until thick and yellow. Turn blender to low and add salad oil very slowly in a thin stream. Blend until sauce emulsifies and thickens. Turn machine up to "mix" or "blend" and add all remaining ingredients. Blend only until thick and smooth.

Place in a tightly covered jar and refrigerate for at least 2 days. This dressing will keep under refrigeration for 2 weeks.

Note: The co-innkeeper suggests a salad of lettuce, spinach, fresh mushrooms, and thinly sliced red onion. Toss with dressing, top with croutons, and serve.

THE CRAIGNAIR

GREEN ONION SALAD DRESSING
Makes about 2 cups

1 bunch scallions (green onions), including green part, chopped
   fine
2 large onions, chopped fine
1 cup mayonnaise
½ cup plain yogurt
¼ cup sour cream
1 tablespoon lemon juice
Salt and freshly ground pepper

continued

Combine all ingredients. Cover tightly and refrigerate overnight so that the flavors can blend together and ripen.

MANCHESTER INN SALAD DRESSING
Makes about 1¹/₂ cups, serves 8

1 egg
1 cup oil
¹/₃ cup wine vinegar
1 clove garlic, crushed
¹/₂ teaspoon dry mustard
Salt and pepper
1 teaspoon dried tarragon
1 tablespoon sugar
Juice and grated rind of 1 lemon
¹/₂ cup grated Parmesan cheese
¹/₂ cup croutons

Place the egg in a blender and blend on medium speed until frothy. Add the oil slowly, drop by drop, adding it more quickly in a slow, steady stream as the sauce emulsifies and thickens. Blend in vinegar, garlic, mustard, salt, pepper, tarragon, and sugar. Add lemon juice and grated lemon rind.

Toss with salad greens of your choice. Figure about 2 cups of loosely packed greens per serving. Add cheese and croutons and toss lightly.

MAPLE SYRUP–CELERY SEED DRESSING
Makes about 1¼ cups

6 tablespoons maple syrup
³/₄ cup oil
¹/₄ cup lemon juice
1 teaspoon salt
¹/₂ teaspoon paprika
¹/₂ teaspoon dry mustard
¹/₂ teaspoon ground ginger
1 teaspoon celery seed

Combine all ingredients in a pint jar and shake well to blend thoroughly. Refrigerate.

When serving, remove from refrigerator at least 30 minutes before use and allow to come to room temperature.

MUSTARD-DILL DRESSING
Makes about 1¹/₂ cups

¹/₄ cup Dijon mustard
¹/₄ cup cider vinegar
³/₄ teaspoon dried tarragon
³/₄ teaspoon dried dillweed
1 cup safflower or sunflower oil
1 tablespoon grated Parmesan cheese
1 tablespoon light cream

In a medium-sized bowl, mix together the mustard, vinegar, tarragon, and dillweed, and let stand for 10 minutes. Slowly add the oil in a thin, steady stream, whisking constantly, until the mixture is emulsified like a thin mayonnaise. Mix in Parmesan cheese and light cream. Refrigerate.

WHITE SALAD DRESSING
Makes 1 cup

³/₄ cup plain yogurt
¹/₄ cup mayonnaise
1 clove garlic, finely minced
2 teaspoons Dijon mustard
1 tablespoon lemon juice
¹/₂ teaspoon pepper
¹/₂ teaspoon salt
1 tablespoon sugar

Mix all ingredients together thoroughly and chill.

The chef says: "For variation, crumbly blue cheese, chopped green onions, or chopped hard-boiled egg may be added."

IV Seafood

Lincoln House
BAKED HALIBUT PARMESAN
Serves 6

3 pounds halibut steaks
1 cup sour cream
½ cup freshly grated Parmesan cheese
½ teaspoon dried dillweed
Salt and freshly ground pepper
¼ cup (½ stick) butter, very soft
Paprika
Lemon wedges

Preheat oven to 375°. Lightly grease a flat baking dish, preferably one that can be brought to the table.

Place halibut steaks in a single layer in baking dish.

In a small bowl, blend together the sour cream, Parmesan cheese, dillweed, salt, pepper, and soft butter. Cover fish with the sauce. Bake for 20 to 25 minutes, or until the fish loses its translucency. Sprinkle lightly with paprika and serve at once, garnished with lemon wedges.

BAKED STUFFED SCALLOPS
Serves 6 to 8

¾ cup (1½ sticks) butter
⅓ cup minced onion
¼ cup minced green pepper
1 teaspoon Worcestershire sauce
5 drops Tabasco sauce
3–4 cups crushed Ritz crackers (about 60 crackers)
1½ tablespoons grated Parmesan cheese
½ teaspoon salt
¼ teaspoon pepper
½ teaspoon curry powder
¼ cup pale dry sherry
1½ cups shellfish: crabmeat, or coarsely chopped uncooked
    scallops, or shrimp, peeled and deveined
1½ pounds sea scallops
Juice of 1 lemon
Salt and freshly ground pepper
2 tablespoons butter
Lemon wedges

Melt 1½ sticks of butter in a small saucepan and cook onion and green pepper in it until soft. Mix in Worcestershire sauce and Tabasco sauce. Remove from heat.

Crush the Ritz crackers in a plastic bag with your fingers or roll them with a rolling pin. The crumbs can be coarse, not as fine as fine breadcrumbs. Measure 3 cups of the crushed crackers (reserving the balance for topping) and combine in a large bowl with the cheese, salt, pepper, curry powder, butter-onion-pepper mixture, and sherry. Toss mixture lightly with your hands. The consistency should be much like poultry stuffing. Fold in the 1½ cups of chopped shellfish and mix well. Refrigerate for half an hour or so to give the mixture time to firm.

Wash the scallops and pat dry with paper towels. If scallops are large, cut them in 2 or 3 pieces; the pieces should be larger than small bay scallops. Sprinkle fresh lemon juice over them and season very lightly with salt and pepper.

Preheat oven to 375°. Butter a large baking sheet.

Scoop up about 2 generous tablespoons of the stuffing and form it in the shape of a large mushroom cap in the palm of your hand. Place cap on baking sheet and continue making caps until all the stuffing is used. You should have between 12 and 16 caps, depending on how large you make them. Place a pile of scallops in each cap, dividing them equally. Sprinkle the remainder of the crushed crackers over each and dot with butter. Bake for 20 minutes. Serve 2 per portion, garnished with a lemon wedge.

BOUILLABAISSE
Serves 4

1/2 cup olive oil
5 tomatoes, peeled and quartered
2 leeks, thoroughly cleaned and coarsely chopped
1 medium onion, thinly sliced
2 cloves garlic, mashed
1 quart fish stock (below)
1 cup dry white wine
2 pinches saffron threads
1 teaspoon dry mustard, or to taste
Salt and white pepper
Hot pepper sauce (Tabasco)
16 fresh mussels, shells closed, well scrubbed and debearded
12 fresh clams, shells closed and scrubbed clean
1/2 pound scrod
1/2 pound halibut
1/4 pound salmon
6 large raw shrimp, peeled and deveined
8 sea scallops

Heat olive oil over moderate heat in a 5- to 6-quart soup pot. Add tomatoes, leeks, onion, and garlic and simmer, stirring, until garlic begins to turn golden. Do not permit it to brown. Add fish stock, wine, saffron, and mustard, and bring to a boil. Reduce heat and cover pot partially. Gently simmer for 5 minutes to blend flavors. Season with salt, pepper, and hot pepper sauce. Set aside 2 cups of soup. Ladle remaining soup into 4 large warmed individual bowls, earthen crocks, or a soup tureen, and keep warm.

Place mussels and clams in soup kettle with the remaining 2 cups of soup. Cut scrod, halibut, and salmon in chunks roughly 2 by 3 inches and add with shrimp and scallops to the soup kettle. Steam in tightly covered pot 5 to 10 minutes, or until clams and mussels open. Discard any that do not open.

Divide fish and shellfish among soup bowls. Serve at once with warm crusty garlic bread.

FISH STOCK
Makes about 3½ cups

1–1½ pounds washed fish bones, heads, and trimmings from any
    white fish
1 quart water
3 stalks celery, thinly sliced (leaves removed)
1 onion, thinly sliced
1 carrot, thinly sliced
½ teaspoon salt
2 dashes white pepper, or to taste

In a 2-quart saucepan, combine all ingredients. Bring to a boil, skim, reduce heat, and simmer, covered, for 25 to 30 minutes, but no longer. (Long cooking can make fish stock bitter.) Cool and strain through a fine strainer. Discard vegetables and bones. The stock may be prepared a day in advance and refrigerated, covered.

CRAB DIJON
Serves 6

2 pounds lump crabmeat
2 tablespoons butter
2 tablespoons all-purpose flour
1½ cups milk
Tabasco sauce
¼ cup Dijon mustard
1½ cups (6 ounces) grated Swiss cheese
2 tablespoons melted butter

Pick over the crabmeat to remove shells and cartilage. Set aside.

Melt butter in a small, heavy-bottomed saucepan and whisk in the flour. Cook about 2 minutes or until it becomes frothy. Remove from heat and add the milk all at once, whisking vigorously to blend well. Return to heat and cook and stir over moderate heat until the sauce is smooth and thickened, about 5 minutes. Stir in 4 or 5 dashes of the Tabasco, and the mustard, and blend well. Remove from heat.

Preheat the oven to 350°. Butter 6 individual ramekins or 1 large au gratin dish.

Combine the crabmeat, grated cheese, and 1½ cups of mustard sauce. Toss gently to keep the crab lumps as whole and firm as possible. Divide into individual ramekins or large baking dish and top with melted butter. Bake for 15 minutes until the cheese is melted and the top is lightly browned.

CRABMEAT AU GRATIN
Serves 4

2 tablespoons butter
2 tablespoons all-purpose flour
1 cup light cream
1 teaspoon Worcestershire sauce
$^1/_4$ teaspoon freshly ground pepper
$^1/_2$ teaspoon salt
1 pound fresh lump crabmeat, picked over
$^1/_2$ teaspoon onion juice*
$^1/_2$ cup (2 ounces) grated Swiss cheese
$^1/_2$ cup fine breadcrumbs
2 tablespoons butter

Preheat oven to 375°. Butter a 1-quart casserole or an au gratin dish, about 5 × 9 inches.

In a heavy-bottomed saucepan, melt 2 tablespoons butter and whisk in the flour. Stir over moderate heat for 2 minutes, until the mixture is bubbly and frothy, but do not let it take on color. Remove from heat and pour in cream all at once, whisking vigorously to blend well. Return to the heat and continue to whisk until the sauce is smooth and thickened. Stir in Worcestershire sauce, pepper, salt, crabmeat, and onion juice. Transfer to baking dish and top with grated Swiss cheese. Sprinkle with breadcrumbs and dot with butter. Bake for 12 to 15 minutes, or until heated through. Run under a hot broiler for a minute to brown the top.

The chef says: "You may substitute lobster meat, scallops, shrimps, etc., for the crabmeat, or a combination of all. This dish may also be portioned out in shells or ramekins and served as an appetizer.

*"To make onion juice, use a garlic press, food processor, or mash with a heavy fork."

CRÊPES ST. JACQUES
Filling for about 16 crêpes

2 cups mushrooms, sliced
3 tablespoons chopped onion
1/2 pound scallops, cut into small pieces
1/2 pound haddock
2/3 cup dry white wine
6 tablespoons butter
6 tablespoons flour
3 cups light cream
1/4 cup clam broth
1/4 cup chopped fresh parsley
Salt and freshly ground pepper
16 cooked crêpes**

In a medium-sized saucepan, simmer together the mushrooms, onion, scallops, haddock, and wine until the haddock loses its transparency and flakes, about 5 minutes. Drain this mixture. Break the haddock into large flakes; transfer mixture to a bowl and set aside.

Using the same pot, melt the butter and stir in the flour, whisking until it bubbles, about 3 minutes. Remove from heat, stir in cream and clam broth, whisking vigorously to blend well, and return to heat. Cook and stir until sauce is smooth and thickened. Add parsley and salt and pepper to taste. Add fish mixture to cream sauce.

Place 1/3 cup of filling in center of cooked crêpes and roll. These may be done in advance and placed on a greased cookie tin, seamside down, to be reheated briefly in a 350° oven for 7 or 8 minutes, until heated through. Dribble a bit of the cream sauce over the crêpes before heating.

**Crêpes (supplied by the editors)*
Makes 20 to 24 crêpes

3 eggs
Pinch of salt
2 tablespoons brandy (optional)
1 cup sifted all-purpose flour
1 2/3 cups milk
1/4 cup oil or melted butter

continued

Beat the eggs until light and add salt and brandy, if using. You may use an electric beater. Beating constantly, add alternately the flour, milk, and oil or melted butter. The batter should be the consistency of heavy cream. If too thick, thin it with a teaspoon or so of water. Let the batter rest at room temperature for 2 or 3 hours. It will work better if the flour has time to expand and absorb the liquid.

When ready to cook, lightly oil or butter a 6-inch skillet. Heat the skillet over medium heat until a drop of water sizzles and bounces off. Add about 3 tablespoons of batter and tilt the pan quickly in all directions to cover the pan in a thin layer. The crêpes should be thin and delicate. Cook over medium-low heat until the underside of the crêpe is delicately browned, about 1 minute. Turn and brown the other side. Repeat until all the batter is used. Brush the pan with oil or butter as needed.

When completely cooled, the crêpes may be stacked one on top of another. They may be prepared a day in advance, wrapped in aluminum foil, and stored in the refrigerator, or they may be frozen, well wrapped, for a long period.

FILLET OF SOLE SUCCESSO
Serves 6

6 fillets of sole (2½ to 3 pounds)
1 cup (2 sticks) butter
2 sweet red peppers, cut into ½-inch strips
½ pound small zucchini, sliced
Salt and freshly ground pepper
¼ teaspoon dried rosemary, crumbled
¼ teaspoon dried basil
1 clove garlic, finely minced
1 small onion, finely chopped
1 stalk celery, chopped
½ pound Italian green beans (or regular beans, cut into 1-inch lengths)
4 tomatoes, peeled, seeded, and chopped
Flour for dredging
2 tablespoons chopped fresh parsley

Rinse fish fillets and pat dry. Set aside.

Heat 2 tablespoons of the butter in a large frying pan and sauté pepper strips gently for 7 or 8 minutes, or until crisp-tender. Transfer to an ovenproof bowl and keep warm.

Heat 3 more tablespoons of butter and add zucchini. Season with salt and pepper, and add rosemary, basil, and garlic. Cook over medium heat for about 5 or 6 minutes, or until crisp-tender but still firm. Add to peppers and keep warm.

Using the same pan, melt 3 tablespoons of butter and sauté onions until they are limp and golden. Add celery and Italian green beans. Cook for 5 minutes over medium heat, stirring gently. Add tomatoes and cook 5 minutes longer. Mix with the other vegetables and keep warm.

Wipe out the frying pan with paper towels and melt the remaining butter. Heat until the butter becomes almost nut colored. Season the fish fillets lightly with salt and pepper and dust lightly with flour. Sauté fish fillets for about 3 minutes on each side. Don't do more at a time than will fit comfortably in a single layer. As the fillets are cooked, place them on the bed of hot vegetables. Sprinkle fresh parsley over all.

FLORENTINE DE MER
Serves 4

> 1 pound scrod, poached
> 2 cups liquid (water, or mixture of water and white wine or
>   lemon juice in any proportion you wish)
> 1/2 teaspoon salt
> 3 peppercorns, crushed
> 2 sprigs parsley
> Pinch of thyme
> Small bay leaf
> 4 sheets phyllo pastry
> 6–8 tablespoons melted butter
> Béarnaise sauce (below)

Rinse fish. An easy way to poach a filleted fish such as scrod is to oven-poach it in a court bouillon. In a small saucepan, combine water (or water and wine or lemon juice), salt, peppercorns, parsley, thyme, and bay leaf and bring to the boiling point. Preheat oven to 350°. Simmer the court bouillon for 10 minutes. Place the fish in a baking dish just big enough to hold the fish snugly (6 × 10 inches is a good size) and pour the liquid over it. The liquid should just cover the fish. To keep the fish moist, cover it with a piece of buttered waxed paper laid directly on top. Poach in the oven for 8 to 10 minutes, or until the fish flakes easily and loses its translucent look. When done, remove the fish with a slotted spoon and place the fish on a linen towel so that it will drain well. Strain the liquid and set aside.

Break up the fish into flakes and add a few tablespoons of Béarnaise to bind it.

Preheat the oven to 425°. Butter a baking dish.

Lay out two sheets of phyllo pastry, one on top of another, and brush with melted butter. Cut down the middle, giving you two strips. Put one-quarter of the fish mixture in the center of each phyllo section. Fold in the edges of the phyllo pastry and roll up. Repeat with the remaining two sheets of phyllo and fish mixture. Place seam-side down on baking sheet and bake for 15 minutes, or until the pastry is browned.

Top with Béarnaise sauce and serve hot.

BÉARNAISE SAUCE
3 egg yolks
2 tablespoons lemon juice
Dash Tabasco sauce
Salt and freshly ground pepper
$1/2$ cup (1 stick) unsalted butter heated to bubbling
2 tablespoons dry white wine
1 tablespoon tarragon vinegar
1 teaspoon dried tarragon
2 teaspoons chopped onion

Put the egg yolks, lemon juice, Tabasco sauce, and a dash of salt and pepper in a blender. Blend just until the eggs are foamy. Heat the butter until it sizzles, but don't let it brown. Remove the insert from the blender lid and, with the machine running, add the hot butter slowly in a thin, steady stream. The sauce will thicken very quickly. Turn off the blender and cover it with a towel to keep the sauce warm.

In a small saucepan, combine the wine, vinegar, tarragon, and onion with about 2 tablespoons of the court bouillon. Cook the liquid over a low flame to reduce it to 1 tablespoon. It will take only a minute or so, so don't go off and leave it. Scrape it into the blender mixture at medium speed. If sauce is too thick, add the court bouillon, half a teaspoon at a time, until the proper consistency is reached.

FRENCH SAUTÉED SOLE
Serves 4

1/2 cup all-purpose flour
Salt and freshly ground pepper
2 eggs
4 6- to 8-ounce sole fillets
Clarified butter (page 90)
Juice of 1 lemon
1/4 cup dry white wine
2 tablespoons chopped fresh parsley
1 tablespoon Worcestershire sauce

Mix flour with salt and pepper and spread on a square of waxed paper. In a shallow bowl, beat the eggs well. Dip both sides of the fish in the flour, shaking off the excess, and then dip into the beaten eggs, letting the excess drip back into the bowl.

Heat enough clarified butter to cover the bottom of a large frying pan. When it is hot, add the fish fillets. Shake the pan gently to keep the fish from sticking. When golden brown on one side, which will take no more than 3 or 4 minutes, and just before turning, squeeze the lemon juice into the pan. When the second sides are cooked, add the white wine before removing the fillets. Remove the cooked fillets from the pan and keep warm.

Leave the frying pan on the stove and add chopped parsley and Worcestershire sauce to the hot butter remaining in the pan. Let foam for 10 seconds and pour over fish.

FRESH BOSTON SCROD À LA MAISON
Serves 6 to 8

8 6-ounce fillets Boston scrod
1 cup mayonnaise
1 cup buttermilk
$1/3$ cup lemon juice
1 or 2 cloves garlic, finely minced or pushed through a garlic
    press
Salt and freshly ground pepper
2 cups fine breadcrumbs
Lemon wedges

Preheat oven to 450°. Grease a large baking sheet and place baking rack in upper third of oven.

Rinse fish fillets and pat dry with paper towels. Set aside.

In a shallow bowl, mix together the mayonnaise, buttermilk, lemon juice, garlic, and salt and pepper, and blend well. Spread the breadcrumbs on a sheet of waxed paper.

Dip the fillets in the batter mixture, letting the excess drip back into the bowl, then dip into the breadcrumbs, using your fingers to make them adhere. Bake for 12 to 15 minutes, until crisp. Serve with lemon wedges.

GRANE'S
FAIRHAVEN

JANE'S BAKED FISH WITH CRABMEAT SAUCE
Serves 8

3 pounds haddock fillets
$1/2$ cup (1 stick) butter or margarine
1 large onion, minced
2 cups seasoned croutons
1 cup Ritz cracker crumbs (16 to 18 crackers)
$1/4$ teaspoon poultry seasoning
$1/4$ cup sweet pickle juice
Salt and freshly ground pepper
$1/2$ cup sour cream
$1/4$ cup salad dressing, such as Miracle Whip

SAUCE
4 tablespoons butter
4 tablespoons flour
2 cups milk
1/2 cup dry sherry
1 cup crabmeat, picked over
Salt and freshly ground pepper

Rinse fish fillets, pat dry, and set aside. Preheat oven to 425°. Grease a large shallow baking pan — a 9 × 11-inch will do — preferably one that can be used for serving.

Heat butter in a saucepan and sauté onion until tender. Remove from heat and add croutons, cracker crumbs, poultry seasoning, pickle juice, and salt and pepper to taste. Toss well. Line the bottom of the baking pan with this mixture. Place fish fillets on top. Combine the sour cream and salad dressing and spread evenly over the fish fillets. Sprinkle lightly with salt and pepper and bake for 20 minutes.

Prepare the sauce while the fish is baking. In a saucepan, heat the butter and whisk in the flour. Cook for 2 minutes, whisking, until bubbly. Remove from heat and add the milk all at once, whisking it in vigorously to blend well. Return to heat and cook and stir until the sauce is thick and smooth. Add sherry, crabmeat, and salt and pepper to taste. Heat through but do not boil. Pour some of the sauce over the fish and serve the remainder in a sauce boat.

LITTLENECKS AND SHALLOTS IN BROTH
Serves 4 to 6

3 dozen littlenecks in shells
6 tablespoons clarified butter (page 90)
2 cups chopped shallots
1 clove garlic, chopped
2 cups dry white wine
4 cups chicken broth
1/2 cup chopped fresh parsley

continued

Scrub clams well with a stiff brush and rinse one by one under cold running water. Discard any that are open.

In a large pot, heat butter and sauté the chopped shallots until they become transparent. Add chopped garlic and white wine. Cook briskly for 10 to 15 minutes, or until the wine is reduced by about one-third and the alcohol evaporated. Add chicken broth and bring to a boil. Add the clams and cover the pot. Steam until the clams open, 3 to 5 minutes. Do not overcook the clams or they will be tough and rubbery. Discard any that remain closed even after giving them an extra minute or so to open.

Divide clams in soup plates, cover with broth, and sprinkle with chopped parsley. Serve with cheese toast or hot garlic bread.

MUSSELS CASINO AND BILLI BI SOUP
Serves 4 to 6

4–5 pounds mussels in shells
2 small onions, chopped
2 cloves garlic, chopped
2 sprigs parsley
Freshly ground pepper
Dash cayenne pepper
1/2 bay leaf
1/2 teaspoon thyme
1 cup dry white wine
Garlic salt
Chili sauce
8 strips bacon, cut into small squares
2 cups heavy cream (approximately)
1 egg yolk, lightly beaten
2 tablespoons butter

Scrub the mussels well under cold running water, using a stiff brush. Yank out the beard with your fingers or pliers. Place the mussels in a large kettle with the onions, garlic, parsley, pepper, cayenne, bay leaf, thyme, and wine. Cover and bring to a boil. Steam just until the shells open, about 5 minutes, shaking the kettle a couple of times to redistribute the mussels. Drain mussels, reserving the liquid. Discard any mussels that do not open.

To prepare the Mussels Casino, discard the top shell of each mussel. Arrange mussels in their bottom shells on a cookie sheet. Sprinkle each with garlic salt, dab on ½ teaspoon of chili sauce, and top each with a piece of raw bacon. Broil until bacon is crisp. Serve immediately.

For the Billi Bi Soup, strain the reserved liquid through a double thickness of cheesecloth and measure. Add an equal amount of heavy cream. Heat to the point where a film forms on top, but do not allow to boil.

Remove from heat. Stir a little of the liquid into the beaten egg yolk and return the egg yolk to the kettle, stirring it in slowly. Add the butter and heat just long enough for the soup to thicken a bit. Do not let it boil. Serve hot or cold. Serves 4.

The chef says: "This is an elegant two-in-one dish."

MUSSELS IN CREAM
Serves 4

SAUCE
½ cup (1 stick) butter
½ cup all-purpose flour
4 cups half-and-half
2 tablespoons Worcestershire sauce
1 tablespoon minced onion
1 clove garlic, minced
¼ teaspoon salt
Dash of white pepper

MUSSELS
40 mussels in shells
1 cup (2 sticks) butter, cut into small pieces
1 cup dry white wine
2 tablespoons minced fresh parsley

continued

In a 2-quart saucepan, heat the butter and stir in the flour with a wire whisk. Cook over low heat, whisking, for 2 or 3 minutes, until the mixture is bubbly, but don't let it change color. Remove pan from heat and, when the *roux* has stopped bubbling, add the half-and-half all at once and beat it vigorously with the whisk to blend smoothly. Return to moderate heat and stir in Worcestershire sauce, onion, garlic, salt, and pepper. Continue to cook and whisk until the sauce is thickened and smooth, 10 to 12 minutes longer, and then simmer slowly, stirring occasionally, 15 minutes longer. Strain sauce and set aside.

Scrub mussels well with a stiff brush and clip off beards with scissors. Place mussels in a heavy 8-quart or larger pot. Add butter and wine and heat until butter is melted. Cover pot and steam over medium heat about 5 minutes, or until the mussels open. Discard any that do not open even after you give them a little extra time. When the mussels are open, you may remove the empty half of the shell or not, as you prefer.

Arrange mussels in a large tureen or in individual bowls. Add cream sauce and parsley to liquid in the pot and heat through. Pour sauce over mussels. Serve with warm, crusty French bread to sop up every drop of the delicious sauce.

ANDOVER INN

MUSSELS PROVENÇALE
Serve 4 per portion as appetizer; 8 as main course (serves 6)

4 dozen mussels in shells
$\frac{1}{2}$ cup water
5 shallots, finely minced
2 cloves garlic, finely minced
$\frac{1}{4}$ cup finely minced fresh parsley
$\frac{1}{2}$ teaspoon salt
Freshly ground pepper
1 cup (2 sticks) butter at room temperature
2 egg yolks
1 cup breadcrumbs

Scrub mussels well with a stiff brush and clip off the beards with scissors. Place the mussels in a large kettle. Pour over them ½ cup water and cover tightly. Steam over medium heat. Shake the kettle a few times (with your hands protected by heavy pot holders) so that the mussels change their levels and cook evenly. Steam until the shells open, 5 minutes or so. If any do not open even after you give them a little extra time, discard them. Loosen the mussels from the shells, discard the empty half shells, and replace the mussels in the remaining half shells.

In a small bowl, blend together shallots, garlic, parsley, salt, pepper, softened butter, egg yolks, and breadcrumbs. Cover mussels in the shells with the mixture and arrange on a baking pan. Bake in a 375° oven for about 10 minutes, or until heated through.

Gateways Inn
OLD BOSTON HADDOCK PUDDING
Serves 6

2¹/₂ pounds fresh haddock fillets
Salt and white pepper
2–3 tablespoons lemon juice
1–2 tablespoons Worcestershire sauce
3 medium potatoes, unpeeled
2 tablespoons butter
1 large onion, sliced or diced
3 medium eggs, beaten
¹/₂ cup sour cream
¹/₂ cup milk
Pinch nutmeg
¹/₂ cup buttered breadcrumbs

Sprinkle the haddock fillets with salt, pepper, lemon juice, and Worcestershire sauce. Let stand for 45 minutes.

Partially cook the unpeeled potatoes: they should be just slightly tender, but still firm. When cool enough to handle, peel and slice.

Preheat oven to 400°. Butter a 3-quart casserole or baking dish. Arrange the potatoes and haddock in layers in casserole.

Melt the butter in a skillet and sauté the onion until transparent. Do not brown. Spread over the haddock-and-potato mixture.

Combine the eggs, sour cream, milk, and nutmeg, and pour over the contents of the casserole. Cover with buttered breadcrumbs. Bake for 25 to 30 minutes.

The chef says: "Instead of fresh fish, you may substitute smoked or kippered fish (finnan haddie)."

OYSTERS VICTORIA
Serves 4 or 5

3 cups (about 1¹/₂ pounds) cooked baby shrimp
3 cups (about 1¹/₂ pints) fresh shucked oysters, drained

MORNAY SAUCE
5 tablespoons butter
5 tablespoons all-purpose flour
2¹/₂ cups light cream
1 cup (4 ounces) shredded medium Cheddar cheese
¹/₂ cup freshly grated Parmesan cheese

Preheat the oven to 350°. Grease an ovenproof au gratin baking dish.

Line the bottom of the baking dish with the baby shrimp. Cover the shrimp with the oysters, making sure there are no small pieces of shell present.

Melt the butter in a heavy-bottomed saucepan. Whisk in the flour and cook for 3 minutes, stirring until bubbly and frothy, but do not let it take on color. Remove from heat and add the cream all at once, whisking vigorously to blend well. Return to moderate heat and continue to cook and stir until the sauce becomes thick and smooth. Remove from heat and add the cheeses, stirring, until melted and blended.

Pour sauce over seafood and bake until heated through — about 15 to 20 minutes. Do not overcook or the oysters will toughen. Run under the broiler for a minute or two to brown the top, if desired.

The chef says: "Other cheeses may be substituted for the Cheddar and Parmesan in the Mornay sauce."

PAELLA ZINGARA
Serves 4 or 5

6 tablespoons oil
3-pound chicken cut into 8 pieces
Salt and freshly ground pepper
1 cup chopped onion
¹/₄ pound sausage, sliced
¹/₂ cup diced green pepper
1 teaspoon finely minced garlic
2 cups uncooked long-grain rice
1 cup chopped tomatoes (peeled and seeded if fresh, or canned
    Italian plum tomatoes)
1 3¹/₂-ounce jar pimientos, chopped
¹/₄ cup sliced pitted olives
1¹/₂ cups cooked or canned chick peas
4 cups chicken broth
Several pinches saffron threads, dissolved in 2 tablespoons hot
    chicken stock
12–16 mussels or littleneck clams in their shells, well scrubbed
¹/₂ pound raw shrimp, shelled and deveined
Chopped fresh parsley

Heat oil in a large skillet with an ovenproof handle, a 14-inch paella
pan, or a large braising pot. Brown the chicken pieces well. Sprinkle
lightly with salt and pepper. Set aside and keep warm.
    Preheat oven to 375°.
    Sauté the onion, sausage, green pepper, and garlic for 3 minutes.
Add the rice and stir for 1 minute. Add the tomatoes, pimientos,
olives, chick peas, and chicken broth, blending well. Stir in the dissolved saffron threads. Add the reserved chicken pieces, and more salt
and pepper to taste. Cover tightly and bake for 15 minutes. Add the
mussels or clams, and shrimps and continue baking covered for another
15 minutes, or until the liquid is absorbed, the shellfish opened, and
the chicken tender. Sprinkle top with parsley and serve.

SCALLOPS SAUTÉED WITH HERBS
AND VEGETABLES
Serves 6

¹/₄ cup each julienne strips of leeks, carrots, celery, and fennel (if available)
6 tablespoons butter
¹/₂ cup dry white wine
2 pounds bay scallops, or sea scallops cut in thirds
1 tablespoon finely chopped fresh sorrel or spinach
1 tablespoon finely chopped fresh parsley
2 teaspoons finely chopped fresh tarragon and basil leaves, or ¹/₂ teaspoon each of dried
1 large clove garlic, crushed
Salt and freshly ground pepper
1¹/₂ teaspoons all-purpose flour
1 tablespoon butter at room temperature
6 puff pastry shells, baked
Garnish: minced fresh parsley

Cut the vegetables into julienne strips ¹/₈ inch wide and about 1¹/₂ inches long. Heat 2 of the tablespoons of butter in a large frying pan and stir-fry for 1 minute. Add wine and simmer for 3 minutes. Remove from pan and keep warm.

Wipe out the frying pan with paper towels and heat the remaining 4 tablespoons of butter. Pat the scallops dry. Add to the hot butter and cook and stir until almost done, when they begin to lose their translucency and become opaque, about 3 minutes. Add herbs, seasonings, and vegetables in wine. Stir well.

In a saucer, blend together the flour and soft butter. Push scallops and vegetables to the side of the pan and whisk in butter and flour. Cook and stir until bubbly and blend sauce with the contents of the pan. Cook and stir until slightly thickened. Taste and correct seasonings.

Spoon into puff pastry shells and sprinkle with chopped parsley.

SCAMPI IN DILL SAUCE, GLAZED WITH HOLLANDAISE
Serves 4

6 tablespoons butter
3 tablespoons chopped shallots
2 pounds large fresh shrimp, shelled and deveined
¼ cup dry white wine
¼ cup veal stock (p. 91) or beef broth
¼ cup fresh dillweed, chopped
1 cup heavy cream
1 cup Hollandaise sauce (below)
Chopped fresh parsley

Heat the butter in a large skillet; add the shallots and shrimp and sauté for 2 minutes. Turn the shrimp, add the wine and veal stock or beef broth, and sauté for an additional 2 minutes, just until the shrimp turn pink. Remove the shrimp to a warmed shallow baking dish that can be used for serving, and set aside.

Bring the wine and stock or broth to a lively boil and cook until it is reduced by half. Lower the heat, add the dillweed and cream, and simmer until slightly thickened. Remove from heat and blend in a cup of Hollandaise sauce. Pour over shrimp. Place under preheated broiler, keeping a careful watch so that it doesn't burn. Glaze until a nice golden brown, about 30 seconds. Garnish with fresh parsley and serve immediately.

HOLLANDAISE SAUCE
(A recipe for a Hollandaise made in a blender appears on page 93.) Makes about 1½ cups.

4 egg yolks
1 cup (2 sticks) unsalted butter at room temperature, cut into small pieces
½ teaspoon salt
¼ teaspoon white pepper
Juice of ½ lemon

continued

Lightly whisk the egg yolks in a stainless steel mixing bowl. Place over very low heat and whisk until the mixture thickens and becomes creamy, removing the pan from the heat occasionally as you whisk to prevent the yolks from scrambling. Remove from heat and whisk in the softened butter, one piece at a time, blending completely before adding the next piece. Continue whisking until the sauce is the consistency of light mayonnaise. Blend in salt, pepper, and lemon juice.

SCROD À LA JANE
Serves 4

4 8-ounce scrod fillets
1 teaspoon dried basil
1 teaspoon lemon juice
2 cups half-and-half or light cream
Salt and pepper
2 tablespoons butter
1 large onion, thinly sliced
1 medium green pepper, chopped
4 slices bacon, crisp cooked and crumbled

Preheat broiler.

Lightly grease a shallow baking dish large enough to hold the fish fillets in a single layer. Place the scrod in the dish, sprinkle with basil and lemon juice, and broil until just half cooked, 6 or 7 minutes. Remove from broiler and heat oven to 350°.

Pour the half-and-half over the fish and sprinkle with salt and pepper. Continue cooking in the oven for about 15 minutes, or until fish is cooked through.

While the fish is baking, heat the butter in a medium-sized skillet and cook the onion and green pepper until tender, tossing frequently.

Serve the fish garnished with the sautéed onion and green pepper, topped with crumbled bacon.

SEAFOOD STROGANOFF
Serves 4 to 6

4 tablespoons butter
3 tablespoons all-purpose flour
1½ cups chicken broth
1 tablespoon Worcestershire sauce
¼ teaspoon salt
Few dashes Tabasco sauce
1 clove garlic, finely minced
½ cup finely chopped onion
½ pound mushrooms, sliced
½ pound fresh lump or backfin crabmeat, picked over
½ pound medium shrimp, shelled, deveined, and cooked
1 cup sour cream

Heat the butter in a heavy-bottomed saucepan. Whisk in the flour and cook, stirring constantly, for about 2 minutes, or until the mixture is bubbly and frothy, but do not let it take on color.

Remove from the heat and pour in the chicken broth, whisking vigorously to blend well. Return to heat and bring to a slow boil, stirring. Reduce the heat and continue to cook and stir until the sauce is smooth and thickened, 5 minutes or longer. Add Worcestershire sauce, salt, Tabasco, garlic, onion, and mushrooms, and cook over low heat 10 to 15 minutes longer, or until onion is tender. Stir in crabmeat and shrimp and heat through. Taste and correct seasoning.

Just before serving, stir in sour cream and heat, but do not allow to come to a boil. Serve over fluffy boiled rice or in patty shells.

ANDOVER INN

SOLE PANDITTA
Serves 6

CURRY SAUCE
5 tablespoons butter
1 medium onion, finely diced
1 red bell pepper, finely diced
2 cloves garlic, finely minced
Dash of cayenne pepper
1¹/₂ tablespoons turmeric
1¹/₂ tablespoons ground ginger
1¹/₂ tablespoons ground coriander
1¹/₂ teaspoons cinnamon
3 tablespoons all-purpose flour
1¹/₂ cups fish stock (p. 62) or chicken broth
¹/₂ teaspoon sugar
¹/₂ tablespoon lemon juice
Salt
¹/₂ cup (or more) coconut milk*

6 fillets of sole (2¹/₂ to 3 pounds)
Flour for dredging
5 tablespoons butter
2 ginger stems,* finely chopped
2 bananas, sliced
3 tablespoons sliced almonds

For the sauce, heat 2 of the tablespoons of butter in a medium-sized saucepan and add the chopped onion, diced bell pepper, garlic, and a few dashes of cayenne pepper. (People who like an incendiary curry can be more lavish with the cayenne.) Sauté the vegetables, stirring often, until they are tender. Add the turmeric, ginger, coriander, and cinnamon, and mix well. Add the remaining 3 tablespoons of butter and stir until melted. Mix in the flour and blend well. Cook for 2 minutes and add fish stock or chicken broth. Cook and stir until the sauce is smooth and thickened. Add sugar, lemon juice, and salt to taste. Stir in the coconut milk and heat together for a few minutes. Strain sauce through a fine strainer and discard the solids. Taste and correct seasoning. Return to the saucepan and keep warm.

Rinse the fish fillets and pat dry with paper towels. Spread the flour on a square of waxed paper.

Heat 3 tablespoons of the butter in a large frying pan. Dip the fish lightly in the flour and sauté over moderately high heat until delicately browned on one side. Turn and cook the other side. You will probably have to cook the fish in batches, so keep the cooked pieces warm in a 200° oven.

While the fish is cooking, melt the remaining butter in another frying pan and quickly sauté the ginger stems, sliced bananas, and almonds, turning frequently, until lightly browned and heated through.

To serve, pour the curry sauce over the fish and top with the fruit-and-nut mixture.

*Jars of ginger stems preserved in syrup and cans of coconut milk are available in specialty grocery shops.

TOMATOES AND VEGETABLES WITH SHRIMP
Serves 6 to 8

1/4 cup olive oil
2 small onions, quartered and thinly sliced
2 cloves garlic, minced
5 large tomatoes, peeled, seeded, and chopped
2 green peppers, coarsely chopped
6 ounces fresh mushrooms, sliced
1 cup tomato sauce
1/2 cup cold water
1/4 cup dry vermouth
Salt and freshly ground pepper
1/2 teaspoon dried thyme, crushed
1/2 teaspoon dried marjoram, crushed
1 bay leaf
1/2 teaspoon ground turmeric
2 pounds raw shrimp, or 1 pound cooked shrimp, shelled and
    deveined

Heat oil in a large skillet. Add onions and garlic and sauté until tender, but do not brown. Add the tomatoes, green peppers, mushrooms, tomato sauce, and water. Stir and simmer for 5 minutes.

Add vermouth, salt and pepper, thyme, marjoram, bay leaf, and turmeric. Cover and simmer for about 20 minutes, stirring occasionally. Remove bay leaf.

If shrimp are raw, add to sauce and cook 2 to 3 minutes, or until they turn pink. If shrimp are cooked, add to sauce and just heat through. Taste and correct seasoning.

V $Meats$

VEAL

HUNTER-STYLE VEAL WITH SAUCE CHASSEUR
Serves 6

12 pieces thinly sliced veal (approximately 2 ounces each)
Salt and freshly ground pepper
6 thin slices Swiss cheese
6 thin slices ham
1½ cups fresh breadcrumbs
6 tablespoons (or more) oil

SAUCE
2 tablespoons butter
3 shallots, chopped
1 cup sliced mushrooms
½ cup dry white wine
2 tablespoons brandy
1½ cups brown sauce**
½ cup tomato sauce
Garnish: minced fresh parsley

Flatten the slices of veal between 2 pieces of waxed paper with a meat
pounder until very thin. Season lightly with salt and pepper. Place 1
slice of Swiss cheese and 1 slice of ham on 6 pieces of veal, trimming
if necessary to leave a slight border of the meat uncovered. Cover each
with the remaining slices of veal. Press the edges of the meat together
to make them adhere. Spread the breadcrumbs on a square of waxed
paper and dip both sides of the filled veal slices in the breadcrumbs,
pressing them in firmly with your fingers.

Film a large sauté pan with about ¼ inch of oil, and heat. Sauté
as many of the meat pieces as will fit in one layer. Sauté until golden
brown; turn carefully and sauté the other side, a total of 7 or 8 minutes

for both sides. Don't worry if some of the cheese melts and runs out. Keep meat warm until all is done.

Using the same pan, heat the butter and sauté the shallots gently. Add the mushrooms and cook for an additional few minutes. Add the wine and brandy, increase the heat, and cook until sauce is reduced by a third. Add the brown sauce and tomato sauce and simmer until heated through. Serve sauce over browned veal, sprinkled with minced fresh parsley.

**Quick Basic Brown Sauce (Sauce Chasseur) (supplied by the editors)
Makes about 1³/₄ cups

3 tablespoons butter
1 small onion, chopped
1 cup dry red wine
1¹/₂ cups beef broth
¹/₄ teaspoon dried thyme
¹/₂ bay leaf
3 sprigs parsley
2 tablespoons butter
3 tablespoons all-purpose flour
Salt and freshly ground pepper

Melt the butter in a heavy saucepan and add the chopped onion. Cook until the onion turns golden brown. Add the wine and broth and bring to a boil. Add the thyme, bay leaf, and parsley, and boil briskly until the liquid is reduced by one-third.

Knead together the butter and flour to form a ball. (This is called *beurre manié.*) Break off small pieces and add them, a few at a time, to the boiling liquid. Stir continuously with a wooden spoon until the sauce has reached the desired consistency — somewhere between that of light and heavy cream. Add salt and pepper to taste. Strain the sauce, discarding the solids.

SCALOPPINE OF VEAL MARSALA
Serves 4

1 pound veal for scaloppine, thinly sliced
$\frac{1}{2}$ cup all-purpose flour
Salt and freshly ground pepper
6 tablespoons butter
1 medium onion, finely chopped
4–5 tablespoons chopped fresh parsley
Juice of $\frac{1}{2}$ lemon
$\frac{1}{2}$ pound mushrooms, sliced
$\frac{1}{2}$ cup dry Marsala wine
1 cup beef broth

Pound the veal between 2 pieces of waxed paper until very thin. Cut into 1½-inch squares. Combine flour, salt, and pepper on a square of waxed paper.

Heat the butter in a heavy skillet. Dip both sides of the veal pieces in the seasoned flour and shake off excess. (Dip the pieces in flour as you are ready to cook them to keep the flour from becoming soggy, which will prevent proper browning.) When the butter stops foaming, add the veal and brown quickly on both sides. Sauté only as many pieces at a time as will fit in a single layer. Transfer the browned scaloppine to a warmed platter.

Add onions to the skillet and cook until wilted. Add parsley, lemon juice, and mushrooms, and cook an additional few minutes. Add Marsala and beef broth and any of the juices that have collected from the meat. Boil briskly until the sauce is reduced and thickened, scraping up any of the cooking residue stuck to the bottom of the pan. Turn the heat very low and add the scaloppine, basting with the sauce once or twice. Transfer meat and sauce to a warm platter and serve at once.

VEAL AND ASPARAGUS WITH BROWN SAUCE
Serves 4

COGNAC BROWN SAUCE
3 tablespoons butter
2 tablespoons all-purpose flour
1 tablespoon beef base (such as Bovril)
1 cup light cream
½ cup diced ham
3 tablespoons cognac
Salt and freshly ground pepper

1 pound veal cutlets, thinly sliced
1 egg
¼ cup milk
1½ cups fine breadcrumbs
3 tablespoons butter
Juice of ½ lemon
1 tablespoon dry white wine
1 tablespoon chopped fresh parsley
12 asparagus, cooked firm and just tender

For the brown sauce, melt butter in a heavy-bottomed saucepan. Add the flour, and cook and whisk until bubbly, about 3 minutes. Do not let it take on color. Add the beef base, cream, ham, cognac, and salt and pepper to taste. Stir constantly while cooking over medium heat until the sauce is smooth and thickened. Cover top with waxed paper resting directly on the sauce to prevent a skin from forming, and set aside.

Pound the veal cutlets between sheets of waxed paper with a mallet or meat pounder until the slices are about ¼ inch thick. Cut into 4 serving-size pieces.

Beat the egg and milk in a shallow bowl. Spread the breadcrumbs on a square of waxed paper. Dip the cutlets in the egg-and-milk mixture, letting the excess drip off. Then dip into the breadcrumbs. If possible, set aside for 10 to 15 minutes so that the coating can dry.

Heat the butter in a large skillet and sauté the veal cutlets to a golden brown until cooked through, about 3 to 5 minutes on each side. Add lemon juice and wine, and sprinkle cutlets with parsley. While the meat is cooking, gently reheat the sauce over very low heat.

Place each serving of the veal on a dinner plate and arrange 3 asparagus on top. Pour brown sauce over meat and asparagus and garnish with additional parsley. Serve with small boiled new potatoes or rice.

VEAL BIRDS GRISWOLD
Serves 6 to 8

2 pounds veal, thinly sliced
1 cup finely chopped ham
4 shallots, finely chopped
1 clove garlic, finely minced
$1/2$ teaspoon dried rosemary, crumbled
Salt and freshly ground pepper
5 tablespoons clarified butter*
1 cup dry white wine
2 cups chicken broth
$1^{1}/_{2}$ tablespoons all-purpose flour
2 tablespoons chopped fresh parsley

The veal pieces can be approximately 5–6 inches long and $3^{1}/_{2}$–4 inches wide, but it is of no great importance if the sizes vary a bit. Pound the meat slices between 2 pieces of waxed paper to approximate this size.

Mix together the ham, shallots, garlic, rosemary, salt, and pepper. Lay the veal slices flat and spoon the mixture over each slice except for a $1/4$-inch edge all around. Roll up into compact rolls. Secure with toothpicks inserted along the length so that the rolls can be turned while cooking.

Heat the butter in a heavy skillet over medium-high heat. When the butter foam begins to subside, brown the veal birds, turning as often as needed to brown lightly on all sides, about 5 to 7 minutes. Remove rolls and keep warm.

Add the wine to the skillet, turn up the heat, and cook briskly until the wine has been reduced by half, meanwhile scraping up and loosening the brown residue at the bottom of the pan. Add the chicken broth, reserving 3 or 4 tablespoons, and simmer another 15 minutes. Combine the flour and reserved chicken broth in a screw-top jar and shake well until smooth. Stir flour solution into the sauce and cook and stir 5 minutes longer, or until sauce is sufficiently thickened. Taste and correct seasoning.

Return the veal rolls to the skillet and warm them for 3 or 4 minutes, turning them in the sauce. Garnish rolls with chopped parsley and serve with brown rice pilaf.

*The burning point of clarified butter is much higher than that of ordinary butter, so it can be heated to a high temperature without scorching and changing color. To clarify, cut butter into small pieces and melt over moderate heat. Skim off the foam, remove the pan from the heat, and let stand for a few minutes. Skim the clear yellow liquid off the milky residue left on the bottom of the pan. This clear liquid is the clarified butter. It will keep fresh for weeks in the refrigerator.

VEAL LOIN CHOPS WITH CREAM AND CHIVES
Serves 4

4 lean veal loin chops about 1¹/₂ inches thick
Salt and freshly ground pepper
¹/₂ cup all-purpose flour
3 tablespoons butter
¹/₂ cup dry white wine
¹/₂ cup veal stock** or beef broth
1 cup heavy cream
2 tablespoons chopped fresh chives
2 tablespoons unsalted butter
1 teaspoon lemon juice
Garnish: watercress sprigs

Season veal chops lightly with salt and pepper. Dust chops lightly on both sides in flour, shaking off the excess.

Heat butter in a large skillet until very hot. Add the chops and sauté approximately 7 minutes on each side until golden brown. Remove the chops from the skillet, transfer to a serving platter, and keep warm in a 200° oven.

Pour off the excess grease from the skillet, add the wine, and boil rapidly over high heat until reduced by half, scraping up all the browned bits on the bottom of the pan. Add the veal stock or beef broth and continue to cook over high heat until reduced to ½ cup.

Add the cream and reduce heat to low. Simmer slowly until slightly thickened, about 5 minutes. Blend in the chives, unsalted butter, and lemon juice. Taste sauce and correct seasoning, if necessary. Bring the sauce just to a simmer, but do not boil. Pour sauce over the chops and garnish with watercress.

**Veal Stock *(supplied by the editors)*
Makes about 2½ quarts

Veal stock is a useful preparation to have on hand for fine sauces and soups. The high gelatin content of veal bones gives it a unique richness of flavor and body. Veal stock must be prepared in advance of use and it may be frozen.

> 4 pounds cracked raw veal bones (neck and bony parts of shoulder)
> Veal shank
> 1 peeled onion, stuck with 2 cloves
> 2 carrots, scraped and cut in two
> 2 stalks of celery with leaves, cut in two
> 1 bay leaf
> 1 sprig parsley
> 6 crushed peppercorns
> 3 quarts cold water
> 1 teaspoon salt

To lessen the need for skimming (veal gives off a large amount of scum), first place the veal bones and shank in a kettle and cover with cold water. Bring to a boil and boil slowly for 5 minutes. Rinse the bones and meat under cold running water and wipe out the kettle thoroughly. Replace the veal in the kettle and proceed.

Put all the ingredients except the salt in the kettle. Bring slowly to a boil and skim off all the scum that forms on the surface. Reduce the heat so that the stock simmers gently. Skim as needed. Tilt the cover so that the pot is partly covered and cook slowly for 4 hours, or longer, if you have time. Add the salt toward the end of the cooking.

Remove the stock from the heat, strain through a very fine sieve into a bowl. Cool until the fat rises to the top and remove it. Cover the stock when cool and refrigerate or freeze.

Palmer House
VEAL MEDALLIONS ZÜRICHER ART
Serves 4

1–1½ pounds boneless veal fillets
4 tablespoons butter
1 onion, finely chopped
¾ cup all-purpose flour, spread on a square of waxed paper
½ cup dry white wine
½ cup beef broth
6 ounces fresh mushrooms, sliced
Salt and freshly ground pepper
¼ cup light cream
1 tablespoon chopped fresh parsley

Put the meat between 2 pieces of waxed paper on a cutting board and pound with a meat pounder until very thin. Cut into pieces 1½ to 2 inches square.

Melt the butter in a skillet and add the chopped onion. Cook, stirring occasionally, until lightly browned. Remove onion from skillet with a slotted spoon and set aside. Dip the meat pieces lightly in the flour, shaking off the excess, and cook quickly over high heat until the veal is lightly browned on both sides. Don't overcrowd the pan; you may have to do this in batches.

Return the onion to the meat in the pan and stir in wine, beef broth, mushrooms, and salt and pepper. Reduce heat to medium low and cook 3 to 5 minutes longer, stirring occasionally. Remove from heat and stir in cream. Let stand for a few minutes. Transfer to a warm platter and sprinkle with chopped parsley. Serve with noodles or spätzle, if available, and sliced tomatoes.

The chef says: "This is a remarkably simple recipe for a real gourmet treat. However, don't try to double the recipe in the same pan — it doesn't work. If serving eight persons, use two skillets."

VEAL OSCAR
Serves 4

4 5-ounce slices of veal
$^1/_2$ cup all-purpose flour
Salt and freshly ground pepper
4 tablespoons butter
1 cup crabmeat
12 cooked asparagus tips
Hollandaise sauce**

Put the veal between 2 pieces of waxed paper on a cutting board and pound very thin. Combine the flour, salt, and pepper on a square of waxed paper.

Heat the butter in a heavy skillet. Dip the meat slices lightly in the seasoned flour and shake off excess. When the butter stops foaming, add the meat and brown quickly on both sides. (Dip the veal slices in flour only as you are ready to cook them and sauté only as many as will fit on the bottom of the pan without crowding.) If the veal is thin, it will need only a minute or two on each side. Remove to a heated serving platter as the slices are cooked.

Cover each slice of veal with crabmeat and top with 3 asparagus tips. Serve with Hollandaise sauce.

**Quick Blender Hollandaise Sauce (supplied by the editors)
Makes about $^3/_4$ cup

3 egg yolks
2 tablespoons fresh lemon juice
$^1/_2$ teaspoon salt
Dash of Tabasco sauce or cayenne pepper
$^1/_2$ cup (1 stick) unsalted butter, melted and hot

Combine the egg yolks, lemon juice, salt, and Tabasco sauce or cayenne pepper in a blender and blend until eggs are foamy, about 5 seconds. Heat the butter until it sizzles, but do not let it brown. Remove the center insert from the cover of the blender (the cover prevents spattering) and, with the machine running, pour in the bubbling hot butter in a thin steady stream. The sauce will thicken very quickly, in seconds. If it is too thick, stir in 1 or 2 tablespoons of hot water. Taste and correct seasonings. Serve at once.

Snowbill

VEAL PICCATA
Serves 4

1 pound veal for scaloppine, thinly sliced
$\frac{1}{2}$ cup all-purpose flour
6 tablespoons butter
2 tablespoons fresh lemon juice
2 tablespoons finely chopped fresh parsley
Freshly ground pepper
1 lemon, thinly sliced

Pound veal slices between 2 sheets of waxed paper until paper-thin. Dip one side in flour and shake off excess. Heat butter in a large skillet until it foams up. When the foam subsides, place the scaloppine in the hot butter. (Cook only as many pieces at one time as will fit comfortably in the pan without crowding.) Cook the scaloppine until lightly browned on one side; turn and brown the other. If the meat is thin enough, it should be completely cooked in about 1 minute.

Remove veal from the pan and keep warm. Add lemon juice to the butter in the pan and heat quickly. Pour over veal. Then sprinkle with parsley, pepper, and garnish with a thin slice of lemon.

The chef says: "We are best known for our Veal Piccata. Our secret is to buy the very best white, milk-fed veal, and beat the slices paper-thin."

BEEF

BEEF CARBONNADE
Serves 4

2 large onions
2 tablespoons butter
2 pounds lean beef, top round, in 1½-inch cubes
4 slices bread (crusts removed, unless homemade)
3–4 tablespoons dark mustard
German dark beer
Salt and freshly ground pepper
½ teaspoon dried thyme
1 small bay leaf

Peel and chop onions. Heat butter in a heavy kettle or Dutch oven and sauté onions until lightly browned, stirring from time to time. Remove onions from pan with a slotted spoon and set aside.

Sauté the beef quickly in the same pan until browned on all sides. Do not crowd pan; sauté the meat cubes in batches, if necessary. Add more butter if needed. Add the bread, crumbled, and the mustard. Pour the beer over all, just covering the meat. Add salt and pepper to taste, thyme, and bay leaf.

Adjust heat to very gentle simmering, cover, and simmer for 1½ to 2 hours, or until meat is tender. Serve with broad noodles.

The chef says: "Excellent at lunch."

BEEF STROGANOFF
Serves 4 or 5

1–1½ pounds boneless sirloin steak or beef tenderloin, cut in ½-inch-thick slices
⅓ cup all-purpose flour seasoned with ½ teaspoon salt
4 tablespoons butter
1 cup thinly sliced mushrooms
½ cup chopped onion
1 clove garlic, minced
3 tablespoons all-purpose flour
1 tablespoon tomato paste
1¼ cups beef broth
1 cup sour cream
2 tablespoons dry sherry
½ teaspoon dried dillweed
Salt and freshly ground pepper

Cut the meat into strips ¼ inch wide and cut the strips into 2-inch lengths. Dredge the meat strips lightly in the seasoned flour.

Heat 2 tablespoons of the butter in a large skillet. Add half the meat strips and toss them constantly with a wooden spoon until browned on all sides. Remove to a platter using a slotted spoon and brown the remaining meat. Keep meat warm.

Add to the skillet the mushrooms, onion, and garlic. Sauté, stirring, for 4 to 5 minutes, or until the onion is soft. Add more butter if needed. Remove the vegetables from the skillet with a slotted spoon and keep warm.

Add the remaining 2 tablespoons of butter and 3 tablespoons of flour to the skillet and stir well to blend. Stir in the tomato paste and cook and stir for 2 minutes. Slowly add the beef broth and cook and stir over moderate heat until the sauce becomes thick and smooth. Return the meat, with whatever pan juices have formed, and vegetables to the skillet and heat through. Stir in the sour cream, sherry, and dillweed. Taste for seasoning and add salt and pepper as needed. Warm gently without boiling. Serve with cooked broad noodles.

The chef says: "This recipe can be doubled easily, but watch the amounts of sour cream and beef stock used. Half again the amount of each may be sufficient."

CARBONNADE DE BOEUF BOURGUIGNON
Serves 6

3 pounds beef rump, trimmed and cut into 2-inch cubes
1 cup red Burgundy wine
2 whole cloves
1 large bay leaf
8 crushed peppercorns
1 teaspoon salt
2 cloves garlic
4 slices bacon, cut into small pieces
2 cups beef broth
1 large *bouquet garni**
4 carrots, scraped and cut bite-size
2 onions, sliced
³/₄ pound mushrooms, sliced
1 medium turnip, scraped and cut bite-size
Chopped fresh parsley

In a large glass or stainless steel bowl (not aluminum), marinate the meat cubes in the wine, cloves, bay leaf, peppercorns, salt, and one garlic clove for an hour or longer, stirring occasionally. Refrigerate if marinating for a longer time.

In a large skillet, over low heat, cook the bacon until fat is melted. Reserve the fat; remove the bacon bits with a slotted spoon and set aside.

Drain the meat, reserving the marinade. Pat the meat dry with paper towels and add to the skillet with the bacon fat and remaining garlic clove. Sear over high heat, turning meat cubes until well browned. (Don't put more into the pan than will fit in a single layer or the meat won't brown properly.) Discard the garlic clove.

When all the meat is browned, transfer to an ovenproof casserole. Heat the marinade to the boiling point and add to the meat with the beef broth and *bouquet garni*. Bring the mixture to a full boil and boil for 10 minutes. Reduce heat and simmer uncovered slowly for 30 minutes.

Heat oven to 350°. Add carrots, onions, mushrooms, turnip, and bacon bits to the casserole. Cover casserole, transfer to oven, and bake for 1¹/₂ hours, or until meat is tender. Discard *bouquet garni*. Serve in casserole or transfer to a heated bowl and garnish top with chopped parsley. Steamed new potatoes are a good accompaniment.

*A *bouquet garni* is a combination of herbs such as parsley, thyme, bay leaf, and other favorite herbs such as chervil or basil, tied together in a square of cheesecloth for easy removal.

Gateways Inn
FILLET OF BEEF WELLINGTON
Serves 6

2-pound beef tenderloin, well trimmed
Salt and freshly ground pepper
$^1/_2$ teaspoon dry mustard
2 tablespoons clarified butter (page 90)

PÂTÉ
4 tablespoons butter
1 medium onion, finely diced
1 clove garlic, finely minced
1 cup ground veal
$^1/_2$ cup chicken livers, ground or minced
1 pound mushrooms, finely diced
$^1/_4$ cup cognac
1 tablespoon diced truffles (optional)
$^1/_2$ cup liver pâté

2 pounds puff pastry dough
2 eggs, beaten

Trim the beef tenderloin neatly, removing silver skin and tendons. Rub meat with salt, pepper, and dry mustard. Heat the clarified butter in a large skillet or sauté pan and sauté the tenderloin until lightly browned on all sides, turning it with kitchen tongs to brown evenly. Remove from pan and let cool.

Using the same pan for the pâté, heat the butter and sauté the onions and garlic until the onion is limp and transparent. Add the ground veal and chicken livers and cook, stirring, for 5 minutes. Add the mushrooms and sauté 2 minutes longer. Add the cognac, truffles, and liver pâté. Sauté for 3 more minutes, or until the liquid has evaporated. Let cool.

Preheat oven to 450°. Grease a large baking sheet.

On a floured pastry board, roll out the puff pastry to a thickness of ¼ inch. Spread the pâté on the puff pastry ½ inch thick. Place the tenderloin upside down, over it. Spread more pâté over the tenderloin until it is completely coated. Brush the ends of the puff pastry with the beaten egg. Carefully wrap the tenderloin in the pastry, turning in the ends. Press all the seams firmly together.

Place the tenderloin, seam side down, on baking sheet. Brush the pastry with the beaten egg. Cut some decorative pieces from leftover pastry — circles, leaves, etc. — and brush the cut-outs with beaten egg. Place them on the wrapped tenderloin.

Place in hot oven and bake for 20 to 25 minutes or until puff pastry is golden brown.

HUNGARIAN GOULASH
(Hungarian *Gulyás*)
Serves 6 to 8

    2 tablespoons butter
    4 tablespoons oil
    5–6 medium onions, sliced
    1 large clove garlic, finely minced
    3 tablespoons sweet Hungarian paprika
    3 pounds beef (cross rib, chuck, or rump) cut into 2-inch cubes
    Salt and freshly ground pepper
    3 tablespoons cider vinegar
    2½ cups (approximately) water or beef broth
    6 medium potatoes

Heat the butter and oil in a large heavy kettle or a 12-inch sauté pan. Add the sliced onions and sauté over medium heat until golden, stirring them often so they won't stick or scorch. Mix in the garlic and paprika and cook for 2 or 3 minutes. Remove the onions with a slotted spoon and set aside. Add the beef cubes in small batches and brown well on all sides. Add more oil if needed. Sprinkle meat with salt and pepper.

When all the beef cubes are browned, return them to the pan with the onions. Stir in the vinegar and just enough water or beef broth to cover the meat. Cover pot and simmer slowly until the meat is tender when pierced with the point of a knife, about 2 hours. Stir occasionally.

While the meat is cooking, peel the potatoes and cut them into chunks slightly larger than the meat cubes. About 30 minutes before the meat is done, add the potatoes and continue to cook, covered, until tender. Taste and correct seasoning.

The innkeeper says: "Make more *gulyás* than you need — the taste improves with reheating."

MEATBALLS WITH TOMATO SAUCE
Serves 6 to 8 as main course; 12 as appetizer

MEATBALLS
2 pounds lean chopped beef
3–4 slices white bread, crusts trimmed, shredded
2 eggs
1 teaspoon salt
1–2 cloves garlic, crushed or finely minced
1/8 teaspoon dried oregano
2 tablespoons finely minced fresh parsley
1/8 teaspoon dried mint
1/4 cup (approximately) cold water

TOMATO SAUCE
2 tablespoons butter
1 small onion, chopped
3 cups tomato puree
1 6-ounce can tomato paste
Salt and freshly ground pepper

Mix all the meatball ingredients, except the water, together in a large bowl. Use your hands and blend lightly. Add as much water as needed to hold mixture together. Heat oven to 350°.

Form the mixture into balls, rolling them between the palms of your hands. To make the rolling easier, wet your palms from time to time. Make the balls about the size of a walnut or larger, depending on whether you want them for hors d'oeuvres or a main course. Place in a single layer in a shallow, lightly greased baking pan. Bake for about 20 minutes and remove from oven.

Sauce: Melt butter in a saucepan and sauté the onion until transparent. Add remaining ingredients and simmer, covered, for at least 30 minutes. If the sauce seems too thin, uncover for the last 10 minutes. Taste and correct seasoning.

Place meatballs in tomato sauce and simmer slowly until ready to use.

The innkeeper says: "We use the meatballs without the tomato sauce on a buffet table."

STUFFED PEPPERS
Serves 4

4 medium green peppers, tops removed and seeded
2 tablespoons butter
¹/₂ cup finely chopped onion
1 pound extra-lean ground beef
1 cup tomato sauce
1 8³/₄-ounce can whole kernel corn, drained (optional)
2–3 teaspoons chili powder
1 teaspoon salt
³/₄ cup (about 3 ounces) grated sharp Cheddar cheese

Preheat oven to 375°. Cook peppers in boiling salted water for 5 minutes and drain well, cut side down.

In a medium-sized skillet, sauté chopped onion in butter until soft-but not brown. Add meat and sauté, stirring it around, until it loses its raw look. Mix in tomato sauce, optional corn kernels, chili powder, and salt to taste.

Fill drained peppers with meat mixture and place in deep baking dish just large enough to hold the peppers snugly. Add ½ inch of water to bottom of baking dish. Bake for 20 minutes. Sprinkle tops of peppers with grated cheese. Continue to bake another 10 minutes or until cheese is melted and peppers are heated through.

SUKIYAKI
Serves 6 to 8

¼ cup soy sauce
2 tablespoons sugar
½ teaspoon cornstarch
2 teaspoons chicken broth (made with chicken bouillon cube or instant chicken broth powder)
2 tablespoons oil
½ medium cabbage, cut into bite-sized pieces
12 scallions (green onions), cut into 2-inch lengths
1 large carrot, scraped and thinly sliced in rounds
½ pound fresh mushrooms, sliced
¼ pound fresh bean sprouts, rinsed in cold water and drained
2 stalks celery, thinly sliced
1 pound beef steak, very thinly sliced*
½ pound fresh spinach, well washed and drained, torn into bite-sized pieces

Blend soy sauce, sugar, cornstarch, and chicken broth in a small bowl and set aside.

Heat oil in a large skillet over medium-high heat. Add cabbage,

---

*It is essential that the meat be sliced paper-thin for this preparation and thus it is a project for your butcher's slicing machine, rather than the hand of man (or woman). The tip of the sirloin is a popular cut, although any good-quality boneless beef steak can be used. It is also possible to substitute the very thinly sliced rare roast beef from your corner delicatessen if the butcher cannot provide the proper cut.

scallions, and carrot, and stir to blend. Pour soy sauce mixture over vegetables. Cover and simmer 5 minutes.

Add mushrooms, bean sprouts, and celery. Cover and simmer 2 minutes. Stir. Add meat and spinach and simmer 2 minutes. Serve hot with rice.

🏠 Sugar Hill Inn
SUNDAY NIGHT STEAK SANDWICH
Serves 6

$^2/_3$ cup beer
$^1/_3$ cup oil
1 teaspoon salt
1 clove garlic, finely minced
$^1/_4$ teaspoon pepper
2-pound flank steak
2 tablespoons butter
$^1/_2$ teaspoon paprika
Dash of salt
4 cups thinly sliced onion
12 slices French bread, toasted
1 cup sour cream
$^1/_2$ teaspoon horseradish, or more, according to taste
Paprika

In a shallow glass or porcelain-lined dish, combine the beer, oil, salt, garlic, and pepper. Place flank steak in the marinade and cover. Marinate overnight in the refrigerator or for several hours at room temperature.

When ready to cook, melt the butter in a large skillet and blend in the paprika and a dash of salt. Add the sliced onions and cook until tender, but don't let them brown. Stir them from time to time as they cook.

Preheat the broiler. Remove the flank steak from the marinade and pat dry with paper towels. Place on a rack over a drip pan and broil 2 inches from the heat for 4 or 5 minutes on each side for medium, 3 to 4 for rare.

Remove to a carving board and slice thinly on the diagonal across the grain. For each serving, arrange the meat slices over 2 slices of toasted French bread and top with cooked onions. Combine the sour cream and horseradish and spoon over each open sandwich. Sprinkle with paprika.

VIENNESE BEEF CUTLET WITH ONIONS
(Zwiebelrostbraten)
Serves 4 or 5

2 thin slices boneless sirloin steak (1½ to 2 pounds in all)
2 tablespoons oil
Salt and freshly ground pepper
⅓ cup all-purpose flour
3 tablespoons butter
2 large onions, thinly sliced

Place the steaks between 2 pieces of waxed paper and pound with a meat pounder to a thickness of about ¼ inch. Make shallow cuts at 1-inch intervals in the outside rim of fat so the steaks will lie flat and cook evenly.

Heat 2 tablespoons of oil in a large skillet. You may be able to cook only one steak at a time. Sprinkle meat lightly with salt and pepper and dip one side in flour, shaking off excess. Brown the floured side first for about 5 minutes and turn with kitchen tongs to brown the unfloured side. It will need a total of 8 to 10 minutes, depending on the thickness of the meat and your preference for rare, medium, or well done. When done to your liking, keep the cooked steak warm in a 250° oven while you prepare the second. Add more oil if needed.

While the meat is cooking, melt the butter in another skillet, add the sliced onions, and sauté until golden, turning them frequently so they don't scorch or become too brown.

When all the meat is cooked, pour off all but a tablespoon or two of fat from the pan, add about 3 or 4 tablespoons of water to the pan drippings, and with a wooden spoon scrape up all the browned bits on the bottom of the pan. Cook and stir for a few minutes over medium heat until well blended. Transfer steaks to a warmed platter, pour the gravy over, and top with sautéed onions.

The innkeeper says: "Zwiebelrostbraten tastes very good with roasted potatoes or semolina dumplings. *Guten Appetit.*"

YANKEE POT ROAST
Serves 6 (4 pounds); 8 or 9 (6 pounds)

4–6-pound beef roast (bottom, top, or eye round)
Salt and freshly ground pepper
6 tablespoons oil
2–3 stalks celery, chopped
2 carrots, scraped and sliced
1 onion, cut in chunks
1 bay leaf
3–4 fresh tomatoes, or one 1-pound can tomatoes
Water, beef broth, or a combination

GRAVY
4 tablespoons butter
Salt and freshly ground pepper
4 tablespoons all-purpose flour
3 cups stock (reserved from meat)
$1/3$ cup peas
$1/3$ cup carrots cut in small cubes
$1/3$ cup tender string beans, cut in $1/4$-inch slices
1 stalk celery, cut in $1/4$-inch pieces

Preheat oven to 450°. Tie the roast if necessary to keep it in shape. Salt and pepper the meat and place in a heavy kettle, such as a Dutch oven, with the oil. Sear the meat in the hot oven for 30 minutes, turning from time to time to brown evenly.

Add celery, carrots, onion, bay leaf, and tomatoes, and continue cooking for an additional 10 minutes. Remove kettle from oven and add water (or beef broth or a combination) to cover the meat. Do this carefully to avoid spattering. Reduce oven temperature to 325°, cover pot, return to oven, and cook 2 hours or longer, until the meat is easily pierced by a fork. It may need as much as an additional hour, depending on the quality and size of the roast. Turn the meat from time to time.

When the meat is tender, remove it from the kettle and set aside. Strain the stock, pressing it through a strainer to extract all the vegetable juices. Cool the stock and skim fat. (Store overnight in the refrigerator, if possible, for the most complete job of fat removal.) continued

Gravy: In a large saucepan, heat 4 tablespoons of butter. Add salt, pepper, and flour, stirring well to blend. Stir over medium heat until the flour and butter foam and are frothy with little bubbles. Remove from heat and add 3 cups of strained stock, whisking it in quickly and thoroughly. Return to heat and continue to cook and stir until the mixture reaches the desired thickness and is smooth. Taste for seasoning and correct. Add the cubed vegetables and cook 10 minutes or so longer, until they soften slightly.

To serve: About 30 minutes before serving, slice the meat in ¼-inch slices and arrange in a large skillet. Cover with the gravy and vegetables. Cover the skillet and place over low heat until thoroughly heated. Transfer to a warm platter and pour some of the gravy over the meat. Serve the remainder in a gravy boat.

The chef says: "Our first choice is bottom round. We cook Yankee Pot Roast ahead of time and reheat it before serving. The vegetables added to the gravy may be varied as desired."

PORK

CHOUCROUTE
Serves 6

3 pounds sauerkraut
3 tablespoons cooking fat, preferably lard
2 medium onions, coarsely chopped
10–15 juniper berries, crushed*
6 peppercorns, crushed
4–5 slices bacon or salt pork
2 or 3 smoked ham hocks (1–1½ pounds total)
1½–2 cups Riesling wine
6 loin pork chops
3 tablespoons butter
6 frankfurters
12 small new potatoes, peeled

Rinse the sauerkraut well in a colander under cold running water. (This gets rid of the salt in which it was pickled.) Then take up large handfuls and squeeze out as much water as possible. Set aside.

Melt the lard or fat in a large braising pan with a cover. Add onions and cook until limp and transparent, but not brown. Add drained sauerkraut, juniper berries, and peppercorns, and mix well. Push down and line the bottom of the pot with the bacon or salt pork and the ham hocks. Add enough wine to almost cover the sauerkraut. Bring to a boil, cover, and reduce heat. Simmer gently for 1 hour.

Trim some of the fat from the chops. Melt the butter in a skillet and brown the chops quickly on both sides over medium-high heat. Sprinkle chops lightly with salt and pepper and arrange the browned chops on top of the sauerkraut. Pour the pan juices over them. Cover pot and simmer slowly another 2 hours. Add frankfurters and cook 20 to 30 minutes longer.

While this is cooking, boil the peeled potatoes. To serve, arrange the drained sauerkraut in the center of a large platter and surround with pork chops, pieces of the ham hocks, and frankfurters. Serve with potatoes.

*If you can't get juniper berries, substitute 2 tablespoons gin. You can substitute knockwurst or smoked bratwurst or any sausage of your choice for the frankfurters if you wish.

GRANE'S SCRAPPLE
Serves 18 or 20

> 3 cups water
> 1 cup cornmeal
> ¹/₂ cup buckwheat flour
> 1¹/₂ pounds ground pork
> 1 tablespoon each chopped fresh parsley and chives
> ¹/₂ teaspoon dried sage or thyme
> 1 teaspoon garlic powder or 1 clove garlic squeezed through a
>   garlic press
> 1¹/₂ cups chicken broth
> Salt and freshly ground pepper

Mix 1 cup of the water with the cornmeal and buckwheat flour and set aside.

In a large, heavy saucepan, combine pork, herbs, garlic or garlic powder, chicken broth, the remaining 2 cups of water, and salt and pepper to taste. Mix well and bring to a boil. Add the cornmeal mixture slowly, stirring continuously. Simmer uncovered for 20 minutes, stirring occasionally, but be careful since sometimes the bubbles burst, spewing hot meal.

Rinse a 5 × 9-inch loaf pan with cold water. Pack the mixture into the pan and press down to compress. Cool thoroughly. When firm, remove from the pan, wrap in plastic, cover with tinfoil, refrigerate until used. For smaller family-size portions, the loaf can be divided into 2 or 4 parts, each individually wrapped, which can be frozen and used as needed.

To serve, cut into ¹/₄-inch slices, flour lightly, and fry in butter until crisp. Serve with maple syrup or honey, with eggs, or as a base for poultry and other dishes.

ANDOVER INN

PORK LOIN HUNTER STYLE
Serves 6 to 8

3 pounds boneless pork loin
Salt and pepper

MARINADE
2 cups dry white wine
1 tablespoon oil
2 bay leaves
$^1/_2$ onion, sliced
2 cloves garlic, chopped
6 peppercorns, crushed
1 teaspoon juniper berries, crushed

$^1/_2$ cup all-purpose flour spread on a square of waxed paper
3 tablespoons butter
2 cups fresh cranberries
$^1/_2$ cup water
$^1/_2$ cup sugar
3 tablespoons all-purpose flour
3 tablespoons cold water

Trim some of the fat from the meat and discard. Tie the roast with butcher's twine to hold its shape. Sprinkle the meat lightly with salt and pepper.

Combine the marinade ingredients in a stainless steel, glass, or enamel-lined bowl (not aluminum) and mix well. Refrigerate the meat in the marinade for 24 hours, covered, turning it occasionally.

When ready to cook, strain and reserve marinade. Pat the meat dry with paper towels and dredge lightly with flour. Heat the butter in a braising pot, Dutch oven, or ovenproof casserole just large enough to hold the meat. Place the meat in the pan, fat side down. Brown well on all sides, lower the heat, and add the strained marinade. Cover partially and cook slowly for 1$^1/_2$ to 2 hours or until meat can be pierced easily with a fork. Turn and baste meat from time to time.

While the meat is cooking, wash the cranberries. In a small saucepan bring $^1/_2$ cup water to a boil and add the cranberries and sugar. Cook for 7 to 10 minutes, or until the skins burst. Skim off white foam and set cranberries aside. Keep warm.

When the meat is tender, remove to a cutting board and tent lightly with foil. Skim off most of the fat from the pot with a spoon and discard. Dissolve the 3 tablespoons flour in the cold water and add to the sauce. Cook and stir over medium heat, scraping and loosening all the brown particles on the bottom of the pan, until the sauce becomes smooth and thickened. Taste and correct seasoning.

Remove the trussing string from the meat, carve into slices about 3/8 inch thick, and place on a warmed serving platter. Spoon some of the cranberries over the meat slices and cover with the sauce. Serve with Brussels sprouts and fluffy mashed potatoes.

Lincoln House

ROAST LOIN OF PORK WITH CHERRY GLAZE
Serves 5 or 6

4–5-pound pork loin roast
Salt
1 teaspoon dried tarragon (optional)
1/2 cup cherry preserves
1/4 cup dark corn syrup
2 tablespoons vinegar
1/8 teaspoon nutmeg
1/8 teaspoon cinnamon
1/8 teaspoon ground cloves
1/8 teaspoon salt
Few grinds of pepper

Preheat oven to 350°. Trim some of the excess fat from the loin and discard. Rub meat lightly with salt, and tarragon, if desired. Place the loin, fat side up, on a rack in a shallow roasting pan. Roast uncovered for about 25 to 30 minutes per pound, or about 2 to 2 1/2 hours. (The internal temperature, with the thermometer placed in the thickest part, not touching the bone, should register 165°.)

Mix the remaining ingredients together in a small saucepan and simmer gently for 10 minutes.

When the meat is done, transfer it to a carving board and let it rest for 10 minutes. Cut the roast into slices, cutting between the bones. Cover with hot glaze and serve at once.

Edson Hill
MANOR

ROAST LOIN OF PORK FLORENTINE
Serves 6

2½–3 pounds boneless center-cut pork loin
2 tablespoons Dijon mustard
2–3 cloves garlic, minced
Salt and freshly ground pepper
8–10 sprigs fresh parsley
1 cup cooked spinach
Pan gravy**

Preheat the oven to 500°. Place the boned pork fat side down on a cutting board, and with a sharp carving knife, make a cut through the thickest part of the meat from top to bottom. Don't cut all the way through; you want only to open the roast so that it will lie almost flat.

Spread the mustard over the opened loin. Sprinkle with garlic, salt, and pepper. Cover the entire surface with parsley sprigs and a layer of cooked spinach, leaving half an inch or so of the meat at both ends uncovered so that you can make a tidy roll without any of the greens showing.

Take one side of the loin and carefully roll it toward the other, taking care that the stuffing stays where it belongs. You should finish the roll-up step with the fat side facing you. Tie the roast securely with butcher's twine at intervals to keep it in shape.

Transfer the meat to a rack in a shallow roasting pan and place in preheated oven. Immediately reduce the heat to 325°. Roast about 1½ to 1¾ hours, or until a meat thermometer inserted into the center registers 165°. Transfer the meat to a warm platter and tent with aluminum foil while you prepare the pan gravy.

To serve, remove the trussing strings, cut meat into slices, and serve with pan gravy. Hot spicy applesauce or apple slices sautéed with brown sugar and butter are a good accompaniment.

Pan Gravy *(supplied by the editors)*

Pour off from the roasting pan all but a tablespoon or two of fat. Mix well with a tablespoon of flour and add a cup or more of chicken or veal broth. Scrape up all the browned residue on the bottom of the pan and stir and cook until well blended. You can enrich the sauce further with cream or a tablespoon of butter swirled in bit by bit. Taste and correct seasoning.

LAMB

Gatewâys Inn

BRAISED LEG OF SPRING LAMB "PASQUALE"
Serves 6 to 8

18 narrow strips prosciutto, 2 inches long
1 cup dry red wine
2 large cloves garlic, finely minced
1 tablespoon chopped fresh parsley
1/2 tablespoon chopped fresh marjoram, or 1/2 teaspoon dried
6–7-pound leg of lamb, trimmed, boned, and rolled
Salt and freshly ground pepper
1–2 cloves garlic, peeled
6 tablespoons butter
1 cup dry white wine
2 tablespoons tomato paste
4 cups brown stock**
4 tablespoons *beurre manié**

Marinate the strips of prosciutto in the red wine with garlic, parsley, and marjoram for 2 to 3 hours. Remove prosciutto and reserve marinade.

Make slits in the lamb with a sharp, pointed knife and insert the strips of prosciutto in the slits. Rub the meat with salt, pepper, and garlic cloves.

Melt the butter in a heavy braising pot over fairly high heat

Beurre manié, kneaded butter, a simple mixture of flour and butter, is a splendid thickening agent for sauces and sometimes soups. Work together equal quantities of slightly softened butter and flour with a fork or your fingers until they form a thick paste. If you wish, you can use slightly more butter.

One full tablespoon of flour and an equal amount of butter are sufficient to transform 2 cups of liquid into a thin sauce.

until it is golden. Add the lamb and brown on all sides, using kitchen tongs to turn the meat. Add the reserved marinade and the white wine and cook over high heat until the liquid has almost evaporated. Stir in the tomato paste, the brown stock, and enough water if necessary to reach about one-third up the sides of the lamb. Bring to a boil, cover the pot, and reduce the heat to low so that the liquid just simmers quietly. Cook for approximately 1³/₄ hours, or until the meat is tender enough to be pierced easily with a meat fork.

Transfer the lamb to a serving platter and keep warm.

Drop balls of *beurre manié* into the pan liquid while cooking and stirring, until the sauce is thickened to your liking. Simmer for about 15 minutes. Cut the lamb into slices and arrange on a platter. Pour the sauce over the slices and serve hot.

**Brown Stock (supplied by editors)
Makes 6 or 7 cups

1 veal knuckle, sawed into 3 pieces
2–3 pounds beef shin or marrow bones or same weight of equal
   amounts of beef bones and stew meat
2 scraped carrots, cut into quarters
1 peeled onion, cut in half
1–2 cups boiling water
2 quarts cold water
1 stalk celery, sliced, with leaves
1 small white turnip, cut into chunks
¹/₂ teaspoon dried thyme
1 bay leaf
5 sprigs parsley, tied in a bundle
1 clove garlic (optional)
3 peppercorns, crushed
Salt

Heat oven to 450°. Arrange the veal knuckle, meat, and bones in a shallow baking pan and place on center rack in oven for about 10 minutes. Turn the meat and bones a few times. Add the carrots and onions and roast for another 35 to 40 minutes or until they are well browned, turning them from time to time so that they brown evenly and do not scorch.

Remove from oven and transfer the browned ingredients to a soup kettle. Discard any fat in the roasting pan and add a cup or two of boiling water to the pan. Place over heat and scrape up all the browned bits on the bottom of the pan. Add to the soup kettle with the 2 quarts of cold water and slowly bring to a boil. Skim off all the scum that forms. Add remaining ingredients except salt and partially cover the pot. Simmer very slowly for 4 or 5 hours. Continue to skim until the foam turns white. Add more boiling water if the level of the liquid evaporates below the ingredients. Add salt during the last hour of cooking and taste shortly before the stock is finished, adding more salt if needed.

Strain and cool uncovered. When cooled, cover and refrigerate. Freeze leftover stock for future use.

LAMB CURRY
Serves 8

    4 tablespoons butter
    2 large onions, chopped
    1 green pepper, seeded and coarsely chopped
    1 large clove garlic
    1 tablespoon (or more) curry powder
    4 tablespoons all-purpose flour
    2½ cups hot beef or chicken broth
    ½ cup tomato juice
    Juice and rind of ½ lemon
    ½ cup raisins
    Salt and pepper to taste
    4 large cooking apples, peeled, cored, and chopped
    4 cups lamb, cubed and cooked

Heat the butter in a large saucepan or skillet and sauté the onions, green pepper, and garlic until the onions are tender and lightly golden. Discard garlic clove.

Stir in the curry powder and cook for 2 or 3 minutes. (Curry powders vary in intensity, so taste as you go, using more or less according to personal preference.) Add flour, hot broth, tomato juice, lemon juice and rind, and bring to a boil, stirring constantly until smooth and thick. Add the raisins, lower heat, and simmer, covered, for half an hour. Season with salt and pepper to taste. Add the chopped apples and lamb and simmer, covered, for 5 to 10 minutes until the apples are tender but still hold their shape, and the lamb is heated through.

Serve with boiled rice and side dishes of chutney, coconut, and slivered toasted almonds.

The Inn at Mt. Ascutney

PERSIAN LAMB
Serves 6 to 8

5–6-pound leg of lamb, boned, all fat removed, cut into 1½- to
   2-inch cubes
2 medium onions, sliced
Salt and freshly ground pepper
Water
½ cup lemon juice
¾ cup chopped fresh parsley
2 16-ounce cans red kidney beans, rinsed and drained
1–2 tablespoons cornstarch dissolved in 2 to 4 tablespoons water
Garnish: plain yogurt

Preheat oven to 400°. Place the lamb cubes in a shallow roasting pan and roast for 30 minutes, stirring them a few times so they brown evenly. Place the sliced onions over the lamb, sprinkle with salt and pepper, and bake until the onions become transparent and limp, about 15 minutes. Pour off excess fat, if there is any.

Add enough water to barely cover the meat and onions and add lemon juice and parsley. Stir well and cover pan with aluminum foil. Lower the oven temperature to 325° and continue cooking the lamb for 45 minutes, or until tender. Add the drained kidney beans and the cornstarch solution. Place the baking pan over the stove burner and heat through, stirring until the sauce is thickened and smooth. Taste and adjust seasoning.

Serve meat, beans, and sauce on a bed of boiled rice. Top meat with a spoonful of yogurt.

Gateways Inn
RAGOÛT OF LAMB À LA MAISON
Serves 6

8 strips of bacon, cut in 1-inch pieces
2–3-pound leg of lamb, cut in large pieces
6 tablespoons all-purpose flour, seasoned with salt and pepper
3 cloves garlic, minced
2 onions, coarsely chopped
2 cups beef broth or bouillon
1½ cups tomato puree
10 black peppercorns, crushed
3 whole cloves
¼ cup chopped fresh parsley
2 small bay leaves
¼ teaspoon dried rosemary, or 1 sprig fresh
½ teaspoon dried marjoram, or 1 sprig fresh
¾ cup dry white wine
6 small potatoes, peeled and quartered
6 medium carrots, peeled and quartered
1 small stalk celery heart, sliced
2 medium parsnips, peeled, cut into ½-inch slices
Garnish: chopped fresh parsley

Sauté the bacon slowly in a large skillet. Remove bacon pieces with a slotted spoon and set aside. Increase the heat and brown the lamb pieces in the hot drippings. Pour off most of the accumulated fat, and sprinkle the meat with the seasoned flour, tossing well.

In a separate saucepan, combine garlic, onions, beef broth, tomato puree, peppercorns, cloves, parsley, bay leaves, rosemary, and marjoram. Heat until boiling.

Place the meat in a heavy skillet or sauté pan and pour the boiling mixture over it. Simmer covered for 1½ hours, or until the meat is tender and can be pierced easily. Stir occasionally. During the last hour of cooking, add the dry white wine.

While the meat is cooking, cook the potatoes, carrots, celery, and parsnips until tender. Drain well and add vegetables and bacon pieces to the ragoût the last 20 minutes of cooking. Taste for seasoning and correct. Transfer to a warmed bowl and sprinkle with chopped parsley.

GAME

STEWED RABBIT
(Hasenpfeffer)
Serves 6 to 8

MARINADE
2 cups dry white or red wine
1 cup water
$^{1}/_{2}$ cup vinegar
1 tablespoon lemon juice
12 peppercorns, crushed
4 cloves garlic, crushed
$^{1}/_{2}$ teaspoon thyme
$^{1}/_{2}$ teaspoon rosemary
$^{1}/_{2}$ teaspoon marjoram
1 cup celery leaves

2 2$^{1}/_{2}$–3-pound rabbits, cut into serving pieces
4 slices bacon, cut in $^{1}/_{4}$-inch squares
1$^{1}/_{2}$ cups diced onion
1 cup small or quartered mushrooms
3–4 tablespoons butter
Salt
Flour for dredging
$^{1}/_{2}$ cup all-purpose flour
$^{1}/_{2}$ cup sour cream

Mix marinade ingredients together in a large glass or stainless steel bowl (not aluminum) and add rabbit. Cover and marinate in the refrigerator for two days, turning the pieces from time to time.

When ready to cook, remove rabbit from the marinade and pat dry with paper towels. Strain marinade and set aside.

In a large heavy kettle or Dutch oven, cook the bacon, onion, and mushrooms until onion is soft, stirring frequently. Remove vegetables and bacon with a slotted spoon and set aside. Add butter to the pan and heat.

Sprinkle the rabbit pieces lightly with salt. Dredge the rabbit pieces in flour, shaking off the excess. Sauté only as many pieces as will fit in one layer at a time without crowding. Turn them carefully with tongs. When all are browned, return them to the pan with the onion mixture. Add strained marinade, cover pan, and simmer slowly until the meat is tender, when the flesh can be pierced without resistance by the point of a small sharp knife, about 1 hour.

Arrange the rabbit pieces on a heated platter and keep warm. Stir flour into sour cream and add to sauce in Dutch oven. Add salt to taste. Heat and stir over low heat until gravy thickens, but don't let it come to a boil. Spoon sauce over rabbit and serve at once.

SUNDAY SUPPER HERBED RABBIT
Serves 3 or 4

1 cup Corn Chex (or similar cereal) crumbs*
1/4 cup all-purpose flour
1 1/2 teaspoons salt
1 1/2 teaspoons paprika
1/4 teaspoon pepper
1/4 teaspoon dried thyme
1/4 teaspoon dried basil
1 egg
1/4 cup milk
2–2 1/2-pound rabbit, cut into serving pieces
1/2 cup butter

Combine the cereal crumbs, flour, salt, paprika, pepper, thyme, and basil, and spread on a large piece of waxed paper. In a shallow bowl, beat the egg and milk together. Dip the rabbit pieces in the egg-and-milk mixture; then roll in crumb mixture. (Or place crumb mixture in a paper bag and shake rabbit pieces to coat.)

Preheat oven to 400°. Melt the butter in a shallow baking pan just big enough to hold the rabbit pieces in a single layer. Place the rabbit pieces in the melted butter and bake for 25 minutes. Turn rabbit pieces and bake for an additional 15 to 20 minutes or until golden brown and tender.

*Approximately 3 cups of uncrushed Chex cereal will yield 1 cup crumbs. A food processor or blender will make the crumb conversion quick and easy.

VI Poultry

CHICKEN

Mountain Top Inn

BREAST OF CHICKEN BARBADOS
Serves 4 or 5

4 whole chicken breasts (about 2 pounds), skinned and boned
2 eggs
⅓ cup milk
1 cup all-purpose flour, seasoned with salt and pepper
4 tablespoons butter
1 tablespoon honey
2½ ounces dark Jamaican rum

Trim chicken breasts of fat and membranes. Cut chicken into ⅜-inch strips. In a shallow bowl, mix eggs and milk to make an egg wash. Spread the seasoned flour on a square of waxed paper. Dip the chicken strips lightly in the flour to coat, then into egg wash, then into flour. Shake off excess flour.

Heat butter in a large sauté pan over medium heat. Add chicken strips and brown lightly on all sides. Don't put more into the pan than will fit in one layer. If the pan is overcrowded, the chicken strips will steam rather than brown. If you sauté the chicken in batches, keep the first part warm while you complete the remainder. They will take only 2 or 3 minutes a side to cook; turn only once. When all the chicken strips are browned, return them to the pan, add honey, and mix well.

Add the rum carefully. It is flammable and might flare up if carelessly spilled. Cook for 10 minutes longer and serve over boiled rice.

CHICKEN BARBAROSSA
Serves 10 to 12

8 whole chicken breasts (about 4 pounds), skinned and boned
6 tablespoons butter

SAUCE BARBAROSSA
$^1/_2$ cup (1 stick) butter
$^1/_4$ cup minced onion
1 cup sliced mushrooms
2 tablespoons all-purpose flour
$^1/_4$ cup Amaretto liqueur
2 cups light cream
1 tablespoon chopped fresh tarragon, or 1 teaspoon dried
Salt and freshly ground pepper

Wash the chicken breasts, pat them dry, and cut them in two. Trim fat and peel off membranes. Heat the butter in a large heavy skillet and, when bubbly and hot, place the fillets in the pan. Put in only as many as will fit in a single layer without crowding, and brown them quickly. If the heat is steady at medium high, they should take only 2 minutes or so on each side. Continue until all are cooked and keep warm.

Using the same skillet for the sauce, heat the butter and add the onion and mushrooms. Cook until the onion is limp and transparent, stirring often. Stir in the flour until completely absorbed. Stir in the Amaretto and cook for 2 minutes. Add the cream and tarragon and simmer over low heat for 5 minutes. Add salt and pepper to taste.

Return the chicken breasts to the sauce, cover pan, and simmer gently for 15 to 20 minutes. Serve hot with sauce and garnish with fresh tarragon if available, or with minced fresh parsley.

The chef says: "Chicken Barbarossa may be refrigerated for two weeks."

CHICKEN BIBIONI WITH MUSHROOMS
Serves 8

2–3¹/₂-pound fryers, each cut into 8 serving pieces
¹/₂ cup oil
3–4 cloves garlic, finely chopped
2 large or 3 medium onions, chopped
6 tablespoons all-purpose flour
3 cups chicken broth
Salt and freshly ground pepper
³/₄ pound mushrooms, sliced
2 tablespoons chopped fresh parsley
1¹/₂ pounds spaghetti
Freshly grated Parmesan cheese

Each chicken, when disjointed, will yield 8 pieces: 2 legs, 2 thighs, 2 wings, and 2 half breasts. (Save the backbones and necks for your next soup.) Prepare a large kettle with 6 quarts of water and 2 tablespoons of salt and start heating it so that it will be boiling when you are ready to cook the pasta.

Heat the oil in a large skillet and brown the chicken quickly on both sides. Remove the pieces as they are browned. When all are done, pour off all but 2 or 3 tablespoons of oil.

Add the chopped garlic and onions to the skillet and sauté until the onions are just tender. Do not brown. Sprinkle with the flour and stir until oil and onion juice moisten all the flour. Stir in the chicken broth and cook, stirring constantly, until the sauce is smooth and thickened. Add salt and pepper to taste. It should be well seasoned with a strong garlic flavor, as it is served over bland pasta.

Return the chicken pieces to the sauce in the pan and add sliced mushrooms and parsley. Simmer covered for 15 to 20 minutes, stirring occasionally, or until chicken is tender.

Ten minutes or so before the chicken is finished, drop the spaghetti into rapidly boiling water and cook until just tender, to the *al dente* ("firm to the bite") stage. Drain immediately.

Remove the chicken to a warmed platter. Toss the spaghetti with the sauce and serve immediately with lots of grated Parmesan cheese sprinkled over the pasta and the chicken.

continued

The innkeeper says: "Another Palmer House favorite from a little family-run restaurant/hotel about a mile back from the tourist-crowded beach at Bibioni, between Venice and Trieste. We traded a recipe for American apple pie for this one, properly called *Chicken Bibioni con Fungi*. Our Italian and their English were practically nonexistent, so we spent an evening with sign language and a bottle of *grapa* to improve the translation."

Switzer Stübli
CHICKEN CORDON BLEU
Serves 4 to 6

> 6 large half chicken breasts, skinned and boned
> Salt and freshly ground pepper
> 6 thin slices cooked ham
> 6 slices Swiss or Parmesan cheese
> ½ cup all-purpose flour
> 2 eggs, well beaten
> 1½ cups breadcrumbs
> 4 tablespoons butter
> 4 tablespoons oil

Lay the chicken breasts, smooth side down, between 2 sheets of waxed paper. With a meat mallet or a heavy pounder, pound each breast to a thickness of between ⅛ and ¼ inch. Don't worry about tears in the meat; chicken is gelatinous and it will mend. Overlap the edges of the tear, cover the patch with waxed paper, and pound it gently until the meat comes together again.

When ready to assemble, sprinkle the breasts lightly with salt and pepper (smooth side down). Place a slice of ham and a slice of cheese on one half of the breast (trimming the ham and cheese if too large), and fold over the other half of the chicken breast. Pinch and pound the edges tightly to seal. Dip lightly in flour, shaking off the excess, then in egg, then in breadcrumbs, pressing with your fingers to make the crumbs adhere. Place the breaded cutlets on a baking sheet lined with waxed paper and refrigerate for an hour or more to give the crust a chance to dry.

Heat oil and butter in a large heavy skillet and sauté chicken over medium heat, turning frequently, for 10 minutes or so until cooked. The cutlets should be nicely browned on the outside and the cheese melted and runny on the inside.

The innkeeper says: "Our restaurant is rather famous for this."

CHICKEN CRÊPES ÉLÉGANTE
Serves 6 to 8 (2 or 3 crêpes per serving)

6 tablespoons butter
6 tablespoons all-purpose flour
Salt and freshly ground pepper
1/4 teaspoon thyme
2 1/2 cups chicken broth
1 cup milk
1 1/2 cups cooked chicken, cut into 1/2-inch cubes or shredded
1/2 cup sliced mushrooms, sautéed in 1 tablespoon butter
1 tablespoon chopped fresh parsley
2 tablespoons dry sherry
16 crêpes (page 65)

Heat butter in a saucepan. Blend in flour, salt, pepper, and thyme. Cook over low heat until bubbly, about 3 minutes. Remove from heat and stir in chicken broth and milk, whisking vigorously to blend well. Return to heat and cook and stir until sauce is smooth and thickened. Add shredded or cubed chicken, sautéed mushrooms, and parsley. Taste and correct seasoning. Add sherry just before serving and heat through.

Place about 1/3 cup of chicken mixture in the center of each cooked crêpe and roll up. Garnish each crêpe with a small amount of filling and a sprinkle of minced parsley.

CHICKEN ELIZABETH
Serves 6

6 6-ounce boneless, skinless chicken breasts
6 ounces Alaskan King crabmeat
6 teaspoons lobster tomalley (optional)
6 puff pastry patty shells, homemade or frozen (see chef's note)
Egg wash, made with 1 egg beaten with ¼ cup of water
2 cups Hollandaise sauce (below)

Pound the chicken breasts between 2 sheets of waxed paper to a thickness of ¼ inch. Spread 1 teaspoon lobster tomalley on inside of breast. Place 1 ounce of crabmeat in center of breast and roll breast into a small log enclosing the tomalley and crabmeat.

Preheat oven to 400°.

If patty shells are frozen, thaw and roll out to a thickness of ⅛ inch and a diameter of approximately 8 inches. Place a chicken breast in the center of the rolled dough, tuck in the sides, and envelop the dough around the chicken breast. Trim away excess dough if overlapping, and place seam side down on an ungreased baking sheet. Repeat process with remaining 5 chicken breasts and pastry rounds. Lightly brush the tops with egg wash to make the crust shiny. Bake for 20 minutes.

Remove chicken from oven and top with Hollandaise sauce.

HOLLANDAISE SAUCE
6 egg yolks
Juice of 1 lemon
⅛ teaspoon salt
1½ cups liquid clarified butter (see page 90)

In the top of a double boiler over hot, but not boiling, water, beat the egg yolks, lemon juice, and salt until the egg yolks have thickened to the consistency of heavy cream. Slowly whisk in the warm, but not hot, melted butter and whisk until very thick. When the sauce is thick enough to coat the whisk, it is done. Be careful not to let the eggs get too hot or they will curdle.

The chef says: "We prefer to use our own puff pastry, but to make life easy for everybody we have tested this recipe with frozen patty shells and found that it works quite well.

"This recipe was requested by *Bon Appétit* magazine for publication."

CHICKEN EN CROÛTE
Serves 6

3 tablespoons butter
½ cup broccoli flowerets, cut small
1 small onion, diced
½ cup sliced mushrooms
½ cup diced zucchini
1 pound cooked, diced chicken (3–3½ cups)
¼ pound cooked, diced ham
1 cup (¼ pound) grated Cheddar cheese
Dash of curry powder
Pinch of thyme
½ teaspoon dried basil
Salt and freshly ground pepper
12 sheets phyllo pastry
4–5 tablespoons melted butter (or more)
Brown sauce (below)

Heat the butter in a large saucepan and add the broccoli, onion, mushrooms, and zucchini. Cook over medium heat, stirring occasionally, until the vegetables are crisp-tender. Don't overcook. Add the chicken, ham, cheese, seasonings, and herbs and mix well. Taste and correct seasoning.

Preheat oven to 400°. Butter a cookie sheet.

Lay out 2 phyllo sheets, one on top of the other. Brush with melted butter and cover with 2 more sheets of phyllo. (Keep the reserved phyllo sheets covered with waxed paper and a damp towel, as they dry out quickly.) Cut sheets in two. Place ⅙ of the vegetable-and-meat mixture in the center of each half. Working quickly, tuck in the sides and roll up.

Repeat twice more, for a total of 6 rolls. Place the rolls, seam side down, on the cookie sheet and brush tops with melted butter. Bake for 15 to 20 minutes, or until brown and crisp. Top with brown sauce to serve.

BROWN SAUCE
4 cups beef broth
1 cup tomato puree
1/2 cup chopped leeks
2 sprigs parsley
1 teaspoon orange zest (skin of orange only, without the white part)
1/4 cup dry red wine

Combine all ingredients in a heavy-bottomed saucepan and bring to a boil. Reduce heat and simmer, uncovered, for 1 hour. Strain sauce, or if you wish, you may puree it. (This may be more sauce than you need, but you can freeze the balance. Wonderful to have on hand for gravies and other sauces.)

The chef says: "Instead of the phyllo pastry, you can make a rich pie dough [Pâte Brisée, page 199]. Cut the pie pastry into six pieces and roll each into a rectangle. Place filling in the center of each rectangle and fold over, moistening the edges with water to seal tightly. Crimp edges with the tines of a fork and bake as directed."

ANDOVER INN

CHICKEN INDONESIAN STYLE
Serves 4

2 2–2½-pound broilers, split
2 tablespoons oil
½ cup dry Madeira wine
½ cup dry red wine
2 tablespoons wine vinegar
⅓ cup soy sauce
1½ teaspoons cinnamon
½ teaspoon nutmeg
Pinch ground cloves
2 tablespoons light brown sugar
½ cup finely chopped onion

Preheat oven to 425°. Rinse chickens, pat dry, and trim away and discard visible fat. Rub skin lightly with vegetable oil. Arrange chicken halves in a shallow baking pan and bake for 25 minutes, or until the skin is browned.

While the chicken is baking, mix together the remaining ingredients and blend well.

Remove the pan from the oven when the chicken is browned and pour the wine-and-spice mixture over the chickens. Cover the pan tightly with foil, reduce the heat to 350°, and bake for another 30 to 35 minutes, or until chicken is tender. Serve with fluffy boiled rice.

**Combes
Family Inn**

CHICKEN PICCATA
Serves 6 to 8

4 whole chicken breasts, skinned and boned
2 eggs
2 tablespoons milk
3–3½ cups fresh breadcrumbs (8 slices of bread crumbed in
    processor or blender)
½ cup butter
Salt and freshly ground pepper
Juice of 1 lemon
1½ cups chicken broth
Minced fresh parsley
1 thinly sliced lemon

Cut the breasts in two down the middle and trim away fat and membranes. Pound the chicken breasts, smooth side down, between 2 pieces of waxed paper, to about ⅜-inch thickness. Combine eggs with milk in a shallow bowl and beat well. Spread breadcrumbs on a sheet of waxed paper.

Dip chicken cutlets in egg mixture, then in crumbs, pressing them firmly with your fingers to make them adhere. If you have time, refrigerate them for an hour or so on a waxed paper–lined cookie sheet to firm the coating.

Heat butter in a large skillet and, when hot and bubbling, add as many cutlets as will fit in one layer without crowding. If the cutlets are crowded, they will steam instead of sauté. Brown quickly on both sides, sprinkling with salt and pepper as they cook. Each side will take no more than 2 or 3 minutes, just until the coating is lightly browned. Add more butter between batches if needed. Keep the cooked cutlets warm.

When all are done, reduce heat under the skillet. Squeeze the juice of 1 lemon into the pan drippings. Stir in chicken broth, scraping to loosen browned bits from the bottom. Simmer for 15 minutes. Taste and correct seasoning.

Pour sauce over cutlets and serve with a sprinkling of chopped parsley and thin slices of lemon over top.

Avon

CHICKEN PIERRE
Serves 6 to 8

8 half chicken breasts, skinned and boned
$1/2$ cup (1 stick) butter
1 clove garlic, finely minced
$1/2$ cup all-purpose flour
$1/2$ cup dry sherry
$1/2$ pound small whole mushrooms, cleaned and patted dry
Salt and freshly ground pepper
4 scallions (green onions), sliced (white and part of green)
2 small tomatoes, peeled, seeded, and cut into small chunks
2 tablespoons minced fresh parsley

Pound the chicken breasts, smooth side down, between 2 sheets of waxed paper to a thickness of about $3/8$ inch. Mash together the butter and garlic and heat in a large sauté pan. Spread the flour on a sheet of waxed paper and dip the chicken cutlets lightly, shaking each to get rid of the excess flour.

Sauté as many cutlets as will fit in one layer without crowding. Brown quickly on both sides, about 2 minutes. Remove and keep warm as they are done. When all are browned, return to the pan and add sherry, mushrooms, and salt and pepper to taste. Simmer 3 minutes. Add scallions and tomatoes and simmer 2 minutes longer, or until heated through. Transfer cutlets and vegetables with sauce to a heated platter and sprinkle top with chopped parsley. Serve with fluffy rice.

CHICKEN SUPREME À LA EAST WIND
Serves 4

4 half chicken breasts, boned and skinned
6 tablespoons butter
2 tablespoons oil
Salt and freshly ground pepper
Puff pastry*

continued

TARRAGON CREAM SAUCE
3 tablespoons butter
2 tablespoons all-purpose flour
1 cup milk
Salt and freshly ground pepper
1 tablespoon chopped fresh tarragon, or 1½ teaspoons dried
1 tablespoon butter at room temperature

Trim the chicken breasts of fat and membranes. Heat butter and oil in a large sauté pan. When the foaming subsides, add the chicken and brown quickly and evenly on both sides until about half done, approximately 3 minutes per side. Sprinkle lightly with salt and pepper. Let cool in the pan juices.

Preheat oven to 400°. Butter a cookie sheet.

Roll out the puff pastry and cut into 8 squares, each slightly larger than a half chicken breast. Place the cooled breast on a square of puff pastry, cover with about a tablespoon of congealed pan juices, and cover with second square of puff pastry. Press the edges together firmly to enclose the breast and crimp with the tines of a fork. Transfer to baking sheet and bake until puffy and golden brown, about 25 minutes.

For the sauce: Heat the butter in a heavy-bottomed saucepan and whisk in flour. Cook slowly, stirring constantly, for 2 or 3 minutes or until well blended and frothy. Do not let it take on color. Remove from heat, add milk all at once, and stir vigorously. Increase heat to medium and continue to cook and stir until the sauce is thickened and smooth. Remove from heat and add tarragon, salt and pepper to taste, and the tablespoon of soft butter. Stir until butter is melted.

Serve chicken pastries topped with the tarragon cream sauce.

*Puff pastry is generally available in the frozen foods section of supermarkets, for those who choose not to make their own.

CHICKEN WITH BAY
Serves 4

3–3¹/₂-pound chicken, cut into quarters
1 onion, sliced
1 cup hot chicken broth, or 2 chicken bouillon cubes dissolved
    in 1 cup of hot water
¹/₄ cup (¹/₂ stick) butter or margarine
Salt and freshly ground pepper
Paprika
2 bay leaves, broken

Set broiler at medium heat and preheat.

Place chicken quarters in a lightly oiled baking pan big enough to hold them in a single layer — a 10 × 14-inch pan should do it. Distribute onion rings over chicken. Pour broth over the chicken. Dot with butter or margarine; sprinkle with salt, pepper, and paprika. Add broken bay leaves around chicken pieces.

Broil skin side up, 3 or 4 inches from the heat source, until browned. Remove from broiler and baste well with gravy. Set oven heat at 350° and bake for 45 to 50 minutes, or until tender, basting often.

The chef says: "Simple and delicious. Good served hot or cold."

COQ AU VIN
Serves 4 to 6

6 half chicken breasts, boned and skinned
¹/₂ cup (1 stick) butter
2 tablespoons oil
1 cup water
4 tablespoons all-purpose flour
1 cup dry red wine
1 envelope onion soup mix
1 clove garlic, finely minced
3 tablespoons minced fresh parsley
1 bay leaf
¹/₂ teaspoon dried thyme
Salt and freshly ground pepper
¹/₂ pound mushrooms, sliced

Trim halved chicken breasts of fat and membrane and wipe dry with paper towels. Heat 6 tablespoons of butter and the oil in a 12-inch sauté pan or a heavy kettle such as a Dutch oven. When the butter stops foaming, add the chicken breasts and cook over medium-high heat on both sides until golden, about 10 minutes total. Remove chicken breasts with tongs and set aside.

Mix ¹/₂ cup of the water with the flour until smooth. Add to the drippings in the pan with the remaining ¹/₂ cup of water, red wine, onion soup mix, garlic, parsley, bay leaf, and thyme. Cook and stir until smooth and thickened, scraping up all the browned bits on the bottom of the pan. Taste and correct seasoning. Return chicken to pan and spoon sauce over chicken. Cover and simmer gently over low heat for 10 minutes.

While this is heating, in a medium-sized frying pan sauté mushrooms in the remaining 2 tablespoons of butter for 3 or 4 minutes. Add mushrooms to chicken and cook for another 5 minutes or so, or until the chicken is cooked through.

Serve over toast points or fluffy boiled rice.

CRAB-STUFFED CHICKEN BREASTS
Serves 6

6 large half chicken breasts, skinned and boned
Salt and freshly ground pepper
$^1/_2$ cup chopped onion
$^1/_2$ cup chopped celery
3 tablespoons butter
3 tablespoons dry white wine
$^1/_2$ cup stuffing mix
14 ounces crabmeat, picked over
Crushed potato chips
2 tablespoons melted butter

SAUCE
1 envelope Hollandaise sauce mix
$^3/_4$ cup heavy cream
3 tablespoons dry white wine
$^1/_2$ cup (2 ounces) shredded Swiss cheese

Trim halved chicken breasts of fat and membranes. Place between 2 pieces of waxed paper, smooth side down, and pound until flattened and thin. Sprinkle lightly with salt and pepper.

Melt 3 tablespoons of butter or margarine in a saucepan and sauté the onion and celery until tender. Remove from heat. Add the white wine, stuffing mix, and crabmeat and toss. Preheat the oven to 375°.

Divide the stuffing mixture among the chicken breasts and roll up tightly, tucking in the sides to hold the stuffing securely. Coat the rolls in crushed potato chips and place in a greased baking dish. Drizzle with melted butter or margarine. Bake uncovered for 1 hour.

While the chicken is baking, blend the sauce mix and cream. Cook until thick. Add white wine and shredded Swiss cheese. Stir until cheese is melted.

Pour some of the sauce over the finished chicken and serve the remaining sauce in a gravy boat at the table.

DRUNKEN BIRD
Serves 4

4 whole chicken breasts, skinned and boned (about 8 ounces
    each)
Salt and freshly ground pepper
2 large cloves garlic, squeezed through garlic press
1 tablespoon dried oregano
1 8-ounce stick extra sharp cheese
¹/₂ cup dry sherry
¹/₂ cup honey
1 cup walnuts, finely chopped
Garnish: 4 unpeeled orange slices

Preheat oven to 325°. Butter an 8- or 9-inch baking dish.

Trim chicken breasts of fat and membrane. Place each breast, smooth side down, between 2 pieces of waxed paper and pound thin with a meat pounder. Sprinkle breasts lightly with salt and pepper; rub them with garlic and coat with oregano.

Cut cheese lengthwise into 4 sticks. Place a stick of cheese in the center of each breast (on the inner, not the smooth, side) and roll the breast around it, tucking in the ends, to make a tidy sausage-shaped roll. Bake for about 25 minutes or until cooked through.

While the chicken is cooking, combine sherry, honey, and nuts in a small bowl and mix well. Remove the chicken from the oven and ladle about ¹/₄ cup of sauce over each breast. Return to oven for 3 to 5 minutes, or until the sauce bubbles. Serve with a slice of orange for garnish.

HOT CHICKEN SALAD
Serves 6 to 8

4 cups cubed cooked chicken
2 cups coarsely chopped celery
¾ cup mayonnaise
¾ cup cream of chicken soup
2 tablespoons lemon juice
1 teaspoon salt
1 tablespoon grated onion
4 hard-cooked eggs, sliced

TOPPING
1 cup (4 ounces) grated cheese
1½ cups crushed potato chips
⅔ cup toasted slivered almonds

Combine all the salad ingredients in a good-sized bowl and toss well. Transfer to a buttered baking dish — a 9 × 13 inch will do nicely — that can be brought to the table.

Top the salad with layers of cheese, crushed potato chips, and almonds.

Refrigerate overnight. Let come to room temperature before placing in a 400° oven. Bake for 25 to 30 minutes, or until heated through.

Note: This is a personal favorite of the innkeeper, and has appeared in local New Hampshire cook books.

LEMON CHICKEN CASSEROLE
Serves 6

1 large or 2 medium leeks
3 cloves garlic, finely minced
$1/2$ pound mushrooms, sliced
6 tablespoons butter
2 pounds cooked chicken cut into bite-sized pieces
$1/2$ teaspoon black pepper
2 tablespoons tamari sauce*
2 tablespoons dry sherry
2 lemons, thinly sliced, seeds removed

Wash the leek thoroughly to remove all traces of sand and cut into julienne strips 2 to 3 inches long. Heat the butter in a large sauté pan and sauté leeks, minced garlic, and sliced mushrooms, tossing, until the leeks, are crisp-tender and the mushrooms lightly browned, 4 or 5 minutes. Add the cooked chicken, pepper, tamari sauce, and dry sherry, and mix.

Preheat oven to 325°. Butter a 2- to 3-quart ovenproof casserole. Transfer the chicken to the casserole, distributing the lemon slices throughout. Cover with aluminum foil and bake for 25 to 30 minutes, or until the lemon flavor becomes absorbed by the chicken mixture. If you wish, you can remove some of the lemon slices before serving. Serve with boiled rice.

*Tamari sauce is a natural soy sauce made without artificial additives or preservatives. It is salty enough to make additional salt unnecessary.

Aubergine

MEDALLIONS OF CHICKEN WITH PORT AND LEEKS
Serves 4 to 6

1 cup good port
4 cups strong veal stock (p. 91)
$^{1}/_{2}$ cup each chopped celery, carrot, and onion
8 half chicken breasts, boned and skinned
Salt and freshly ground pepper
2 tablespoons butter
1$^{1}/_{2}$ cups loosely packed leeks in fine julienne strips about 2$^{1}/_{2}$
   inches long

Combine port, veal stock, and chopped vegetables in a heavy-bottomed saucepan and cook uncovered over medium-high heat until sauce is reduced and fairly thick. Strain sauce and return to saucepan. Set aside.

Preheat oven to 400°. With a sharp knife, slice the chicken breasts horizontally, making at least 2 slices from each breast. If the breasts are thick, you may be able to divide them in thirds; otherwise, content yourself with 2 slices per half breast. Arrange the slices on a buttered baking sheet, making 4 to 6 groups, each in fan formation. Sprinkle lightly with salt and pepper, butter lightly, and sprinkle with port. Bake for 10 to 12 minutes.

While the chicken is baking, bring the strained sauce to a boil and add julienned leeks. Reduce heat and simmer for 4 to 5 minutes, until the leeks are crisp-tender. Skim as necessary.

To serve, coat warmed plates with leek sauce and place drained chicken medallions on top.

POULET À LA CRÈME D'ESTRAGON
Serves 6 to 8

5–7-pound fine roasting chicken (reserve giblets)
Salt and freshly ground pepper
3–4 sprigs fresh tarragon
6 tablespoons butter (or more)
½ cup dry white wine
1 cup chicken broth
1 cup heavy cream
2 tablespoons finely chopped tarragon leaves

Wipe the chicken inside and out with a damp towel. Season the inside of the bird with salt and pepper and tuck the fresh tarragon into the cavity. Tie the legs together or, better still, truss the bird to help it hold its shape during cooking.

Melt the butter in a heavy braising pan or Dutch oven with a cover. Use enough butter to coat the bottom of the pan generously. Add the chicken, turning it over and over until it is lightly golden on all sides. Use kitchen tongs for this operation; a fork could puncture the skin, which would release precious juices. Add the giblets to the bottom of the pan (not the liver, which would darken the sauce), pour the white wine over the bird, and stir it into the melted butter, loosening all the browned bits at the bottom of the pan. Add the chicken broth and cook, tightly covered, over low heat for 40 to 50 minutes, until tender. The sauce should be pale gold. (It may also be cooked in a pressure cooker. See chef's note.) To test the state of doneness, slit the flesh between the leg and the body. If the juices that run out are clear, the bird is done; if pink, more cooking is needed.

Remove the cooked chicken to a warm place and discard the tarragon. Add the cream to the juices in the pan and cook over low heat until the sauce becomes smooth and thick enough to coat a spoon. Do not allow the sauce to come to a boil or it will curdle. Cut the giblets into pieces and pour sauce and giblets into a blender. Blend at medium speed for half a minute.

Carve the chicken into serving pieces, pour the sauce over, and sprinkle with fresh tarragon.

The chef says: "We have found you really don't need a genuine Avignon hen for this recipe — a plump roasting chicken will do very nicely — but you really should use fresh tarragon.

"We prepare this chicken in a pressure cooker. But never let the pressure go above five pounds — just slightly above zero pressure is best."

SAUTÉED CHICKEN COINTREAU
Serves 8

    4 cups rich chicken broth
    2 oranges, peeled, sliced, and seeded
    2 ounces diced fresh ginger
    4 large whole chicken breasts, boned and skinned
    ¼ pound fresh mushrooms, sliced
    7 tablespoons butter
    ½ cup Cointreau
    ¼ pound pea pods
    Salt and freshly ground pepper

Place the chicken broth, orange slices, and ginger in a saucepan and simmer until reduced to 1 cup. This will take about 1 hour.

Cut the chicken breasts in two, giving you 8 halves, and trim away fat and membranes.

In a large skillet, sauté the mushrooms in 2 of the tablespoons of butter until slightly soft, 3 or 4 minutes. Remove mushrooms with a slotted spoon and set aside. Add 3 tablespoons of butter to the pan and cook the breasts over very low heat for 6 to 8 minutes on each side until tender, but not brown. Do not overcook or they can become stringy. Cook only as many at a time as will fit comfortably in a single layer.

When all the chicken breasts are cooked, return them to the skillet. Heat the Cointreau, ignite it, and pour the flaming liqueur over the breasts. When the flames die out, remove the chicken to a hot platter and keep warm.

Pour the reduced chicken broth mixture into the skillet and increase heat. Cook and stir until sauce thickens and coats the spoon. While the sauce is cooking, blanch the pea pods in boiling salted water for 1 or 2 minutes and drain. Add the cooked pea pods and the remaining

2 tablespoons of butter to the sauce in the skillet and mix well. Taste for seasoning and add salt and pepper as needed. Serve the breasts with a topping of mushrooms and the sauce poured over. Accompany with stir-fried vegetables and boiled rice.

DUCKLING

BREAST OF DUCK SUPREME
Serves 4

2 large boneless duck breasts
2 tablespoons oil
¹/₃ cup raspberry vinegar
1 cup veal stock (page 91)
1 teaspoon sugar
Garnish: pink peppercorns and parsley sprigs

Have your butcher remove bones from 2 large breasts of 2 whole ducks.

Heat the oil over high heat until very hot. Pat each breast dry with paper towels, place in the hot oil, and cook, skin side down, for 5 minutes. With kitchen tongs, turn breasts and cook another 4 to 5 minutes. Remove to heated platter and keep warm.

Pour off all the fat in the pan. Add the raspberry vinegar and boil rapidly until reduced by half, scraping up any browned bits on the bottom of the pan. Add the veal stock and sugar and boil further until the sauce is reduced and slightly thickened.

Serve on heated dinner plates. With a very sharp knife, cut the breasts lengthwise into very thin slices. Divide the slices among 4 plates, forming the slices into fan-shaped arrangements.

Pour the boiling sauce over the duck slices. Garnish with parsley sprigs and sprinkle each serving with a few pink peppercorns.

DUCKLING À L'ORANGE
Serves 2 amply; 4 modestly

4–4¹/₂ pound duck
Salt and freshly ground pepper
¹/₂ bay leaf
¹/₂ onion, sliced
2 oranges
1 lemon
2 tablespoons all-purpose flour
¹/₂ cup dry white wine
1 cup orange juice
1 cup chicken broth
3 tablespoons sugar
4 tablespoons wine vinegar

Preheat oven to 350°. Wipe the duck inside and outside and remove the giblets. Cut off the neck and wings. Trim away the fat from the body cavity and around the neck and discard. Rub the inside of the duck and the skin with salt and sprinkle lightly with pepper. Place the duck on a rack in a shallow roasting pan and bake in preheated oven. Prick the skin from time to time and remove some of the fat from the pan with a spoon or bulb baster. After about 50 minutes, add to the bottom of the roasting pan the giblets, wings, neck, bay leaf, and onion. Roasting time for a well-done duck is from 1³/₄ hours to 2 hours; for medium duck, about 1¹/₂ hours. To test for doneness, wiggle the leg. If it moves easily and the flesh of the thigh feels soft, or if a meat thermometer in the thigh registers 180°, it is done.

While the duck is roasting, remove the colored part of the skin (the "zest") of 2 oranges and 1 lemon with a vegetable peeler and cut into narrow julienne strips. Bring a small saucepan of water to a boil and add the strips. Let them steep in the boiling water for 5 minutes, drain, and set aside. Remove all the white coating from the oranges and slice the oranges. Set aside. Squeeze the lemon and reserve the juice.

When the duck is roasted, remove from oven and keep warm. Drain the fat from the roasting pan. Add the flour to the remaining drippings and, over moderate heat, stir well to blend, scraping up all the browned bits on the bottom of the pan. Add the wine, orange juice, chicken broth, and lemon juice. Boil rapidly until the sauce is reduced to about 10 ounces.

While the sauce is reducing, heat the 3 tablespoons of sugar over medium-high heat in a heavy-bottomed pan. Heat until the sugar turns a light caramel color and completely liquefies. When the sauce has been reduced, strain it over the caramelized sugar, and add the wine vinegar. Stir well, and simmer a few minutes longer. Add the julienne strips of orange and lemon peels and season to taste.

Cut the duckling into halves or quarters. Remove and discard the breast bones. Sprinkle the duck with the orange and lemon rinds and pour enough of the rich brown sauce to glaze the duck. Serve the balance of the sauce in a sauce boat. Garnish with the slices of orange.

WAYSIDE INN DUCKLING IN ORANGE SAUCE
Serves 4

2 4½-pound ducklings
Salt
1 cup currant jelly
3 tablespoons white vinegar
Juice of 1 lemon
½ cup frozen orange juice concentrate
½ cup chicken broth
½ cup brown sauce (page 128), or gravy
2 oranges

Preheat oven to 350°.

Wipe the ducks, remove giblets, and cut off the second joint of the wings and the neck skin. Trim the loose fat from the cavities and around the neck. Rub skin and inside of the ducks with salt. Place ducks on a rack set in a shallow baking pan and roast for 2¼ to 2¾ hours, or until the leg joint moves easily. Spoon off the fat from time to time. Remove ducks from oven and, when cool enough to handle comfortably, remove and discard the backbones, thereby separating the ducks into two halves. Remove the breast and thigh bones.

To prepare the sauce, melt the currant jelly in a heavy saucepan over moderate heat for 15 minutes. Add the vinegar, lemon juice, orange juice concentrate, chicken broth, and brown sauce. Simmer for 10 minutes.

Remove the colored part of the skin (the "zest") of the 2 oranges with a vegetable peeler and cut into narrow strips. Boil the strips in water for 3 minutes. Drain well and add to the sauce. Taste and correct the seasoning. Cut the oranges into slices as a garnish for the platter.

When ready to serve, place duckling halves in a shallow pan in a 450° oven for 6 to 10 minutes until the skin is crisp. Transfer to a heated platter. Cover with orange sauce and garnish with orange slices.

The chef says: "This may be served flaming by pouring an ounce of heated Grand Marnier (or brandy) over the duckling and lighting it as it is brought to the table."

POULTRY STUFFING

You can prepare poultry stuffing in advance and keep it refrigerated, but do not put it into the bird until just before roasting. Even though the stuffed bird is refrigerated, the cold cannot fully penetrate the stuffing in the interior of the bird and there is danger of food-poisoning microorganisms developing in a prestuffed fowl.

Fill the bird only ¾ full because any dressing containing bread or other dry ingredients will swell during cooking. If you have more dressing than the bird can comfortably hold, bake it separately in a greased baking dish for the last 1¼ hours that the bird is in the oven. Baste it 2 or 3 times with the drippings from the bird. Cover with foil if it gets too brown on top.

Figure about ¾ to 1 cup of stuffing for each pound of bird. Bear in mind that stuffed poultry needs about 20 to 30 minutes more cooking time than unstuffed poultry.

Place a little stuffing into the neck cavity, pull the skin over to the back, and skewer closed. Lightly stuff the body cavity and either sew the body cavity closed or close it with skewers and wrap string around the skewers as you would lace shoes.

Gateways Inn

CORNBREAD-APPLE-PECAN STUFFING
Makes enough stuffing for a 12–15-pound bird

3 pounds apples, peeled and cored
1½ quarts water
1 cup dry white wine
Juice of 1 lemon
5 tablespoons butter
4 teaspoons sugar
1 cup diced onions
1 cup diced celery
14 ounces (4 cups) cornbread (below), broken up
2 tablespoons chopped fresh parsley
Pinch nutmeg
2 pinches dried thyme
3 eggs, lightly beaten
½ cup chicken broth
1¼ cups coarsely chopped pecans
Salt and pepper to taste

Slice each apple into 16 slices. Soak slices in water with ½ cup of the wine and lemon juice to prevent discoloration. Drain well and pat dry with paper towels.

Heat 1 tablespoon of butter in a large skillet, add the apples, sugar, and remaining ½ cup of wine, and cook, stirring occasionally, until the apples are just slightly softened, but not mushy. They should retain their shape. Transfer to a bowl and set aside.

Wipe out the pan, heat the remaining 4 tablespoons of butter, and sauté the onions and celery lightly, until crisp-tender.

Break up 4 cups of the cornbread and place in a large bowl. (The remainder of the cornbread can be saved for another occasion.) Add the celery-and-onion mixture and blend well. Mix in the apples and all the remaining ingredients. Toss lightly to blend. Add salt and pepper as needed.

CORNBREAD
2 cups white cornmeal*
1 cup boiling water
2 eggs, separated
1 tablespoon melted butter or lard
$^1/_2$ teaspoon baking soda
$^3/_4$ cup buttermilk
1 teaspoon baking powder

Preheat oven to 350°. Grease an 8-inch square baking dish.

In a large bowl, combine the cornmeal with the boiling water and stir. Beat the egg yolks lightly in a separate bowl. Stir slowly into the cornmeal with the melted fat, the baking soda dissolved in the buttermilk, and the baking powder. Beat the egg whites until stiff and fold into the batter. Transfer to baking pan, smoothing top with a spatula, and bake for 25 to 30 minutes, or until the top is lightly browned and a cake tester comes out dry. Let cool in the pan for 15 to 20 minutes. You will need a little more than half the cornbread to make the 4 cups.

*The fine white cornmeal is favored in the South and in some parts of New England, but if you are unable to find it in your area, you may substitute yellow cornmeal.

Palmer House

OYSTER-PECAN STUFFING FOR A 12–15-POUND TURKEY OR GOOSE

4–5 tablespoons butter or bacon drippings
1 cup pecans, coarsely chopped
2 large onions, chopped
1 green pepper, chopped
4 stalks celery, chopped
$\frac{1}{2}$ pound fresh mushrooms, sliced, or one 4-ounce can sliced
    mushrooms, drained (reserve liquid)
1 gizzard of fowl, chopped
1 tablespoon chopped fresh parsley
1 tablespoon dried thyme
1 tablespoon poultry seasoning
2 bay leaves, crumbled
3–4 slices dry bread, cubed
1 cup dry sherry
1 pint shucked oysters, coarsely chopped, with their liquor
Salt and freshly ground pepper

Heat butter or bacon drippings in a large pot and sauté the pecans, vegetables, gizzard, herbs, and seasonings until slightly soft, but not brown. Toss them frequently. Add the cubed bread moistened with the wine, and the oysters and their liquor. Cover pot and cook gently, stirring often, for 5 minutes. Add salt and pepper to taste. If the mixture is a bit dry, add the liquid from the canned mushrooms or a little water if fresh mushrooms are used.

Remove from heat, cool, and stuff the bird.

The innkeeper says: "We have found that putting the shucked oysters in the freezer for a short time makes the chopping easier and retains more of the liquid.

"This is our own combination of two recipes found in a privately printed book of old New Orleans family recipes that we bought years ago on our honeymoon in New Orleans. It has been a Thanksgiving and Christmas tradition of our family ever since and is a great favorite of our guests."

STUFFING FOR A 5-POUND ROASTING CHICKEN

3 cups cooked mashed pumpkin
$1/2$ cup pumpkin seeds, shelled
$1/2$ cup sunflower seeds, shelled
$1/2$ cup coarsely chopped walnuts
$1/2$ cup raisins
1 cup diced apple
1 cup diced celery
$1/4$ cup cornmeal
Salt and freshly ground pepper

Combine all ingredients and blend well. Stuff into chicken cavity.

VII   Eggs and Cheese

BREEZEMERE CRABMEAT QUICHE
Serves 6 to 8

1 9-inch deep-dish unbaked pastry shell (Pâte Brisée, page 199)
$\frac{1}{2}$ pound fresh crabmeat, picked over and flaked
1 cup (4 ounces) shredded Swiss cheese
1 tablespoon dehydrated onion flakes
4 eggs, slightly beaten
2 cups light cream
$\frac{1}{2}$ teaspoon salt
Dash cayenne pepper
$\frac{1}{4}$ cup grated Parmesan cheese
Paprika

Preheat oven to 450°.

Sprinkle the crabmeat, Swiss cheese, and onion evenly over the pie shell.

Beat the eggs and add cream, salt, and cayenne pepper. Mix well and pour over the crab mixture. Sprinkle Parmesan cheese on top and dust with a little paprika for color.

Bake in 450° oven for 15 minutes. Lower oven temperature to 300° and continue baking for 30 minutes or until a slim knife inserted in the center comes out clean.

BROCCOLI SOUFFLÉ
Serves 4 to 6

1 cup cottage cheese
3 eggs
1¹/₂ cups cooked, chopped broccoli (about 1 pound)
3 tablespoons all-purpose flour
¹/₄ cup (¹/₂ stick) butter, melted
1 cup (4 ounces) grated sharp Cheddar cheese
Salt and freshly ground pepper
1 tablespoon minced onion

Preheat oven to 350°. Grease a 1-quart soufflé dish.

Place the cottage cheese in a bowl. Add the eggs and beat until well blended. Stir in the broccoli. Add the flour and mix well. Add the melted butter and ¹/₂ cup of cheese, salt, pepper, and onion, mixing well.

Transfer to soufflé dish and sprinkle the remainder of the cheese over top. Bake for 30 to 40 minutes, until set and golden on top.

CHEESE AND GRITS SOUFFLÉ
Serves 4 to 6

1 cup grits (regular or instant)
2 eggs, well beaten
2 cups (8 ounces) grated sharp Cheddar cheese
Salt
Dash of Tabasco sauce

Cook the grits according to recipe on package. Remove from heat and cool lightly in same pot.

Preheat oven to 350°. Grease a 1-quart ovenproof baking dish.

Stir beaten eggs vigorously into the cooked grits. Stir in the grated cheese. Add salt to taste and Tabasco sauce. Transfer to the casserole and bake for 1 hour.

CORN-BEAN SOUFFLÉ
Serves 12

1 pound fresh green beans
1 cup (4 ounces) grated sharp Cheddar cheese
¹/₄ cup chopped green chilies
4 cups fresh corn, cut from the cob (about 8 ears)
Salt and freshly ground pepper
8 ounces Monterey Jack cheese, sliced
3 eggs
¹/₃ cup milk
³/₄ cup sour cream
¹/₂ cup chopped fresh chives

Wash the beans and snap off the ends. Cut beans diagonally in fourths. Cook in lightly salted water until crisp-tender. Drain well. Grease a 9 × 13-inch baking dish and layer the beans on the bottom. Cover with a mixture of grated cheese and green chilies. Evenly spread corn over this layer and sprinkle with salt and pepper to taste.

Cut sliced Monterey Jack cheese into strips and place over corn. Beat the eggs and milk together and fold in the sour cream and fresh chives. Pour over vegetable-cheese layer.

Bake in a preheated 350° oven for 45 minutes to 1 hour, or until set and golden on top.

The
  Wildwood
EGG AND SAUSAGE CASSEROLE WITH HERBS
Serves 6

¹/₃ cup butter
1 pound pork sausage, ground
3 cups cubed dry bread
2 teaspoons dried basil
1¹/₂ tablespoons chopped fresh dill, or 1 teaspoon dried dillweed
1 cup (4 ounces) shredded Cheddar cheese
5 eggs
2 cups milk
Salt and freshly ground pepper

Preheat oven to 350°. Melt the butter in a small pan and pour into a 9 × 15-inch baking pan, tilting the pan to all sides so that the butter bathes the bottom and sides of the pan.

Brown the ground sausage in a skillet and set aside.

Layer half the cubed bread in the buttered baking pan and sprinkle with half the basil, dill, and cheese. Then layer with the remaining bread cubes, herbs, and cheese. Sprinkle the browned sausage meat over all.

Beat the eggs well and add the milk, blending well. Season with salt and pepper. Pour over the contents of the baking pan. Bake for 1 hour.

The chef-innkeeper says: "The advantage to this dish is that it can be made the evening before, refrigerated overnight, and then whisked into the oven by a still sleepy-eyed cook in the morning.

"For a subtler taste, use Swiss cheese instead of Cheddar."

The Inn at Mt. Ascutney

EGGS FLORENTINE
Serves 4

4 tablespoons butter
4 tablespoons all-purpose flour
2 cups milk
$\frac{1}{2}$ teaspoon ground mace
1 tablespoon dry white wine
Salt and freshly ground pepper
2 10-ounce packages frozen chopped spinach
8 eggs

Melt butter in a heavy-bottomed saucepan. Whisk in flour and cook and stir for 2 or 3 minutes until the flour and butter foam and bubble. Remove from heat and add the milk all at once, whisking vigorously to blend well. Return saucepan to moderately high heat and bring to a slow boil. Reduce heat and continue to whisk until the sauce is smooth and thickened, 4 or 5 minutes longer. Stir in mace, white wine, and salt and pepper to taste. Set aside.

Cook the spinach quickly and drain well, pressing out all the liquid. Stir 2 tablespoons of sauce into the spinach.

Preheat oven to 325°. Butter an 8-inch square casserole. Place the spinach mixture over the bottom. Make 8 indentations or wells in the spinach. Crack a raw egg into each indentation. Spoon the sauce carefully over the eggs. Place in oven for approximately 10 minutes, or until the eggs are cooked. Serve immediately.

The chef says: "This can be completely prepared four hours or so before it is to be baked, if you wish."

𝕾𝖜𝖎𝖙𝖟𝖊𝖗 𝕾𝖙𝖚𝖇𝖑𝖎
KÄSESCHNITTEN NACH SWITZER STUBLI
(Variation of a grilled cheese sandwich)
Serves 6

¼ cup (½ stick) butter
6 slices fine white bread (preferably homemade)
6 thin slices any kind of cooked ham
6 slices Swiss cheese
6 canned pineapple rings, well drained
6 fried eggs

Heat butter in a skillet and sauté bread slices on both sides. Place sautéed bread on a baking sheet.

Preheat oven to 350°.

Top each bread slice with ham, cheese, and pineapple ring. Place in oven and bake for about 15 minutes, or until cheese is melted. While the sandwiches are baking, fry eggs. To serve, place a fried egg over the pineapple ring.

LEEK TART LYONNAISE
Serves 6 to 8

1 10-inch unbaked tart shell (below)
2 cups coarsely chopped leeks, including a little of the green part
¼ cup (½ stick) butter
4 eggs
1½ cups half-and-half
1½ cups (6 ounces) grated Gruyère or natural Swiss cheese
Freshly grated nutmeg
Salt and freshly ground pepper

Refrigerate the tart shell for 1 hour. Then bake in a preheated 425° oven for 15 minutes and cool.

Sauté the leeks in butter until just softened, but not transparent. Cool. Beat eggs and half-and-half together, blending well. Add the cheese, nutmeg, salt, and pepper, and mix well. Preheat oven to 375°.

Arrange the leeks over the bottom of the baked tart shell. Pour in the egg-cream-cheese mixture and sprinkle with more nutmeg. Bake for 30 minutes or until firm in the center. Cool for 10 minutes before cutting. May be served warm or cold.

PIE OR TART PASTRY
1½ cups all-purpose flour
½ teaspoon salt
½ cup solid vegetable shortening
4–5 tablespoons cold water

Sift the flour and salt into a bowl. Cut in shortening with a pastry blender until the mixture resembles small peas or coarse meal. Sprinkle water over the flour mixture a little at a time and toss with a fork, using only enough water to hold the pastry together. Form into a ball.

Roll out dough on lightly floured surface, rolling from center to outside edge (not back and forth) until dough is ⅛ inch thick. Fit loosely without stretching into pan and flute rim. Prick entire surface with a fork. Refrigerate for 1 hour or place in freezer for ½ hour. Bake in preheated oven for 10 to 12 minutes or until golden. Take a peek after 5 minutes or so to see if any spots have begun to rise. If so, gently push them down. Cool shell before filling.

MOCK HAM AND CHEESE SOUFFLÉ
Serves 8

3 cups bread cubes (crustless; homemade white is best)
1 cup chopped ham
1½ cups (6 ounces) grated sharp Cheddar cheese
1 small onion, grated
Salt and freshly ground pepper
8 eggs
2½ cups milk
¼ cup (½ stick) melted butter
1 tablespoon dry mustard
1 teaspoon chopped chives
½ cup grated Parmesan cheese
Paprika

Butter a large (2–3 quart) soufflé dish well and spread 1 cup of bread cubes over the bottom. Sprinkle with half the ham, half the Cheddar cheese, and half the grated onion. Sprinkle with salt and pepper.

Repeat with 1 cup of bread cubes, and the remaining ham, Cheddar cheese, and grated onion. Sprinkle the remaining cup of bread cubes over the top.

Beat the eggs well, and stir in the milk, melted butter, mustard, and chives. Pour over the ingredients in the soufflé dish.

Sprinkle top with grated Parmesan cheese. Refrigerate overnight. Let come to room temperature when you are ready to cook. Bake in a preheated 350° oven for 1 hour. Sprinkle with paprika and serve.

The innkeeper says: "Even the atmosphere loves this one. The aroma lingers on and on."

ONION PIE
Serves 10 as appetizer course; 6 to 8 as main course

CRUST
2 cups all-purpose flour
$^1/_2$ cup cold water
$^3/_4$ cup (1$^1/_2$ sticks) melted margarine
$^1/_2$ teaspoon salt
$^1/_4$ teaspoon pepper

FILLING
1 16-ounce Spanish onion, thinly sliced
3 tablespoons butter
6 eggs, beaten
1 tablespoon minced fresh parsley
Salt and freshly ground pepper
1 cup heavy cream
1 cup (4 ounces) grated Swiss cheese

Preheat oven to 400°. Grease a deep 10-inch pie dish or 2-inch-deep quiche pan, or a metal torte pan, which the French call a *tourtière.*

Beat together the crust ingredients, which will form a rather spongy dough, in contrast to the conventional pie dough. Roll out on a floured surface with a well-floured rolling pin and fit loosely into the pie dish. Bring the crust well up the sides of the dish and flute the edges. Prick the bottom and sides well with a fork. Bake for 20 minutes and remove from the oven.

While the crust is baking, sauté the onion in the butter until tender and soft, but not brown. Stir frequently. The onion should take about 15 minutes.

Beat the eggs well in a large bowl and stir in the parsley, salt and pepper, cream, and grated cheese. Add the cooked onion and blend well. Pour into the hot crust and bake for 20 to 25 minutes, or until the top is lightly browned and the filling set. Let rest for 15 minutes before serving.

POTATO OMELET
Serves 4 to 6

5–6 medium potatoes (about 2 pounds)
½ cup (or more) oil
1 large onion, thinly sliced
6 eggs, beaten
Salt and freshly ground pepper

Peel the potatoes and slice very thinly. Heat about ½ inch oil in a deep 10-inch skillet. Fry the potatoes until golden and almost done, turning them often. Add the sliced onion and cook, stirring, until softened. Pour off excessive oil, if present, and add the beaten eggs that have been seasoned with salt and pepper. Cover the pan and lower the heat. Cook until the bottom is set, 12 to 15 minutes. Cover the pan with a large plate (using oven mitts or pot holders to protect your hands) and invert the pan to flip the omelet. Slide the omelet back into the skillet until completely cooked, about 1 minute.

Slide the omelet onto a serving platter, cut into wedges, and serve at once.

The chef says: "Accompany with a green salad, crusty French bread, and a dry white wine or rosé."

Switzer Stübli

SWITZER KÄSE FONDUE
(Cheese Fondue)
Serves 4

1 clove garlic
1¼ cups very dry white wine
1¼ pounds Emmentaler cheese, grated
1 teaspoon cornstarch
¼ cup Kirsch
1 pinch baking soda
1 pinch salt
Freshly ground pepper
Bread cubes

Rub a heavy earthenware casserole (what the Swiss call a *caquelon*) with a garlic clove and add the white wine and grated cheese. Place over medium heat and stir with a wooden paddle until the cheese melts into the wine. Dissolve the cornstarch in the Kirsch and add to the casserole when the cheese has melted into a creamy mixture.

Keep stirring until the wine and cheese are well blended with the cornstarch and Kirsch. Add a pinch of baking soda. This will make it foam a bit.

Season generously with freshly ground pepper and very little salt. (The cheese may be salty enough.) Keep stirring with a figure-eight motion and it will not become stringy.

Place the casserole over an alcohol burner or candle warmer and serve with plenty of crusty bread cubes and long-handled forks. Each person dips a bread cube spiked on the end of the fork into the melted cheese.

VIII Vegetables

Switzer Stübli
BARBARA'S BAKED TOMATOES
Serves 8

8 medium tomatoes
2 medium white potatoes, peeled, cut into small cubes, and
    cooked until just tender with a bit of salt
1 small onion, chopped
¼ pound Gruyère cheese, cut into small cubes
¼ pound Emmentaler or raclette cheese, cut into small cubes
1 tablespoon chopped fresh parsley
Freshly ground pepper

Wash the tomatoes, cut off the tops, and scoop out more than half of
the pulp, leaving a good-sized cavity. (Save the pulp for your next
sauce or soup.) Turn the tomato halves upside down, giving them
time to drain.
   Preheat oven to 350°.
   Toss together lightly the remaining ingredients, being generous with
the pepper. Fill the tomatoes with the potato-cheese mixture and place
them in a baking dish. Bake for about 20 minutes, or until the filling
is hot and bubbly.

The Inn- at Mt. Ascutney
BEETS WITH ORANGE SAUCE
Serves 4

½ small onion, sliced
1 16-ounce can sliced beets
1 tablespoon frozen orange juice concentrate
2 teaspoons cornstarch diluted in a tablespoon of water
Salt and freshly ground pepper

Cook the onion in a small amount of water in a saucepan until tender. Drain and return the onion to the pan.

Add the beets with their liquid and the orange juice concentrate. Bring to a boil. Stir the cornstarch solution into the beets and cook and stir until the sauce is thickened and shiny. Season to taste.

THE CRAIGNAIR
ENGLISH-STYLE CAULIFLOWER
Serves 4

1 medium cauliflower (about 1½ pounds)
2 tablespoons butter
1 tablespoon chopped fresh chives
1 tablespoon chopped fresh parsley
Salt and freshly ground pepper

Wash cauliflower and trim away all but 2 rows of leaves. Steam in a steamer basket over boiling water, or cook, top down, in a covered pot in 2 inches of boiling salted water. Boil until tender. The whole head will take 15 to 25 minutes, depending on the age and size of the head. When tender, drain and place on platter. The leaves may also be eaten.

In a small pot, melt the butter, add the chives, parsley, salt, and pepper, and pour over the cauliflower.

GREEN BEAN CASSEROLE
Serves 8

¼ cup (½ stick) butter
2 tablespoons all-purpose flour
1 teaspoon salt
Freshly ground pepper
1 teaspoon sugar
1 teaspoon grated onion
1 cup sour cream
2 12-ounce packages frozen French-style green beans, cooked
  and drained
2 cups (½ pound) grated Cheddar cheese
½ cup cornflake crumbs

Preheat oven to 350°. Grease a shallow 2-quart baking dish.

In a large saucepan, heat 3 tablespoons of butter and stir in flour. Cook and stir over low heat until bubbly, about 3 minutes. Remove from heat and stir in salt, pepper, sugar, onion, and sour cream. Add the drained beans and blend well. Transfer to casserole. Cover with cheese and top with cornflake crumbs mixed with the remaining tablespoon of butter, melted.

Bake for 30 minutes.

Note: This is a personal favorite of the co-innkeeper and has appeared in local (North Sutton, New Hampshire) cook books.

MINTED PEAS
Serves 4 or 5

1/4 cup green onions (scallions), finely chopped
3 tablespoons butter
2 pounds shelled fresh peas
2 tablespoons water
1 teaspoon sugar
1 tablespoon minced fresh mint leaves, or 2 teaspoons dried
   mint, crushed
1 teaspoon lemon juice
1/4 teaspoon salt

In a medium-sized saucepan, sauté the onions in butter until tender but not browned. Add the peas, water, sugar, mint, lemon juice, and salt. Cover pot and cook until the peas are just tender, about 10 minutes. Watch them carefully to make sure they do not scorch; add a bit more water if necessary. Garnish with extra mint leaves.

Switzer Stübli
MIXED VEGETABLES AU GRATIN
Serves 8

1 small cauliflower
1 bunch broccoli
2 cups sliced celery
6 carrots, scraped and sliced
3/4 cup fine breadcrumbs
2 cups (1/2 pound) grated Emmentaler cheese
1 cup light cream
2 eggs, well beaten with a fork
Salt and freshly ground pepper
2 tablespoons butter

Separate the cauliflower and broccoli into flowerets. Trim away the tough outer part of the broccoli stems, leaving about 2 inches of stem.

Cook the vegetables in lightly salted water until just tender. Since they all need slightly different cooking times, it is best to cook them separately, thus avoiding the danger of overcooking. They should be crisp-tender. The cauliflower and carrots may need about 10 minutes; the broccoli and celery, 7 or 8. As soon as they reach the proper degree of doneness, drain them well and place in a buttered shallow baking dish, preferably one that can be used for serving. Sprinkle the bread-crumbs evenly over them.

Preheat oven to 350°.

Mix together the Emmentaler cheese, light cream, beaten eggs, and salt and pepper. Pour over the vegetables. Dot with butter and bake for about 20 minutes or until the top is browned.

The chef says: "I make almost any vegetable or combination of vegetables this way."

NOISETTE POTATOES
Serves 4 to 6

3–5 large white potatoes
Salt
6 tablespoons butter
2 tablespoons chopped fresh parsley

Peel the potatoes and drop immediately into a bowl of cold water. With a 1-inch melon-ball cutter, cut the potatoes into balls, dropping them immediately back into the cold water. You should have about 50 balls.

Drain the potato balls well and place them in a pot, such as a large skillet, in which they will fit in a single layer. Add water to cover, and salt. Bring to a boil and simmer for 1 minute — no more. Drain well and pat skillet dry with paper towels.

Heat the butter in the skillet and add the potatoes. Cook, stirring and shaking the pot so that the balls brown evenly. Cook them over relatively high heat for 12 to 15 minutes, until nicely browned. Sprinkle with salt and chopped parsley and serve hot.

ORANGE-GLAZED CARROTS
Serves 6

1¹/₂ pounds carrots, scraped and thinly sliced
1 tablespoon butter
1 tablespoon light brown sugar
1¹/₂ teaspoons cornstarch
¹/₄ teaspoon salt
¹/₄ teaspoon ground mace
Freshly ground pepper to taste
¹/₂ cup orange juice
¹/₂ teaspoon grated orange rind

Cook the carrots in a covered saucepan in 2 inches of salted water until crisp-tender, about 13 minutes. Drain.

Using the same saucepan, melt the butter or margarine and stir in the brown sugar. Mix together in a small bowl the cornstarch, salt, mace, pepper, orange juice, and orange rind. Add to the sugar mixture and stir over medium heat with a whisk until thickened, about 3 minutes. Add the carrots and bring to a boil. Serve immediately.

 Sugar Hill Inn

POTATOES DELMONICO EN CASSEROLE
Serves 4 to 6

¹/₄ cup (¹/₂ stick) butter
3 tablespoons all-purpose flour
1¹/₂ cups milk
Salt and freshly ground pepper
1 small clove garlic, squeezed through garlic press, or 1 teaspoon
    garlic powder
¹/₂ cup (2 ounces) grated cheese (Swiss, Cheddar, Fontina, etc.)
4 cups cold cooked potatoes, sliced ¹/₄ inch thick
Paprika

continued

Preheat oven to 400°. Grease a heavy baking dish that can be used for serving.

In a medium-sized saucepan, heat the butter and whisk in the flour, whisking until bubbly, about 2 or 3 minutes, but do not let it brown. Remove from heat and whisk in the milk, beating vigorously to blend well. Return to moderate heat, add salt, pepper, and garlic, and cook and stir until sauce is thickened and smooth. Add the grated cheese and stir until melted.

Place the potatoes in the baking dish and pour sauce over them. Mix gently with a wooden spatula in order not to break up the potato slices. Sprinkle the top with paprika. Bake for 20 minutes.

POTATOES O'BRIEN
Serves 8 to 10

6 russet potatoes, peeled and cubed
6 tablespoons butter
3 tablespoons all-purpose flour
2 cups milk
¹/₂ cup finely diced green pepper
3 tablespoons diced pimiento
1 teaspoon salt
Freshly ground pepper
1 cup (4 ounces) shredded sharp Cheddar cheese
Few grains of cayenne pepper
¹/₂ cup Ritz cracker crumbs

Cook the potatoes in salted water until just tender and drain. Melt 4 tablespoons of butter in a saucepan. Stir in the flour and cook, stirring, for 3 minutes. Remove from heat, stir in the milk, and blend well. Return to the heat and bring to a boil. Stir and cook until thickened. Add green pepper, pimiento, salt, pepper, cheese, and cayenne and mix. Pour the sauce over the potatoes and blend carefully.

Preheat oven to 400°. Butter an 8-inch square baking dish.

Transfer the potatoes to baking dish. Heat the remaining 2 tablespoons of butter and mix with the cracker crumbs. Sprinkle the buttered crumbs over the potatoes and bake for 15 minutes or until hot and bubbly.

The chef says: "A good way to use leftover potatoes."

Switzer Stübli

RÖSTI
(Swiss Potatoes)
Serves 4

2 pounds unpeeled white potatoes
2 tablespoons oil
Salt

Scrub potatoes and place them, unpeeled, in a large saucepan and cover with water. Bring to a boil and boil potatoes for 9 to 10 minutes. Drain thoroughly and allow potatoes to cool. (Potatoes may be cooked a day in advance, if desired.) When ready to use, peel the potatoes and shred them in a coarse shredder, such as one used for cabbage.

Heat the oil in a large, heavy, well-seasoned skillet. When hot, put in the shredded potatoes and sprinkle with salt. Cook over low heat, turning frequently, until potatoes are slightly yellow and soft. Press the potatoes with a spatula into a flat cake.

Cook until the bottom of the potatoes is crusty and brown, 10 to 15 minutes. Make sure they are not sticking to the bottom of the pan. Add a little oil if needed. Flip the rösti over and brown on the other side. When both sides are crusty and brown, serve in a heated serving dish.

Jay Village

SICILIAN BROCCOLI
Serves 4

2 pounds broccoli
¼ cup (½ stick) butter
4 medium shallots, thinly sliced
2 cloves garlic, crushed and chopped
Grated Parmesan cheese
Garnish: lemon slices

Wash broccoli and divide it into large flowerets, leaving about 4 inches of stem. Peel the stems, removing the thick outer covering. (When the stems are peeled, they will cook as quickly as the flowerets, thus avoiding tough stems or overcooked flowerets.) Boil a large quantity of salted water and add the broccoli. Cover and cook for 5 minutes, until the broccoli is still bright green and slightly tender. Drain carefully and plunge into cold water to set the color. Drain again.

Heat the butter in a large skillet and add shallots and garlic. Cook until the shallots are a bit soft, but not browned. Add the broccoli and sauté, stirring gently, until heated through. Transfer to a warm serving platter and sprinkle broccoli with grated Parmesan cheese. Garnish with lemon slices.

SPINACH-STUFFED ONIONS
Serves 4

4 jumbo white onions (about 2 to the pound)
1/4 cup mayonnaise
1 tablespoon lemon juice
1/4 cup sour cream
Pinch ground nutmeg
Salt and freshly ground pepper
1 pound fresh spinach with stems removed

Skin and cook the onions in boiling water until tender, 50 to 60 minutes. Cool thoroughly. Remove the curved tops of the onions with a straight slice across. Trim the root area carefully, leaving the bottom intact so that the filling will stay in. Remove and reserve the center of the onions, leaving enough layers of the outside for a firm shell.

Chop the reserved onion. Combine mayonnaise, lemon juice, sour cream, nutmeg, salt, and pepper. Blend half of this mixture with the chopped onions.

Cook the spinach in the water clinging to the leaves after careful washing. Cook only until wilted, 1 to 2 minutes. Drain well in a sieve, pressing out all the moisture against the side of the sieve or between the palms of your hands. Chop and combine with the onion mixture. Taste and adjust seasoning if necessary.

Preheat oven to 350°. Grease a shallow baking dish.

Mound the spinach mixture in the onion shells and place in baking dish. Cover onions with the remaining mayonnaise sauce. Bake for 30 minutes.

The chef says: "This is a delicious accompaniment to beef."

 Sugar Hill Inn

STUFFED ZUCCHINI
Serves 4 to 6

3 zucchini
1 10-ounce package frozen chopped spinach, cooked and drained
2 tablespoons all-purpose flour
$^{1}/_{2}$ cup milk
Salt
$^{1}/_{3}$ cup (about 1$^{1}/_{2}$ ounces) shredded Cheddar cheese
4 slices cooked bacon, crumbled

Scrub zucchini well and trim off ends. Cook whole in boiling salted water for 10 to 12 minutes, until slightly tender. Drain and cut in half lengthwise. Scoop out centers, leaving a firm shell. Chop the centers and add to cooked chopped spinach.

Preheat oven to 350°. Grease a shallow baking dish large enough to hold the 6 zucchini shells.

In a small saucepan, blend the flour and milk and add the spinach mixture. Cook and stir until thickened. Place the zucchini halves in baking dish and sprinkle the cavities with salt. Spoon the spinach mixture into the zucchini shells. Sprinkle tops with shredded cheese and crumbled bacon. Bake for 15 to 20 minutes, until heated through.

SWEET AND SOUR RED CABBAGE
Serves 6 to 8

1/4 cup bacon drippings
8 cups shredded red cabbage (about 2 pounds)
4 cups cubed apples, unpeeled
1/2 cup firmly packed light brown sugar
1/2 cup cider vinegar
Salt and freshly ground pepper
1 teaspoon caraway seeds
1/2 cup water

Heat the bacon drippings in a large skillet or Dutch oven. Add all the remaining ingredients. Cook over low heat, covered, stirring occasionally. For crisp cabbage, cook 15 minutes; for soft, tender cabbage, cook 25 to 30 minutes.

The chef says: "The cabbage may be made the day before using and reheated."

THREE-WAY SQUASH
Serves 8

4 small yellow straightneck squash, scrubbed, unpared, and
   thinly sliced
1 medium onion, quartered and thinly sliced
Salt and freshly ground pepper
4 small zucchini, scrubbed, unpared, and thinly sliced
1 pound banana squash, pared and very thinly sliced
1/2 cup (1 stick) butter, melted
1 cup grated Parmesan cheese
1 cup sour cream
2 tablespoons minced chives or green onions (scallions)

Grease a 9 × 13-inch baking dish. Preheat oven to 375°.

Place the yellow squash in a layer in the bottom of the pan, cover with a thin layer of onion and a sprinkling of salt and pepper. Next, add a layer of the zucchini, onion, salt, and pepper; and finally the banana squash, onion, salt, and pepper. Pour melted butter evenly over the top. Cover tightly with foil and bake for 20 minutes. While the squash is baking, mix together the grated cheese, sour cream, and minced chives or onions, and blend well.

After 20 minutes, or when the squash is tender, remove pan from oven and take off foil. Spread the sour cream mixture over the top. Place under the broiler about 5 inches from the heat. Broil, watching carefully to make sure it doesn't scorch, until the topping is lightly browned and heated through, about 5 to 8 minutes.

TURNIPS OR RUTABAGAS AU GRATIN
Serves 6 to 8

2 pounds small white turnips or young rutabagas, peeled and
   diced
1 cup chicken broth
$\frac{1}{4}$ cup ($\frac{1}{2}$ stick) butter
3 tablespoons all-purpose flour
1 cup milk
1 cup half-and-half
Salt and freshly ground pepper
$\frac{2}{3}$ cup (about 3 ounces) grated natural Swiss cheese
2 tablespoons Ritz cracker crumbs

Cover the turnips or rutabagas with water and bring to a boil. Cook for 5 minutes and drain. Add chicken broth to turnips and simmer until vegetables are very tender. Drain and set aside.

Preheat oven to 375°. Grease a 2-quart baking dish.

In a medium-sized saucepan, melt 3 tablespoons of the butter. Add the flour and cook, stirring, for 3 minutes until bubbly. Remove from heat and add the milk and half-and-half, whisking them in vigorously to blend well. Return to heat and continue to cook, stirring, until the sauce thickens, about 10 minutes. Add salt and pepper to taste and mix in the cheese, stirring until melted.

Combine cheese sauce with the turnips or rutabagas. Turn into baking dish. Sprinkle with cracker crumbs and dot with the remaining tablespoon of butter. Bake for 10 minutes or until browned on top.

The chef says: "If refrigerated before serving, return to room temperature and bake in a 375° oven until heated through and well browned on top."

IX Breads

BANANA BREAD
Makes 1 loaf

3 very ripe bananas
1 cup sugar
1 egg
3 tablespoons oil
1 teaspoon vanilla extract
2 cups cake flour
1 teaspoon baking soda
1 teaspoon salt

Preheat oven to 400°. Grease and lightly flour a loaf pan.

Peel the bananas and mash them in a large mixing bowl. Add the sugar, egg, oil, and vanilla extract, and beat until the batter is well blended. Beat in the flour, baking soda, and salt, and beat until the batter is smooth. Pour into prepared loaf pan and place in oven. Immediately reduce oven temperature to 350°. Bake approximately 45 minutes or until a cake tester inserted in the middle comes out dry. Remove from pan and cool on a rack.

BERKSHIRE APPLE PANCAKE
Serves 4

2–3 tart apples (greenings, Granny Smith, etc.)
Juice of ½ lemon
2 eggs, well beaten
2 cups all-purpose flour
3 teaspoons baking powder
½ teaspoon salt
3 tablespoons sugar
1⅓ cups milk
½ teaspoon vanilla extract
½ teaspoon cinnamon
¼ cup (½ stick) butter
Topping: brown sugar and maple syrup

Peel and quarter apples. Remove core and slice each quarter into thin slices. Sprinkle with lemon juice to keep from darkening and set aside.

In a medium-sized bowl, mix together the beaten eggs with all remaining ingredients except butter. Blend well.

Preheat oven to 450°.

Heat 2 tablespoons of the butter in a 10- or 11-inch frying pan with a heatproof handle that can go into the oven. Add half the apples and cook and stir in the butter until both sides are lightly golden. Spread the apple slices evenly over the bottom of the pan. Pour over half the batter, spreading it evenly over the apples. Place in oven and bake for 7 to 8 minutes. With your hands well protected with oven mitts, remove pan from oven, invert pancake on a plate, and slide back into frying pan, uncooked side down. Bake 6 to 7 minutes longer, or until nicely browned and puffy. Transfer to warmed platter.

Repeat with remaining butter, apples, and batter. Serve pancakes warm with brown sugar sprinkled over top, and maple syrup.

BLUEBERRY MUFFINS
Makes 12 muffins

1 cup all-purpose flour
$^1/_2$ teaspoon salt
1 teaspoon baking powder
$^1/_2$ teaspoon baking soda
2 eggs
1 cup sour cream
5 tablespoons butter
1 cup light brown sugar, firmly packed
1 cup old-fashioned oats
1 cup blueberries, fresh or frozen (do not defrost)

Preheat oven to 375°. Butter a 3-inch-muffin pan generously.

In a small bowl, combine flour, salt, baking powder, and baking soda, first setting aside a couple of tablespoons of flour to coat the blueberries.

In a large bowl, beat 2 eggs with sour cream until well blended. Melt the butter with the brown sugar and beat into the egg mixture. Stir in the oats.

Fold in the flour mixture, stirring only enough to dampen the flour. The mixture should not be smooth. Toss the blueberries in the reserved flour and stir them into the batter. Spoon into the muffin tins, filling them two-thirds full. Bake for 25–30 minutes, until brown and puffy. Cool and remove from baking tin.

BRAN MUFFINS
Makes 24 to 30, depending on size of muffin cup

2¹/₂ cups All-Bran cereal
1¹/₂ cups raisins
1 cup boiling water
¹/₂ cup sugar
¹/₂ cup oil
1 cup molasses
2 eggs, well beaten
2 cups buttermilk
2¹/₂ cups all-purpose flour
2¹/₂ teaspoons baking soda
¹/₂ teaspoon salt

Preheat oven to 400°. Grease 2 muffin tins.

Place 1 cup of the bran cereal in a small bowl. Add the raisins and pour over the cup of boiling water. Set aside.

In a large mixing bowl, stir together the sugar, corn oil, molasses, beaten eggs, buttermilk, and the remaining 1¹/₂ cups of dry bran cereal.

In another bowl mix together the flour, baking soda, and salt until blended and stir into the egg-buttermilk mixture. Stir only until flour is absorbed. Do not overbeat.

Stir in the cooled bran mixture and blend well. Spoon into greased muffin tins, filling the cups two-thirds full. Bake for exactly 20 minutes. Cool on rack in pan for about 5 minutes. Remove from muffin tins and allow to cool completely on wire rack.

Note: This batter can be stored in a covered glass jar in the refrigerator for up to two months, so it is not necessary to bake the entire recipe at one time.

BUNDT PAN CORN BREAD
Makes one 10-inch bread

1 cup yellow cornmeal
1 cup sour cream
3 teaspoons baking powder
2 eggs
1/2 cup oil
1 16-ounce can creamed corn
1 1/2 teaspoons salt

Preheat oven to 350°. Butter a bundt pan generously.

In a large bowl, mix all the ingredients together and blend well. Pour into bundt pan and bake for 40 to 45 minutes, or until top is lightly browned and a cake tester comes out dry.

Remove from oven and let stand 10 to 15 minutes. Invert on a round serving dish and serve while hot.

THE CRAIGNAIR

CORN BREAD
Makes an 8-inch square bread

1 16-ounce can whole kernel corn (reserve liquid)
Milk
1/2 cup cornmeal
2 tablespoons bacon drippings
1/2 teaspoon salt
2 eggs, well beaten
1 teaspoon baking powder

Drain corn and pour liquid into a measuring cup. Add sufficient milk to make 1½ cups of liquid. In a medium-sized pot, add the liquid to the cornmeal and cook over moderate heat, stirring constantly, until thick. Remove from heat. Add bacon drippings, salt, and corn kernels. Stir and allow to cool.

Preheat oven to 350°. Grease an 8-inch square baking dish.

Add beaten eggs and baking powder to corn mixture and blend. Transfer to baking pan and bake for 35 minutes. Cool on wire rack. Cut into squares when cooled.

IRISH SODA BREAD
Makes 1 loaf

$^1/_3$ cup sugar
3$^1/_2$ cups all-purpose flour
1 teaspoon salt
3$^1/_2$ teaspoons baking soda
10 tablespoons (1$^1/_4$ sticks) butter
2 cups buttermilk
1 cup raisins (optional)

Preheat oven to 350°. Grease and lightly flour an 8 × 4 × 2-inch loaf pan.

Blend together the sugar, flour, salt, and baking soda. Cut in the butter with a pastry blender until it has the consistency of coarse cornmeal. Make a well in the center and pour in the buttermilk. Mix with a fork until all is well blended. If the dough seems too damp, add more flour. Mix in the raisins, if desired.

Transfer the batter to the loaf pan and bake for 50 to 60 minutes or until well browned and a cake tester comes out clean. Let the loaf cool for 15 minutes, then turn out onto a wire rack.

The
 Wildwood
PEACH POINT MUFFINS
Makes 12 muffins

1 egg
³/₄ cup milk
¹/₄ cup oil
¹/₂ cup peach butter* (plus additional for topping)
1¹/₂ cups all-purpose flour
1 tablespoon baking powder
³/₄ teaspoon salt
¹/₂ – ³/₄ cups Grape-Nuts or 1 cup granola

Preheat oven to 425°. Butter a muffin tin generously.

Beat the egg in a small mixing bowl. Beat in milk, oil, and peach butter. Set aside.

Put 1 cup of flour into a large mixing bowl. Place the remaining half cup of flour in a sifter with the baking powder and salt, and sift into the large bowl with the rest of the flour. Add the Grape-Nuts or granola.

Stir the egg-and-milk mixture and add all at once to the flour mixture. Stir just until the dry ingredients are moistened. Check the bottom of the bowl to make sure all the flour is incorporated.

Divide the batter evenly in the muffin tin. Spoon a dollop or "point" of peach butter into the top of each muffin. Bake for 15 minutes, or until golden and puffy on top. Do not overbake.

Remove from pan and cool slightly before serving.

The innkeeper-chef says: "Delicious with additional peach butter or any other preserve."

*Apple butter or other fruit preserves may be substituted for the peach butter.

POPOVERS
Makes 8

4 tablespoons solid vegetable shortening
1 cup all-purpose flour
¹/₄ teaspoon salt
1 cup skim milk
3 large eggs

Preheat oven to 375°. Place 1¹/₂ teaspoons shortening in bottom of each of 8 custard cups (or you may use muffin tins, filling every other cup to give the popovers the room they need to expand). Place cups in the heated oven for 5 minutes before filling.

Combine flour and salt in a medium-sized bowl. Stir in milk. Beat in eggs until well blended. Fill cups two-thirds full and bake for 45 to 50 minutes until puffed and browned. (If using individual cups, place them on a baking sheet.) Do not open the oven door during the baking — a blast of cold air can deflate the popovers. Absolutely no peeking! Make a small slit in the side of each popover to allow steam to escape. Serve immediately.

The chef says: "This recipe may be doubled or tripled successfully. For some reason, I like to make my batter for popovers three or four hours in advance or even a day ahead. A quick stir or two with the whisk, and the batter is reconstituted. This recipe has *never* failed."

POPPY SEED BREAD
Makes 3 loaves

4 eggs
2 cups sugar
1 14-ounce can evaporated milk
1¹/₂ cups oil
3 cups all-purpose flour
4 teaspoons baking powder
1 teaspoon salt
¹/₂ cup poppy seeds

Preheat oven to 350°. Grease three 4 × 8-inch loaf pans.

Beat eggs until light and thick; add sugar and continue beating. Gradually add evaporated milk and oil, beating well. Sift flour, baking powder, and salt together and add to egg-milk mixture, beating continuously. Stir in poppy seeds. Pour into loaf pans and bake for 1 hour, or until cake tester comes out clean and dry.

Cool on wire racks.

Note: This bread freezes very well.

The
Wildwood
PUMPKIN CHRISTMAS BREAD
Makes 3 loaves

5 cups all-purpose flour
1 cup light brown sugar, firmly packed
3 cups sugar
3 teaspoons baking soda
1 tablespoon ground cloves
1 tablespoon cinnamon
2 teaspoons nutmeg
$1/2$ teaspoon rum flavoring (optional)
1 cup oil
1 29-ounce can pumpkin
2 cups walnuts or pecans, coarsely chopped

Preheat oven to 325°. Grease 3 loaf pans well.

In a large bowl, mix together the flour, brown and white sugar, soda, cloves, cinnamon, and nutmeg. In another bowl, blend together the remaining ingredients. Combine and beat well until thoroughly blended and smooth.

Divide batter evenly among the 3 loaf pans and bake for $1 1/2$ hours. Turn out onto racks and cool thoroughly.

The chef says: "A great bread to make ahead and freeze for Christmas giving or carefree buffet serving. If freezing, wrap cooled bread first in plastic wrap, then in foil. Be adventurous and try adding optional rum flavoring."

The
  Wildwood
STEAMED BOSTON BROWN BREAD WITH RAISINS
Makes 2 loaves

1 cup yellow cornmeal
1 cup plus 2 tablespoons whole-wheat flour
1 cup rye flour
1 teaspoon baking soda
1 teaspoon salt
1 cup raisins
³/₄ cup molasses
1¹/₂ cups buttermilk

Mix and sift the dry ingredients into a large bowl, reserving the 2 tablespoons of whole-wheat flour. Toss the raisins in the reserved flour and add to the flour mixture with the molasses and buttermilk, stirring well.

Grease the insides of two 1-pound-size baking cans; cleaned coffee cans are excellent. Line the bottoms of the cans with rounds of greased waxed paper or baking parchment. Fill ²/₃ full with batter.

Place the cans on a rack inside a large kettle with a lid. Add warm water until it comes up to the middle of the cans. Cover the kettle and bring water to a boil. Continue at an easy boil for 2 or 3 hours, or until well done. Add water as needed.

Serve 1 loaf to your hungry family or friends; wrap the other in foil and store. You may then use the Stage Two procedure to make it as moist and delicious as the first loaf.

Stage Two: To serve extra-moist brown bread at a later date, place the bread in a colander that will fit above another pot, making a double boiler with holes to allow the steam to really penetrate the bread. Steam for 15 to 30 minutes and serve.

The innkeeper-chef says: "The trick to the exquisite moistness of our brown bread is that it is steamed twice — once as it is made and again right before serving." (See *Stage Two,* above.)

STRAWBERRY PANCAKES
Makes about 12 pancakes

5 eggs
$^1/_3$ cup sugar
$^1/_4$ cup ($^1/_2$ stick) butter, melted
2 cups milk
$2^1/_4$ cups all-purpose flour
1 heaping teaspoon baking powder
2 cups fresh strawberries, washed and sliced
Maple syrup

Whisk the eggs with the sugar until light and fluffy. Add butter and milk and whisk well. Sift the flour and baking powder and fold into the egg-milk mixture. Do not beat. The batter may be slightly lumpy.

Heat the griddle to the point where a drop of water will bounce off.

Pour batter onto the hot griddle to the desired pancake size and immediately place the sliced strawberries on the pancake. Turn the pancake before the bubbles in the batter burst.

Serve with whipped butter and warm maple syrup.

The chef says: "These pancakes look attractive if they are served so that the strawberries are visible."

YANKEE CORN STICKS
(Corn Pone)
Makes about 24 corn sticks

1 cup all-purpose flour
3 tablespoons sugar
2 teaspoons baking powder
$^3/_4$ teaspoon salt
1 cup yellow cornmeal
1 egg, well beaten
1 $8^3/_4$-ounce can cream-style corn
$^3/_4$ cup milk
2 tablespoons oil

continued

Preheat oven to 425°. Preheat cast-iron corn-stick pans or small-sized muffin tins in oven. When heated, grease generously.

In a large bowl, combine flour, sugar, baking powder, and salt, and mix well. Stir in yellow cornmeal. In another, smaller, bowl, blend together the well-beaten egg, corn, milk, and oil. Add to dry ingredients and stir only until just moistened. Fill the preheated and greased pans two-thirds full of batter. Bake for about 20 minutes.

Combes Family Inn

ZUCCHINI BREAD
Makes 2 loaves

3 eggs
2 cups sugar
1 cup oil
2 cups zucchini, unpeeled, seeded, and shredded
3 teaspoons vanilla extract
3 cups all-purpose flour
1 teaspoon salt
1 teaspoon baking powder
1 teaspoon baking soda
1 tablespoon cinnamon
1 cup coarsely chopped walnuts

Preheat oven to 350°. Grease two 9 × 5 × 3-inch loaf pans.

In a large bowl, beat eggs until light and fluffy. Add sugar, oil, zucchini, and vanilla extract, and mix lightly but until well blended. In a separate bowl, combine flour, salt, baking powder, baking soda, and cinnamon, and mix well. Stir the flour mixture into the egg-zucchini mixture, stirring until well blended. Fold in nuts. Divide batter evenly between the two loaf pans and bake for 1 hour, or until a cake tester comes out dry. Turn out onto wire rack to cool. Let cool completely before slicing. This bread freezes well.

The innkeeper says: "When zucchini is plentiful, I shred and freeze it for use during the winter months."

GRANE'S
FAIRHAVEN

DOWN EAST ANADAMA BREAD
Makes 2 loaves

3½ cups water
½ cup (1 stick) margarine
1 cup molasses
1 cup fine cornmeal
7 cups all-purpose flour
2 packages dry yeast (2 tablespoons)
1 tablespoon salt

Bring water to a boil in a large pan. Add margarine and molasses and stir until margarine is melted. Slowly add cornmeal, stirring constantly. Simmer over low heat for 20 minutes, stirring occasionally. Cool 20 minutes.

In a large bowl, mix 3 cups flour with yeast and salt. Add cornmeal mixture and beat 2 minutes with electric beaters. Add 3 more cups of flour and turn out onto a lightly floured surface. Knead with the remaining cup of flour until smooth and elastic, about 10 minutes.

Place in a greased bowl, turning once to coat top. Cover loosely with a towel or plastic wrap and let rise in a warm place until double in bulk, about 45 minutes to an hour.

Turn out on a lightly floured surface and punch down. Let it rest for 10 minutes. Divide dough in half.

Shape and place in 2 greased 9-inch loaf pans. Cover and allow to rise until double, about 1 hour.

Bake in a preheated 400° oven for 45 minutes or longer, until the bread tests done. (To test, take out 1 loaf, protecting your hands with pot holders or asbestos gloves. The bottom should be browned and, when tapped, it should sound hollow. If the bottom seems soggy and does not give a hollow sound, return to the oven and check every 5 minutes.)

MARY'S PUMPKIN BREAD
Makes 2 loaves

$^1/_4$ cup honey
1 cup scalded milk (temperature about 110°)
$^1/_2$ cup warm water (temperature about 110°)
$^1/_4$ cup ($^1/_2$ stick) butter, melted
2 teaspoons salt
2 packages dry yeast (2 tablespoons)
1 teaspoon cinnamon
$^1/_2$ teaspoon nutmeg
1 1-pound can pumpkin
1 cup whole-wheat flour
2 eggs, well beaten
5–6 cups unbleached all-purpose flour

Place the honey, scalded milk, warm water, melted butter, and salt in a large mixing bowl and gently stir in the yeast. In 5 or 10 minutes, the mixture will bubble, letting you know that the yeast has been "proofed." At that point, add the cinnamon, nutmeg, pumpkin, and whole-wheat flour. Mix thoroughly and beat in the eggs.

Mix in the unbleached flour 1 cup at a time, using only as much as is necessary to make the dough come together and away from the sides of the bowl. This is a soft dough and will be a little sticky.

Cover the bowl and let rise in a warm, draft-free spot for about 45 minutes, until double in volume. Punch down, knead for 1 or 2 minutes, and shape into 2 loaves, either on a greased baking sheet or in 2 standard-sized greased bread pans. Cover and let rise again until double, about 45 minutes.

Preheat oven to 375°. Bake for 45 minutes to 1 hour. Bread should sound hollow when tapped on the bottom.

OATMEAL BREAD
Makes 2 loaves

2 cups water
1 cup quick oats (not instant)
1¹/₂ tablespoons butter
1 package dry yeast (1 tablespoon)
¹/₂ cup lukewarm water
¹/₂ cup molasses
2 teaspoons salt
4²/₃ cups all-purpose flour

Bring 2 cups of water to a boil. Remove from heat and stir in the oats. Add the butter and let stand for 1 hour.

In a large bowl, soak the yeast in ¹/₂ cup of lukewarm water for 5 minutes. Stir until yeast is dissolved. Add molasses, salt, and oatmeal mixture. Stir thoroughly, and gradually stir in the flour. Reserve the last ²/₃ cup until you see how much you need. When the dough begins to leave the sides of the bowl, turn it out onto a lightly floured board or counter top. The dough should be as soft as possible without being too sticky to handle. Dip your hands lightly in flour and knead the dough for 8 minutes. Place the dough in an oiled bowl, turning it to coat the top. Cover the bowl with a light towel and let the dough rise in a warm spot until doubled in bulk, about 1 hour.

Punch down the dough, knead for 1 or 2 minutes, and shape into 2 loaves. Place on a greased baking sheet, cover with a towel, and let rise again until doubled in size, 45 minutes to 1 hour.

Bake in a preheated 375° oven for 35 minutes. Cool on wire racks.

PARMESAN CHEESE ROLLS OR BREAD
Makes 16 rolls or 2 loaves

3½–4 cups all-purpose flour
2 packages dry yeast (2 tablespoons)
2 tablespoons sugar
2 teaspoons garlic salt
1 teaspoon Italian seasoning
1 cup milk
½ cup water
2 tablespoons butter
1 egg, well beaten
¾ cup grated Parmesan cheese
2 tablespoons melted butter

In a large mixing bowl, combine 1½ cups of flour, yeast, sugar, salt, and Italian seasoning. Mix well.

In a saucepan, heat the milk, water, and butter until just warm — not hot — and the butter melts. Add to the flour mixture. Add the egg and, with an electric beater, beat at low speed for 1 minute. Increase to medium speed and beat for 3 minutes.

By hand, blend in ½ cup of the grated cheese and enough of the remaining flour to make a firm dough. When the dough begins to leave the sides of the bowl, turn it out onto a lightly floured board or counter top. Sprinkle it lightly with flour to keep it from sticking to the work surface. Knead the dough for 5 minutes or until it becomes satiny and elastic. Place the dough in a greased bowl, turning it to coat the entire surface.

Preheat the oven to 200°–225° for 1 minute and turn off. Cover the bowl and place it in the warm oven for 15 minutes.

Punch down the dough and divide into 16 pieces, if making rolls. Form into balls and dip tops into melted butter and the remaining quarter cup of Parmesan cheese. Place in a well-greased 9 × 13-inch pan, cover, and let rise for 10 minutes. Bake in a preheated 375° oven for 20 to 25 minutes, until golden brown. When done, remove from baking pan and cool on racks.

If making bread, divide dough in half, following directions above, and bake in 2 well-greased 8-inch bread pans.

PECAN ROLLS
(Sticky Buns)
Makes 12 to 15 rolls

1 package dry yeast (1 tablespoon)
1 teaspoon sugar
$^1/_4$ cup warm water
$^1/_3$ cup hot milk
$^1/_2$ teaspoon salt
2 tablespoons sugar
2 tablespoons butter
1 egg
1 tablespoon grated lemon rind
2 cups all-purpose flour
$^2/_3$ cup dark corn syrup
1 cup pecans, coarsely broken
6 tablespoons melted butter
1 cup light brown sugar
1 tablespoon cinnamon

In a small bowl, stir the yeast and sugar into the warm water and let stand to dissolve. In a large bowl, combine the hot milk, salt, sugar, and butter, and stir until the butter melts and the mixture cools. Stir in the egg and lemon rind. Add the dissolved yeast and the flour to the mixture and blend. Turn out onto a lightly floured board and knead gently for approximately 5 minutes, adding more flour if the dough is sticky, until it can be easily handled. Knead until smooth and elastic. Put the dough in a greased bowl, turning to coat the entire surface, and cover bowl. Let rise in a warm place for about 1½ hours, or until doubled in bulk.

Lightly grease a baking pan 7½ × 8½ × 2 inches. Cover the bottom of the pan with a mixture of corn syrup and pecans. Punch down the dough and roll it into a rectangle about ¼ inch thick. Brush with melted butter. Mix together the brown sugar and cinnamon and sprinkle evenly over the buttered dough. Roll like a jelly roll, starting on the long side, and cut into ¾-inch slices. Place the slices in the baking pan over the corn syrup–nut mixture. Let rise for 1 hour. Preheat oven to 350° and bake for ½ hour. When rolls are done, invert onto a buttered cookie sheet. Serve warm.

POPCORN BREAD
Makes 3 loaves

1 cup boiling water
1 cup cold milk
1½ packages dry yeast (1½ tablespoons)
¾ cup sugar
4 cups popped corn
1 teaspoon salt
3 eggs
⅓ cup melted butter
7 cups all-purpose flour
Melted butter for crust

Combine the water and milk in a large mixing bowl and stir in yeast and sugar. Let stand about 10 minutes until surface is bubbly (proofing).

Pick through the popcorn and discard any unpopped kernels. Run the popcorn through a blender or food processor until it is the consistency of cornmeal. Add to the mixture in the bowl with the salt. Beat in the eggs and melted butter and gradually work in all the flour. Turn out on a lightly floured surface and knead for 10 minutes or so, until the dough is smooth and elastic.

Grease a large bowl and put the dough into it, turning to coat the entire surface. Cover and let rise in a warm spot, usually 25 to 30 minutes. Punch it down while still in the bowl. Cover and let rise once more.

Turn out onto a floured surface and separate into 3 pieces. Shape into loaves and place in 3 greased 9 × 5-inch loaf pans. Cover and let rise until doubled in size, about 1 hour.

Bake in a preheated 350° oven for 35 to 40 minutes or until golden brown and tests done. Remove from oven and brush melted butter over top.

$\mathcal{X}$ $\mathcal{G}$rains, $\mathcal{P}$asta, and $\mathcal{L}$egumes

BAKED BEANS
Serves 12 or more

2 pounds red kidney beans (or another dried bean of your choice)
4 teaspoons dry mustard
1 cup light brown sugar
³/₄ cup molasses
Salt
1 medium onion, thinly sliced
2 tablespoons vinegar
6 strips uncooked bacon

Soak the beans overnight in cold water to cover.

Drain the beans and add fresh water to cover, and bring to a boil. Cover the pot, lower the heat, and simmer for 45 minutes, or until just tender.

Preheat the oven to 325°. Drain the beans when tender, reserving the liquid. Place the beans in a 3-quart bean pot. Combine the mustard, sugar, molasses, salt, onion, and vinegar, and mix with the beans. Push in the strips of uncooked bacon, distributing them evenly. Add reserved cooking liquid, covering the beans by ¹/₂ inch. Cover the bean pot tightly.

Bake for 5 to 6 hours, or until tender. Check periodically to make sure the beans are moist, and add bean liquid as needed.

BREEZEMERE GRANOLA
Makes about 15 cups

5 cups oatmeal
1 cup slivered almonds
1 cup chopped walnuts
1 cup sesame seeds
1 cup wheat germ
1 cup shredded coconut
1 cup sunflower seeds
1 cup safflower oil
1 cup honey
1 cup raisins
1 cup dried currants

Preheat oven to 300°.

Combine the first 7 ingredients in a large bowl and mix well.

Heat the oil and honey until just warm. Pour over the dry ingredients and mix well. Spread out in a thin layer in several shallow pans such as large roasting pans or jelly-roll pans and bake for 45 minutes or until lightly browned. Stir occasionally with a spatula.

Cool and add the raisins and currants. Store in a tightly covered container in the refrigerator. This will keep for weeks when properly stored. Serve with milk or yogurt.

The
Wildwood
NORWEGIAN NOODLE PUDDING
Serves 8

$^1/_2$ pound medium-width noodles
$^1/_2$ cup (1 stick) butter
$^1/_2$ teaspoon cinnamon, or to taste
$^1/_2$ cup raisins
$^1/_2$ cup sugar
Pinch of salt
3 teaspoons almond extract, or to taste
3 eggs
2 cups milk

Boil the noodles in salted water until just barely tender. They will finish cooking in the oven so they should be slightly underdone. Strain the noodles in a colander, rinsing with cold water. Drain well and place in a bowl.

Melt the butter and put half in a large casserole or baking dish, tilting the dish so that sides and bottom are greased. Preheat the oven to 350° and place the empty casserole in the oven.

Add cinnamon, raisins, sugar, salt, and almond extract to the well-drained noodles. In a separate bowl, beat the eggs, add milk, and beat again until well blended. Add to the noodles with the remainder of the melted butter. Stir well.

Pour into the heated casserole and bake until the top is golden brown, 1 hour or longer.

The innkeeper-chef says: "This can be served hot, or it is delicious cold the next day. We serve it warm as a special breakfast treat."

PASTA WITH SAFFRON AND CRAB AUBERGINE
Serves 4

2 tablespoons dry vermouth
$^1/_4$ teaspoon crushed saffron threads
1 cup dry white wine
$^1/_2$ cup minced shallots
2 cloves garlic, sliced thin
2 tablespoons dried basil
1 teaspoon dried tarragon
1 cup heavy cream
3 tablespoons minced fresh parsley
3 tablespoons minced fresh basil, or 1 tablespoon dried
Salt and freshly ground pepper
1 pound lump crabmeat, picked over
1 pound fettuccine

Combine the dry vermouth and saffron in a small bowl and set aside.

In a stainless steel or enamel saucepan (not aluminum), combine dry white wine, shallots, garlic, basil, and tarragon. Bring to a boil and cook briskly over high heat until the wine is almost completely evaporated.

While this is cooking, bring to a boil 4 quarts of salted water for the pasta in a large pot.

When the wine has cooked down and evaporated, add the cream and simmer over low heat for 10 minutes, stirring occasionally. Strain the mixture through a fine sieve and return to saucepan, discarding the solids. Bring to a boil over moderate heat and stir in the saffron mixture, parsley, basil, and salt and pepper to taste. Reduce heat and keep warm.

When the water in the pasta pot reaches a lively boil, add the pasta and cook *al dente* — "firm to the bite."

Add the crabmeat to the cream sauce, blend carefully so as not to break up the lumps, and simmer over low heat only until the crabmeat is heated through.

Drain the pasta in a colander, place in a heated serving bowl, and toss with the hot crabmeat sauce. Serve at once.

Switzer Stübli
POLENTA
Serves 4 or 5

3 tablespoons butter
1 medium onion, chopped
2 cups water
1 teaspoon salt
1 cup cornmeal
1/2 cup grated Parmesan cheese

In a small skillet, melt the butter and sauté the onion until soft. Set aside.

Bring the water and salt to a boil in a saucepan and add the cornmeal in a very thin stream, stirring with a wooden spoon or paddle constantly until the mixture is thick and soft — about 15 minutes.

Add the sautéed onions with whatever butter is in the skillet. Stir over low heat until well mixed and bubbling hot. Add the grated cheese, stirring constantly, and serve when the cheese has melted.

Switzer Stübli
SWISS RISOTTO
Serves 5 or 6

1⅓ cups uncooked rice (not instant)
6 tablespoons oil or butter
1 medium onion, chopped
4½ cups chicken broth
¼ teaspoon ground nutmeg
Freshly ground pepper
¾ cup (3 ounces) grated Swiss cheese

Put the rice, oil or butter, and chopped onion in a large skillet over high heat. Stir constantly for about 3 or 4 minutes until the rice turns opaque and the onion turns yellow.

Add the chicken broth and stir. Add the nutmeg and a few grinds of pepper. Bring to a boil, reduce heat, and cook over medium heat for about 20 minutes. *Do not cover.*

When almost all of the liquid has been absorbed, remove from heat and add the grated Swiss cheese. Stir gently with a fork until the cheese is melted. Serve in a heated serving bowl.

The chef says: "Here is an old Swiss trick. If you cook with cheese, rinse pots and plates with cold water before you use hot dishwater when cleaning up."

XI Pies, Cakes, Cookies, and Bars

PIES

ANNA'S PIE
Makes a 9-inch pie

2 eggs
1 cup sugar
¹/₂ cup (1 stick) butter, melted
³/₄ cup milk
³/₄ cup light corn syrup
1 cup flaked coconut
³/₄ cup uncooked oatmeal (old-fashioned or quick-cooking)
1 unbaked 9-inch pie shell (Pâte Brisée, page 199)
Sweetened whipped cream (optional)

Preheat oven to 350°.

In a large bowl, beat eggs until light. Add sugar, melted butter, milk, and corn syrup, and blend well. Stir in coconut and oatmeal. Pour into the unbaked pie shell and set on a cookie sheet or piece of aluminum foil, since the filling might bubble over. Bake for 1 hour, or until set and the crust nicely browned. Serve at room temperature with a dab of whipped cream for a few additional calories!

The innkeeper says: "Our cook was with us for over ten years. Before that, she ran an inn of her own. We won't tell her age, but she was well past the age most people consider 'retirement' when she came to our inn. She has now retired again, but only from paid employment. This pie is one of her specialties, so we call it simply 'Anna's Pie.'"

Aubergine

APPLE CUSTARD TART
Makes a 9- to 10-inch tart

Pâte Brisée**
4 to 5 apples, peeled, cored, and thinly sliced (Granny Smith,
    greenings, McIntosh, or Cortland)

CUSTARD
3 eggs
¼ cup sugar
1 cup heavy cream
2 tablespoons dark or amber rum

½ cup walnuts, finely chopped

Prepare the Pâte Brisée.

Place sliced apples in water to which a few tablespoons of lemon
juice have been added. (Spin apple slices in salad spinner or blot well
with paper towels before using.)

For custard, place eggs and sugar in a mixing bowl and beat until
well blended. Stir in heavy cream and rum.

Preheat the oven to 350°.

Assemble the tart as quickly as possible. Arrange the well-dried apple
slices over the bottom of the baked pie shell in one layer in concentric
circles, one slice overlapping another like roof shingles. Be generous
with the apple slices; they shrink a bit during baking.

Place the tart on a baking sheet and pour custard over evenly.
Sprinkle top with chopped walnuts and bake until custard is just set,
about 40 to 45 minutes. Serve warm or at room temperature.

***Pâte Brisée (supplied by the editors)*
Makes a single 9- or 10-inch crust

½ cup (1 stick) unsalted butter
1½ cups all-purpose flour
½ teaspoon salt
1 tablespoon sugar
3–4 tablespoons ice water

continued

Cut the butter into ¹/₄-inch bits and refrigerate to chill well. Mix the flour, salt, and sugar in a large mixing bowl. Add the cold butter and mix with your fingertips until the mixture resembles coarse meal. Add 3 to 4 tablespoons of ice water and mix with your fingertips just until the mixture forms a ball. Don't overblend. Wrap in waxed paper or plastic wrap and refrigerate for 30 to 40 minutes or until firm.

Let the dough come to room temperature and roll out on a lightly floured surface until it measures about 12 inches in diameter and is ¹/₈ inch thick. Ease the dough without stretching into a buttered 9- or 10-inch tart pan or pie plate and press it gently into sides and bottom of the pan. Trim off excess pastry. Prick the dough all over, sides and bottom, with a fork. Refrigerate for 30 minutes before baking.

To keep the bottom of the shell from lifting during baking, line the shell with foil or waxed paper and weight it with 4 or 5 cups of dried beans or raw rice, which can be stored in a jar and used repeatedly.

Bake in the center of a 400° preheated oven for 15 to 18 minutes, or until the shell is lightly golden. Remove weights and foil lining and allow to cool.

CHOCOLATE BUTTER CREAM PIE
Makes a 9-inch pie

³/₄ cup butter
1 cup plus 2 tablespoons sugar
3 squares (3 ounces) unsweetened chocolate
3 eggs
1 teaspoon vanilla extract
1 baked 9-inch pie shell (Pâte Brisée, page 199)
Garnish: whipped cream

Cream the butter and sugar until light and fluffy. Melt the chocolate over hot water and cool slightly. Blend into the butter-sugar mixture.

Beat in the eggs, one at a time, and beat 3 to 5 minutes after each egg. Mix in vanilla extract. Check for taste — if the mixture is at all grainy, continue to beat until satiny smooth.

Pour into baked pie shell and chill until firm. Garnish with whipped cream.

The chef says: "An extremely rich dessert."

CHOCOLATE CHIP PIE
Makes an 8-inch pie

CRUST
16 Oreo cookies
¼ cup (½ stick) butter at room temperature

FILLING
32 large marshmallows (½ pound)
¾ cup milk
¼ teaspoon salt
1 square (1 ounce) unsweetened chocolate, grated
¾ cup heavy cream
1 teaspoon vanilla extract
¼ cup finely chopped nuts
Garnish: sweetened whipped cream (optional)

Preheat oven to 350°. Butter an 8-inch pie plate.

Grind, blend, or process Oreo cookies, filling and all, until they are uniformly fine crumbs. You will need about 1¼ cups of crumbs. Place in a bowl with softened butter and mix well. Press crumb mixture over bottom and sides of pie plate. Bake for about 8 minutes, or until the crust is firm. Remove from oven and cool.

For the filling, put the marshmallows, milk, and salt in the top of a double boiler and heat and stir over boiling water until the marshmallows are melted. Transfer to a bowl, cool, and chill.

Grate the chocolate, using the coarse side of the grater, and set aside. Whip the cream until stiff. Fold the grated chocolate, whipped cream, vanilla, and nuts into the chilled marshmallow. Spoon into the baked pie shell and chill for 3 to 5 hours, or overnight, until firm. Serve with additional whipped cream over top, if desired.

CRANBERRY CHIFFON PIE
Makes a 9-inch pie

4 ounces cream cheese at room temperature
1 cup whole cranberry sauce
1 cup heavy cream
$\frac{1}{2}$ cup sugar
1 baked 9-inch pie shell, cooled (Pâte Brisée, page 199)
Garnish: whipped cream or whole cranberry sauce flavored with
   Kirsch

With an electric mixer, mix cream cheese and cranberry sauce at high speed until blended. Slowly add heavy cream and sugar, continuing to whip until thickened. Pour into piecrust. Cover with plastic wrap and freeze for 5 or 6 hours, or longer.

Remove pie a few minutes before serving and garnish, as preferred.

CRANBERRY-RAISIN PIE WITH WALNUT CRUST
Makes a deep 9-inch pie

CRUST
1 cup coarsely chopped walnuts
$\frac{1}{2}$ cup all-purpose flour
$\frac{1}{3}$ cup sugar
$\frac{1}{4}$ cup ($\frac{1}{2}$ stick) melted butter

FILLING
$1\frac{1}{2}$ cups sugar
6 tablespoons all-purpose flour
$\frac{1}{4}$ teaspoon salt
4 cups (1 pound) fresh cranberries
$1\frac{1}{2}$ cups ($\frac{1}{2}$ pound) raisins
$\frac{1}{4}$ cup ($\frac{1}{2}$ stick) butter
$1\frac{1}{2}$ cups water
1 teaspoon almond extract

Preheat oven to 350°. Lightly grease a deep 9-inch pie plate. With the metal chopping blade in place in the food processor, process the walnuts, turning on and off rapidly a few times, until coarsely chopped. Add the flour, sugar, and melted butter, and process until you have a very fine, silky crumb mixture. Press the crumbs firmly over the bottom and sides of the pie plate and bake until very slightly brown, 12 to 15 minutes. Remove from oven and cool to room temperature.

Combine all the filling ingredients except the almond extract in a large saucepan. Cook over low heat, stirring often, until the mixture becomes thick and glossy, about 20 minutes. Remove from heat and stir in almond extract. Cool to room temperature.

To bake, preheat oven to 350°. Pour the filling into the crust and bake for 30 minutes. Serve warm with ice cream or whipped cream.

FROZEN LEMON PIE
Makes a 9-inch pie

CRUST
1¼ cups cornflake crumbs
⅓ cup melted butter
3 tablespoons sugar

FILLING
3 eggs, separated
½ cup sugar
⅓ cup fresh lemon juice
1 tablespoon grated lemon rind
1 cup heavy cream, whipped
Garnish: sweetened whipped cream

Mix together the crust ingredients and press firmly over sides and bottom of a 9-inch pie plate. Place in freezer to firm for 15 to 20 minutes.

To prepare the filling, beat egg yolks with ¼ cup of sugar until thick and lemon colored. Add lemon juice and rind and blend well.

In another bowl and using clean, dry beaters, beat egg whites until soft peaks form. Slowly add the remaining ¼ cup sugar and beat until stiff, glossy peaks form. Fold beaten egg whites into the egg yolk mixture. Whip cream until it mounds softly and fold in.

Pour into chilled pie shell and freeze 6 to 8 hours before serving. Garnish with sweetened whipped cream.

𝔖notohill

HOLIDAY PUMPKIN PECAN PIE
Makes a 9- or 10-inch pie

1 cup sugar
¼ teaspoon ground ginger
¼ teaspoon nutmeg
⅛ teaspoon ground cloves
1 teaspoon cinnamon
½ teaspoon salt
1 tablespoon all-purpose flour
1½ cups cooked and mashed pumpkin, fresh or canned
3 eggs, beaten
2 teaspoons light molasses
1½ cups light cream
2 tablespoons light rum
½ cup coarsely chopped pecans
1 deep unbaked 9- or 10-inch pie shell (Pâte Brisée, page 199)

TOPPING
¼ cup (½ stick) butter
¾ cup light brown sugar
¾ cup chopped pecans

Preheat oven to 425°.

In a large bowl, combine the sugar, spices, salt, and flour. Mix with the pumpkin and add the beaten eggs, molasses, cream, rum, and nuts, blending well. Pour into the unbaked pie shell and bake for 10 minutes. (If you prefer, you may bake at 350° for 20 minutes.)

Prepare the topping while the pie is in the oven. Mix together the butter, brown sugar, and chopped pecans until crumbly.

After the first 10 minutes (or 20 minutes, if baking at 350°), remove the pie from the oven and sprinkle with topping. Replace in oven and continue baking for 25 to 30 minutes, or until the filling sets.

The chef says: "Can be eaten with vanilla ice cream, but it's really nice alone."

LEMON SPONGE PIE
Makes a 9-inch pie

1 cup sugar
3 tablespoons all-purpose flour
3 eggs, separated
¼ cup melted butter
3 tablespoons (or more) lemon juice
Grated rind of 1 lemon
1½ cups milk
1 unbaked 9-inch pie shell (Pâte Brisée, page 199)

Preheat oven to 450°.

In a large bowl, mix sugar and flour. Beat in lightly beaten egg yolks, butter, lemon juice, and rind. Stir in milk. You might taste it at this point to see if it is lemony enough for you. If you like it more tart, add another tablespoon or so of lemon juice.

In another bowl, beat the egg whites until stiff, but not dry. Gently fold them into the batter. Pour carefully into the unbaked shell and bake for 10 minutes. Reduce heat to 325° and bake approximately another 25 minutes, or until a cake tester inserted in the middle of the pie comes out dry. Cool on rack.

"MY" PECAN PIE
Makes a 9-inch pie

1 cup light corn syrup
1 cup dark brown sugar
$^1/_3$ cup melted butter
1 heaping cup pecans, coarsely broken
$^1/_2$ cup walnuts, coarsely broken
3 eggs, lightly beaten
$^1/_2$ teaspoon vanilla
Pinch salt
Sweetened whipped cream (optional)
1 unbaked 9-inch pie shell (Pâte Brisée, page 199)

Preheat oven to 350°.

Mix together all the ingredients (except the whipped cream) in the order in which they are listed, and blend well. Pour into the unbaked pie shell and bake for 50 to 60 minutes, or until the filling is firm. Cool on rack. Serve with whipped cream, if desired.

Lincoln House
RHUBARB CUSTARD PIE
Makes a 10-inch pie

2 eggs
3 tablespoons milk
2 cups sugar, or 1 cup honey
6 tablespoons all-purpose flour
$^1/_2$ teaspoon ground ginger
Few gratings of fresh nutmeg
4–5 cups cut-up rhubarb, fresh or frozen and thawed
1 unbaked 10-inch pie shell with top crust**

Preheat oven to 375°.

In a medium bowl, beat the eggs until frothy and add all the remaining ingredients except the rhubarb. Beat until the mixture is light and very fluffy. Add the rhubarb and mix well.

Pour into the unbaked pie shell. Add the top crust and crimp edges firmly together. Prick top crust well. Bake 50 to 60 minutes, until nicely browned. Cool before serving.

**Pastry for 10-inch Double Piecrust *(supplied by the editors)*

3 cups all-purpose flour
$^1/_2$ teaspoon salt
1 stick ($^1/_2$ cup) plus 1 tablespoon cold butter, cut into bits
$^1/_4$ cup solid vegetable shortening
1 egg and 1 egg yolk, lightly beaten
3–4 tablespoons ice water

Combine flour and salt in a large bowl. Cut in butter and shortening and mix with your fingertips until the mixture resembles coarse meal. Stir in the egg and egg yolk and enough water to hold the dough together. Divide dough in unequal halves — one slightly larger than the other for the bottom crust. Flatten disks of dough, wrap each in waxed paper, and chill in the refrigerator for an hour or more before rolling out.

SOUR CREAM APPLE PIE
Makes a 9-inch pie

2 tablespoons all-purpose flour
$^3/_4$ cup sugar
$^3/_4$ teaspoon cinnamon
$^1/_8$ teaspoon salt
1 egg
$^1/_2$ teaspoon vanilla extract
1 cup sour cream
6 medium apples, pared, cored and thinly sliced
1 unbaked 9-inch whole-wheat crust, chilled (below)

continued

TOPPING

$^1/_3$ cup all-purpose flour
$^1/_3$ cup sugar
$^3/_4$ teaspoon cinnamon
$^1/_4$ cup ($^1/_2$ stick) butter

Preheat oven to 400°.

Sift together into a large bowl the flour, sugar, cinnamon, and salt. Stir in the egg, vanilla extract, and sour cream. Fold in the sliced apples and spoon mixture into the pie shell.

Bake for 15 minutes. Reduce heat to 350° and bake 30 minutes longer.

While the pie is baking, combine the flour, sugar, and cinnamon for the topping. Blend in the butter with a pastry blender until crumbly. Sprinkle topping over pie, increase heat to 400°, and bake 10 minutes longer.

WHOLE-WHEAT CRUST
Makes two 9-inch crusts

2$^1/_4$ cups sifted whole-wheat flour
$^1/_2$ teaspoon salt
$^3/_4$ teaspoon baking powder
10$^1/_2$ tablespoons shortening
6$^1/_2$ tablespoons cold water

Sift the measured sifted flour again with the salt and baking powder into a bowl. Cut in the shortening and work with your fingertips or a pastry blender until the mixture resembles small peas or coarse meal. Add cold water, a little at a time, and only enough to make the mixture form a ball. Wrap in waxed paper or plastic and refrigerate for at least 30 minutes, or until firm.

Divide in two and roll out half the dough on a lightly floured surface. Roll out as thinly as possible — about $^1/_8$ inch thick. Ease the dough into a 9-inch pie plate and chill. Fill and bake as directed above.

(Unbaked pie dough will keep in the refrigerator, tightly wrapped in plastic wrap or foil, for at least 4 days.)

**Combes
Family Inn**

STRAWBERRY TRIUMPH PIE
Makes a 9-inch pie

1 quart strawberries, hulled
3 tablespoons cornstarch
1 cup sugar
2 tablespoons lemon juice
1 baked 9-inch pie shell (Pâte Brisée, page 199) or crumb crust**
Sweetened whipped cream

Crush half the berries and place in a small saucepan. Stir in cornstarch, sugar, and lemon juice. Cook, stirring constantly, until mixture comes to the boil and becomes clear and thick. Remove from heat.

Cut the remaining berries in halves and fold in. Turn into the baked pie shell or crumb crust and chill 3 to 5 hours. Top with whipped cream.

If desired, the pie can be frozen for a different taste.

The innkeeper says: "I usually pick the strawberries myself. Besides turning the berries into strawberry jam, this is the most popular way of using the fruit."

**Crumb Crust (supplied by the editors)*

Mix 1½ cups of fine crumbs — graham crackers or vanilla wafers — with ⅓ cup melted butter. Blend well and pat evenly and firmly over the sides and bottom of a greased pie plate. Bake in a 250° oven for 8 to 10 minutes, or until the crust looks firm. Cool before filling.

Snowbill

WONDERFUL PIE
Makes an 8- or 9-inch pie

3 egg whites at room temperature
1 cup sugar
12 soda crackers, finely crumbled
1 teaspoon vanilla extract
1 teaspoon baking powder
1 cup coarsely chopped walnuts
1 cup heavy cream
Confectioners' sugar

Beat the egg whites until soft peaks form. Add the sugar gradually, beating constantly, until stiff but not dry — the meringue should look shiny and glossy. Gently fold in the soda cracker crumbs. Fold in vanilla extract, baking powder, and chopped walnuts.

Preheat oven to 350°. Grease an 8- or 9-inch pie pan. Pour the meringue mixture into pie pan and bake for 30 minutes. Remove from oven and let cool.

Beat cream until stiff, and sweeten slightly with confectioners' sugar. Top the cooled pie with whipped cream and refrigerate for about 5 hours.

The chef says: "Everyone wonders what this is. It is so simple to make, but is always a hit. You may make the meringue a day ahead."

BLUEBERRY BOY BAIT
Makes a 9 × 13-inch cake

2 cups all-purpose flour
1¹/₂ cups sugar
2 teaspoons baking powder
1 teaspoon salt
²/₃ cup margarine or oil
1 cup milk
2 eggs

TOPPING
2–3 cups blueberries
1 cup sugar
1 teaspoon cinnamon

Preheat oven to 350°. Grease and lightly flour a 9 × 13-inch baking pan, tapping out the excess flour.

Combine the first 7 ingredients in a large bowl and, with an electric beater, beat for 3 minutes. Pour batter into cake pan.

Arrange on top of the batter at least 2 cups of blueberries. Combine the sugar and cinnamon and sprinkle over top.

Bake for 40 to 50 minutes, or until a cake tester comes out dry. Cut into squares and serve with whipped cream as dessert or without cream for breakfast. May be reheated, if desired.

The chef says: "Half this recipe can be made and baked in an 8-inch square pan."

CHEESECAKE
Makes a 9-inch cake

GRAHAM CRACKER CRUST
1 cup fine graham cracker crumbs
Dash cinnamon
3–4 tablespoons melted butter
2¹⁄₄ pounds cream cheese at room temperature
1 cup confectioners' sugar
3 tablespoons cornstarch
¹⁄₂ cup sour cream
3 eggs
2 egg yolks
¹⁄₂ cup light or heavy cream
Grated rind of 1 lemon

Grease a 9-inch square cake pan. Mix together the graham cracker crumbs, cinnamon, and enough melted butter to moisten the crumbs and make them hold together. Spread the mixture over the bottom of the pan, patting it down firmly. Place in freezer for 15–20 minutes to become firm.

Put the cream cheese, sugar, cornstarch, and sour cream in a mixing bowl and blend thoroughly. *Do not whip!* Preheat oven to 375°.

In another bowl, mix together the eggs, egg yolks, cream, and lemon rind, and add gradually to the cheese mixture until thoroughly blended. Transfer mixture to the crust-lined cake pan.

Set the pan on a cookie sheet with sides. Film the bottom of the cookie sheet with water and bake for 45 to 55 minutes. Test for doneness by inserting a toothpick in the center of the cake. When pulled out, the toothpick should be clean. Let the cake cool, cut, and enjoy it!

CHERRY WALNUT BARS
Makes 48 bars

2½ cups sifted all-purpose flour
½ cup sugar
1 cup (2 sticks) butter at room temperature
2 eggs
1 cup light brown sugar, firmly packed
½ teaspoon salt
½ teaspoon baking powder
½ teaspoon vanilla
½ cup maraschino cherries, drained and chopped (reserve juice)
½ cup walnuts, coarsely chopped

ICING
1 tablespoon butter at room temperature
1 cup confectioners' sugar
3 tablespoons cherry juice (approximately)
Coconut

Preheat oven to 350°.

Mix together the flour and sugar. Add the butter cut into small pieces and, with your fingertips, blend until crumbly. Press evenly over the bottom of a 13 × 9 × 2-inch baking dish. Bake for 20 minutes, or until the crust is very lightly browned.

While the crust is baking, combine eggs, brown sugar, salt, baking powder, and vanilla, and beat with an electric mixer for 5 minutes. Drain and chop the maraschino cherries, reserving the juice. Add the chopped cherries and nuts to the egg-and-sugar mixture and mix well. Remove crust from oven and pour the egg-and-sugar mixture into it. Return to the oven for an additional 25 minutes. Remove from the oven and cool on a cake rack.

To prepare the icing, in a small bowl beat together the butter, confectioners' sugar, and enough cherry juice to make it easily spreadable. Frost the cooled cake with the icing and sprinkle with shredded coconut. When frosting has set, cut into 48 small bars.

Note: This is a personal favorite of the co-innkeeper and has appeared in local New Hampshire cook books.

CHOCOLATE CHIP SQUARES
Makes 10 to 12 squares

1 cup (2 sticks) butter
½ cup sugar
½ cup light brown sugar
2 eggs, separated
1 teaspoon vanilla
2 cups all-purpose flour
¼ teaspoon salt
1 teaspoon baking powder
¼ teaspoon baking soda
1 6-ounce package chocolate chips
1 cup light brown sugar (for meringue)

Preheat oven to 350°. Butter a 9-inch square or 8 × 10-inch baking pan.

In a large bowl, cream butter and the two sugars until fluffy. Separate the eggs, setting the whites aside, and beat the yolks lightly. Add beaten yolks to the butter-sugar mixture. Stir in vanilla. In a separate bowl, combine the flour, salt, baking powder, and baking soda. Add to the egg mixture and stir only until smooth and blended.

Spread the batter evenly in the baking pan. Sprinkle the chocolate chips over the top and press gently into the mixture.

Beat the egg whites in a good-sized bowl until foamy. Gradually add the brown sugar and beat until the meringue stands in stiff peaks. Spread the meringue evenly over the batter. Bake for 20 to 25 minutes, or until a cake tester comes out dry. Do not overbake.

Cool on cake rack. Cut into squares when cooled.

The chef says: "Very rich and very good."

CINNAMON COFFEE CAKE
Makes a 9-inch cake

1½ cups sugar
½ cup chopped pecans
1 tablespoon cinnamon
½ cup (1 stick) butter
2 eggs
1 teaspoon vanilla
1 tablespoon lemon juice
2 cups all-purpose flour
½ teaspoon baking powder
1 teaspoon baking soda
½ teaspoon salt
1 cup sour cream

Preheat oven to 350°. Butter bottom and sides of a 9-inch square baking pan.

In a small bowl, mix together ½ cup of sugar, nuts, and cinnamon, and set aside.

In a large bowl, cream the butter and remaining cup of sugar until light and fluffy. Stir in the eggs and mix well. Add the vanilla and lemon juice. In a separate bowl, combine the flour, baking powder, baking soda, and salt, and mix well. Add alternately to the egg mixture with the sour cream, ending with the flour, stirring only until well blended.

Spread half the batter in the baking pan. Sprinkle with half the cinnamon-nut mixture. Cover with the remaining batter and sprinkle top with the remaining cinnamon-nut mixture. Bake for 35 to 45 minutes, or until a cake tester inserted in the middle comes out dry. Cool on a cake rack. When cool, cut into squares.

COCONUT CREAM CAKE
Makes 24 or more squares

$^3/_4$ cup ($1^1/_2$ sticks) butter
2 cups sugar
3 eggs, separated
1 teaspoon vanilla extract
3 cups all-purpose flour
3 teaspoons baking powder
$^1/_2$ teaspoon salt
1 cup milk
Fluffy white icing**
Freshly grated coconut

Preheat oven to 350°. Butter an 8 × 12-inch baking pan.

In a large bowl, cream the butter and add sugar gradually, beating until smooth and fluffy. Add the egg yolks, one at a time, beating well after each yolk is added. Beat in the vanilla extract.

Sift the flour, baking powder, and salt together. Add the dry ingredients alternately in 3 parts with the milk, ending with the flour, and beating only until well blended.

In a separate bowl, beat the egg whites until stiff, but not dry. Stir one-third of the beaten egg white into the batter and gently fold in the remaining egg white. Spoon into the prepared cake pan and spread the batter evenly with a spatula. Bake 25 to 30 minutes, or until a cake tester comes out dry.

Cool in the pan on a rack. When completely cool, frost with fluffy white icing and sprinkle with freshly grated coconut. Cut into squares to serve.

**Fluffy White Icing (supplied by the editors)*

1 egg white
1 cup sugar
1 teaspoon vanilla extract
$^1/_4$ teaspoon cream of tartar
$^1/_2$ cup boiling water

Combine all ingredients in a medium-sized bowl. Beat at high speed with an electric beater for 10 minutes.

EATON WILD BLUEBERRY CHEESECAKE
Makes a 10-inch cake

1½ pounds cream cheese
1 14-ounce can sweetened condensed milk
4 eggs, separated
1 cup sour cream
1 tablespoon confectioners' sugar
1 teaspoon vanilla extract
1 teaspoon freshly grated lemon rind
½ teaspoon salt
Graham cracker crust**

BLUEBERRY GLAZE
1 16-ounce can wild blueberries with 1 cup juice
Juice of 1 lemon
3 tablespoons cornstarch
1 pint fresh wild blueberries

Preheat oven to 275°.

In an electric mixer, beat together cream cheese and condensed milk. Continue to beat, increasing speed, and add egg yolks, one at a time, beating well after each addition, until the mixture is very smooth. Lower speed slightly and add sour cream, confectioners' sugar, vanilla extract, and grated lemon rind.

In a separate bowl, beat egg whites with salt until they are stiff but not dry. Fold them gently into the cheese mixture. Transfer the batter into a 10-inch springform pan lined with graham cracker crust. Bake for 1 hour, turn off heat, and *do not open oven door* for at least 2 hours, so that the cake cools gradually and does not crack.

Refrigerate for at least 12 hours.

Top with blueberry glaze: Drain can of blueberries (or 2 cans if you do not have fresh wild blueberries to add later). Blend 1 cup of the blueberry syrup, lemon juice, and cornstarch in a small pan. Bring rapidly to a boil, stirring constantly, and boil for about 3 minutes. Set aside to cool slightly. Stir in reserved canned blueberries and the pint of fresh blueberries.

When the mixture is cool enough to start to set, spoon over cake and return to refrigerator for at least 1 hour. Remove from the refrigerator and run a knife around the sides of the cheesecake. Remove sides and transfer to serving platter.

The innkeeper says: "Eaton, New Hampshire, has hundreds of acres of wild blueberries, most of which are picked for commercial canning. The town itself owns a large wild blueberry tract, and the proceeds go toward offsetting our property taxes."

**Graham Cracker Crust (supplied by the editors)*

1²/₃ cup fine graham cracker crumbs
¹/₂ cup (1 stick) butter, melted
¹/₄ cup sugar

Prepare the crumbs by rolling the graham crackers between sheets of waxed paper or whir them in a blender or food processor. They should be uniformly fine.

Melt the butter over low heat, remove from heat, and mix in the crumbs and sugar, blending well.

Preheat the oven to 350°. Grease bottom and sides of a 10-inch springform pan. Transfer crumb mixture to pan and pat evenly and firmly over the sides and bottom. Bake for 8 to 10 minutes, or until the crust looks firm. Cool before filling.

FRESH PEACH GENOISE AUBERGINE
Makes a 4-layer 9-inch cake

¹/₂ pound fresh ripe peaches, peeled, for puree
6 eggs at room temperature
²/₃ cup sugar
¹/₄ teaspoon salt
1 cup cake flour, sifted
5 tablespoons clarified butter (page 90)

BUTTERCREAM
5 egg yolks
²/₃ cup sugar
¹/₃ cup water
1 cup (2 sticks) unsalted butter at room temperature

Garnish: fresh peach slices, blanched

To peel the peaches, drop them into boiling water for 1 minute, then plunge them into cold water. The skins should slip off readily. Slice the peaches and puree them in a food processor fitted with the steel blade, or in a blender. Scrape into a bowl and set puree aside.

Preheat oven to 350°. Butter two 9-inch round cake pans and lightly dust only the bottom of the pans with flour.

Break the eggs into a 3 or 4-quart mixing bowl and place over a saucepan containing 2 inches of hot but not boiling water. The bottom of the bowl must not touch the water and the water must never rise above a simmer. Start beating the eggs immediately with an electric beater. Add the sugar slowly in a regular stream. Add the salt. Beat at high speed for 15 minutes, or until the mixture triples in volume and is very light. Remove the bowl from the heat. Place the already sifted flour in a sifter and sift in one-third at a time, folding it in gently but thoroughly. Fold in half the clarified butter and fold only until butter is incorporated; fold in ¼ cup peach puree and repeat with the remainder of the butter.

Divide the batter equally between the 2 cake pans and bake for about 25 minutes, or until a cake tester inserted in the center comes out clean and dry. Place the pans on a rack, cool for 5 minutes, cover with racks, and invert. Remove pans, cover with racks and invert again to cool right side up.

Buttercream: In a large bowl and using an electric mixer, beat the egg yolks at medium speed for 10 minutes, or until they are light and thick. In a small saucepan, combine sugar and water. Bring the mixture to a boil and boil over moderate heat, stirring and washing down any sugar crystals clinging to the sides with a brush dipped in cold water. Cook until it reaches the soft ball stage or a candy thermometer registers 240°. With the electric mixer at high speed, pour the hot syrup in a thin stream over the egg yolks and beat until completely cooled and the mixture forms soft peaks. Beat in slightly softened butter cut into bits and 3 tablespoons of the peach puree. Beat until smooth.

To assemble, split the 2 layers in half horizontally. Place 1 layer on a serving dish and spread it with ⅓ cup of the buttercream. Top with another layer, spread with buttercream, and continue with the remaining 2 layers. Spread the remaining buttercream over the sides and top of the cake.

Garnish the cake with peeled peach slices that have been cooked briefly, 1 or 2 minutes, in a syrup of 1½ cups water and 1½ cups sugar.

GERMAN PLUM KUCHEN
(Zwetschkenkuchen)
Makes a 10-inch kuchen

2 cups sifted all-purpose flour
2 tablespoons sugar
1 teaspoon baking powder
³/₄ cup butter at room temperature
2 tablespoons water
1 egg, beaten
1 teaspoon vanilla extract
2¹/₂ pounds fresh Italian prune plums
4–5 tablespoons butter
³/₄ cup sugar
2 teaspoons cinnamon
1 teaspoon cornstarch

Mix together the sifted flour, sugar, and baking powder. With your fingertips, rub in the softened butter cut into small pieces until well incorporated with the flour mixture. Combine water, beaten egg, and vanilla extract in a cup and add to the mixture. Knead into a pastry dough and press into a 10-inch quiche or flan pan or a 10 × 15-inch cookie sheet with low sides.

Preheat oven to 425°.

Cut the plums in half and remove stones. Press plum halves close together, cut side up, into the pastry. Dot the plums with butter and sprinkle liberally with a mixture of the sugar, cinnamon, and cornstarch.

Bake for 20 to 30 minutes, or until pastry is golden brown and plums tender.

The innkeeper says: "Canned or sweet, overripe plums will not do in this recipe. This delectable dessert can be made only three or four weeks out of the year when the tart little Italian prune plums are available fresh in the market. A Canadian friend of ours in Germany obtained the recipe from her old German landlady."

HOT FUDGE PUDDING CAKE
Makes a 9-inch square cake

1 cup all-purpose flour, sifted
2 teaspoons baking powder
$^1/_4$ teaspoon salt
$^2/_3$ cup sugar
2 tablespoons cocoa
$^1/_2$ cup milk
2 tablespoons oil or melted butter
1 cup coarsely chopped nuts

TOPPING
$^3/_4$ cup light brown sugar
4 tablespoons cocoa
$1^3/_4$ cups hot water

Preheat oven to 350°. Butter a 9-inch square pan.

Sift together sifted flour, baking powder, salt, sugar, and cocoa. Place in a medium-sized bowl and stir in milk, liquid shortening, and nuts, and mix well. Spread batter in prepared cake pan.

For the topping, combine the brown sugar and cocoa, mix well, and sprinkle evenly over the batter. Pour the hot water over. Bake for 45 minutes. The cake will rise to the top and the sauce will settle to the bottom. Cut into 9 squares, and serve each portion generously covered with the fudge sauce. Serve warm.

Switzer Stübli
MAILANDERLI
(Christmas Butter Cookies)
Makes approximately 75 cookies

$^1/_2$ cup (1 stick) butter at room temperature
$^3/_4$ cup sugar
Juice and grated rind of 1 lemon
2 eggs
$2^1/_2$ cups all-purpose flour
1 egg yolk for glaze

continued

Cream the butter and sugar until light and fluffy. Add the lemon juice (a tablespoon of Kirsch may be substituted for the lemon juice if you like), grated rind, and eggs, and blend thoroughly.

Stir in the flour, adding a bit more if the dough is sticky and difficult to work with your hands. Knead the dough until it is smooth and clears your fingers. Wrap the dough in waxed paper and chill at least 4 hours or overnight.

Preheat oven to 350°. Grease a baking sheet and lightly flour, tapping out the excess flour.

Roll out the chilled dough between 2 sheets of waxed paper to a thickness of ¼ inch. Cut with small cookie cutters, which are dipped in flour before each cut. Place cookies on prepared tin 1 inch apart. Brush tops with beaten egg yolk for color.

Bake for 12 to 15 minutes or until golden. When cool, place in a tightly covered cookie tin.

The innkeeper says: "These are a must for family and friends over the Christmas holidays. They should be made at least a week in advance of using and kept in a cookie tin with a tight lid."

MOCHA LOG
Makes a 10-inch log

4 eggs
³/₄ cup sugar
¹/₂ teaspoon vanilla
¹/₄ cup sifted all-purpose flour
¹/₄ cup dry cocoa
¹/₄ teaspoon baking powder
¹/₄ teaspoon salt
Confectioners' sugar

COFFEE CREAM FILLING
2 cups heavy cream
¹/₄ cup confectioners' sugar
1 tablespoon instant coffee granules (not freeze-dried)
1 teaspoon vanilla
1 square (1 ounce) semisweet chocolate

Butter a 15 × 10 × 1-inch jelly-roll pan, line with waxed paper, and butter the paper. Or use baking parchment to line the pan, if you have it; it does not have to be buttered. Preheat the oven to 350°.

Beat the eggs by hand or with an electric beater until light and lemon colored. Gradually beat in sugar and continue beating until the mixture is very thick and ribbony, about 10 minutes. Stir in vanilla. Sift together the flour, cocoa, baking powder, and salt, and fold in.

Spread the mixture evenly to all edges of the prepared pan. Bake on the center shelf of the oven for 25 minutes, or until the top springs back when lightly pressed.

Have ready a clean kitchen towel sprinkled with sifted confectioners' sugar. Remove the cake pan from the oven and invert the pan onto the towel so that the cake falls out. Carefully peel off the paper from the cake and cut off any crisp edges. Wrap in the towel and let cool. When cooled, roll the cake starting from the long side, lifting the towel to help start the cake rolling.

In a large chilled bowl, whip the cream until soft mounds form. Add the confectioners' sugar, coffee granules, and vanilla, and beat until it is stiff and can hold its shape after beaters are lifted.

Unroll the cake carefully and spread the top evenly with half the cream. Reroll and transfer, seam side down, to a long serving platter. Frost with remaining cream. With a vegetable parer, coarsely shave the semisweet chocolate and sprinkle it over the cake.

Chill roll for at least 1 hour or longer, until serving time. Slice crosswise into inch-thick servings.

RHUBARB CRUNCH
Makes 6 to 9 squares or bars

2 pounds rhubarb
1 cup sugar
2½ teaspoons all-purpose flour

TOPPING
1 cup all-purpose flour
1 teaspoon baking powder
¼ teaspoon salt
1 cup sugar
⅓ cup oatmeal
2 teaspoons butter
1 egg, lightly beaten
Sweetened whipped cream (optional)

Preheat oven to 375°. Butter a 9-inch square pan.

Wash the rhubarb and trim away stem ends and leaves. Peel it if it is very tough. Cut into 1-inch pieces. You should have about 4 cups. Mix together the sugar and flour and blend well with the rhubarb. Spread over the bottom of the baking pan.

With a fork, mix until crumbly the flour, baking powder, salt, sugar, oatmeal, butter, and beaten egg. Sprinkle topping over rhubarb, patting it down. Bake for 40 minutes or until topping is lightly browned and baked through. Test it with a fork. If it isn't browning enough, turn up the oven heat toward the end.

Serve with sweetened whipped cream, if desired.

Switzer Stübli
RÜBLI TORTE
(Carrot Cake)
Makes an 8-inch cake

2/3 cup grated raw carrots, firmly packed
1 cup finely ground almonds
3/4 cup breadcrumbs
1/2 teaspoon mace
1/2 teaspoon cinnamon
1 teaspoon ground ginger
1 teaspoon baking powder
6 eggs, separated
1 1/4 cups sugar
2 teaspoons grated lemon rind
1 tablespoon Kirsch or lemon juice

GLAZE
1 cup confectioners' sugar
1 tablespoon water
1/2 teaspoon lemon extract

In a large mixing bowl, mix together carrots and almonds. In another bowl, mix breadcrumbs with the spices and baking powder. Add to the carrots and almonds and blend well.

In a separate bowl, beat the egg yolks until thick and lemon colored. Gradually add, while beating, the sugar, lemon rind, and Kirsch or lemon juice. Continue beating until thick. Fold into the carrot-breadcrumb mixture.

Preheat oven to 350°. Grease the bottom of an 8-inch springform pan. Line with waxed paper and grease the paper and sides of the pan. Sprinkle bottom and sides with fine breadcrumbs, tapping out excess.

In a clean, dry bowl, using clean, dry beaters, beat the egg whites until stiff, glossy peaks form. Fold into the cake mixture. Pour the mixture into the prepared springform pan and bake for 1 hour, or until a cake tester inserted into the center comes out dry. Cool on a cake rack. Remove from pan when cool.

In a small bowl, mix together the confectioners' sugar, water, and lemon extract until smooth. Glaze the cooled cake with the mixture.

SACHERTORTE
Makes an 8- or 9-inch cake

³/₄ cup (1¹/₂ sticks) butter at room temperature
6¹/₂ squares (6¹/₂ ounces) semisweet chocolate
³/₄ cup sugar
8 eggs, separated
1 cup sifted all-purpose flour
2 additional egg whites
2–3 tablespoons apricot jam

ICING
¹/₃ cup water
1 cup sugar
7 squares (7 ounces) semisweet chocolate

Preheat oven to 275°. Grease and lightly flour an 8- or 9-inch spring-form pan, tapping out the excess flour.

Cream the butter until light and fluffy. Melt the chocolate in the top of a double boiler and cool. Add the melted chocolate and sugar to the butter, stirring well. Add the 8 egg yolks one at a time, beating well after each addition. Fold in the flour gradually.

In a separate bowl, beat the 10 egg whites until stiff, glossy peaks form. Fold the meringue gently into the chocolate batter until no white streaks show.

Pour into springform pan and bake for 1 hour. Let stand on a cake rack for 10 minutes and remove rim. When thoroughly cool, trim a thin slice off the top so that the top is perfectly level. Invert the cake on a cake rack and remove the springform base. Heat the apricot jam a little to make it easily spreadable, and spread a thin layer over top surface of cake.

For the icing, place water and sugar in a small, heavy saucepan over high heat. Do not stir, but swirl the pan gently by its handle until sugar has dissolved and the liquid is clear. Cover pan and boil rapidly for a moment or two. Uncover the pan when bubbles begin to thicken, and cook to the thin thread stage, about 270° on a candy thermometer. (In the absence of a candy thermometer, you may use the cold water test. Spoon out ¹/₂ teaspoon or so of the syrup and drop it into a cup of cold water. Work it with your fingers, and if it separates into hard threads that bend when removed from the water, it is done.)

Melt the chocolate in the top of a double boiler and beat in the sugar syrup slowly. Stir constantly until thick enough to spread. Transfer the cake to a serving platter. Spread icing over sides and top, covering the layer of apricot jam.

The innkeeper says: "It is traditional to serve Sachertorte with whipped cream."

SCOTCH SHORTBREAD
Makes 2 dozen small cookies

^{1}/₂ cup (1 stick) butter at room temperature
1^1/₃ cups sifted all-purpose flour
^{1}/₃ cup sugar
Sugar for sprinkling

Preheat oven to 325°. Line a cookie sheet with waxed paper or baking parchment.

Cream the butter until light and fluffy. Combine with the flour, using your fingertips. Add the sugar and knead the mixture until it is a very smooth ball.

On a lightly floured surface, roll out the dough to a thickness of ^{1}/₂ inch. Cut into small shapes and place on cookie sheet. Prick the tops of the shortbread in several places with a fork.

Bake for approximately 10 minutes. The shortbread should only be *lightly* browned. Sprinkle with sugar.

Remove from the pan and cool on a rack. Store in an airtight container. Keep in a cool place but not in the refrigerator. The shortbread improves with keeping.

The chef says: "An alternative is to roll the dough to form a round cake about ^{1}/₂ inch thick. This will take longer to bake but again it should not be allowed to become more than lightly brown."

WINNIE'S CHOCOLATE FUDGE CAKE
Makes a 9-inch 2-layer cake or 9 × 13 rectangle

1 cup (2 sticks) butter at room temperature
2 cups sugar
2 eggs
2 teaspoons vanilla extract
2¼ cups all-purpose flour, sifted
1½ teaspoons baking powder
½ teaspoon baking soda
½ teaspoon salt
½ cup cocoa
1 cup buttermilk
1 cup boiling water
Chocolate icing**

Preheat oven to 350°. Grease two 9-inch round cake pans or a 9 × 13-inch cake pan. Sprinkle lightly with cocoa, coating the bottom and sides. Tap out any excess.

In a large bowl, cream butter and sugar until light and fluffy. Beat in the eggs one at a time and beat well. Beat in vanilla.

Sift together the sifted flour, baking powder, baking soda, salt, and cocoa. Stir the dry ingredients into the butter-sugar mixture alternately with the buttermilk, beating after each addition until batter is smooth. Stir in the boiling water. Pour into the prepared pans or pan.

Bake for 30 to 35 minutes for the layers or 40 to 45 minutes for the rectangle, or until a cake tester comes out dry.

Cool on a rack for 7 to 10 minutes. Turn out of pans onto a rack and cool completely. Frost with chocolate icing.

**Chocolate Icing *(supplied by the editors)*

3 squares (3 ounces) unsweetened chocolate
3 tablespoons butter
1½ cups confectioners' sugar
½ cup milk or water, heated to boiling point
1 teaspoon vanilla extract

Melt the chocolate and butter in a small saucepan over low heat, being careful not to scorch the chocolate. Remove from heat and stir in the confectioners' sugar and the heated milk or water and beat until smooth. Stir in vanilla extract. Spread while still warm on the cooled cake.

XII Desserts

BAKED APPLES
Serves 4

4 Cortland apples
Raisins
4 tablespoons light brown sugar
2 teaspoons butter
$^1/_4$ cup maple syrup
Heavy cream

Preheat oven to 350°. Wash and core the apples, but don't go all the way through to the bottom. Scrape out all the seeds. Place a few raisins in each cavity and pack 1 tablespoon of brown sugar on top of the raisins. Dot the tops of the apples with butter and drizzle maple syrup over each.

Place apples in an ovenproof dish with $^1/_2$ inch boiling water on the bottom. Bake for 30 minutes or until apples are tender but not mushy. Serve warm with pan juices and heavy cream.

BLUEBERRIES WITH DUMPLINGS
Serves 6 to 8

1 quart fresh blueberries
1 cup sugar
2 cups all-purpose flour, sifted
4 teaspoons baking powder
1 teaspoon salt
1 tablespoon shortening at room temperature
$^2/_3$ cup milk

In a good-sized kettle with a cover, combine the washed and drained blueberries and sugar. Bring to a boil.

Into a mixing bowl, sift together the flour, baking powder, and salt. Cut in the shortening with a pastry blender until the mixture resembles rice kernels. Quickly stir in the milk with a fork until just blended.

Drop the batter by tablespoons into the boiling berries. Cover the kettle tightly and cook over medium heat for 20 minutes.

Serve the dumplings and hot stewed blueberries with vanilla ice cream.

The Inn at Mt. Ascutney

CHOCOLATE ASCUTNEY
Serves 6 to 8

1 10-ounce pound cake
3 tablespoons brandy
2 tablespoons wild cherry brandy
2 tablespoons Triple Sec
1 6-ounce package semisweet chocolate chips
$1/4$ pound shelled pecans
2 cups heavy cream

Thinly slice three-quarters of the pound cake. Line a $1^1/2$-quart mixing bowl with the slices, one slightly overlapping the other, over the bottom and sides.

Mix together the brandies and the Triple Sec. Reserve 1 tablespoon for the top of the dessert. Sprinkle the rest over the cake in the mixing bowl.

Melt half the chocolate chips in a bowl placed over a pan of hot water or over low heat, watching carefully to make sure the chocolate doesn't scorch. Place the remainder of the chocolate chips and the pecans in the food processor and chop coarsely.

Whip the cream until it holds in stiff peaks. Fold the chopped pecans and chocolate chips into the whipped cream.

Fill the cavity of the mixing bowl with half the whipped cream mixture. Fold the melted chocolate chips into the remaining whipped cream and fill the rest of the cavity with this mixture. Smooth the top with a spatula.

Slice the remaining cake and cover the top of the cream mixture completely. Pour the reserved tablespoon of brandies over the top. Cover with plastic wrap and refrigerate for 1 or 2 days.

To serve, run a knife between the cake and the bowl. Place a serving plate over the top of the bowl and invert. Presto — Chocolate Ascutney.

The innkeeper says: "This should look like a single standing mountain, which Mount Ascutney is. The inspiration for this dessert was the mountain which we overlook."

CHOCOLATE RUM SAUCE
Makes 2 cups

1½ cups light corn syrup
½ cup cocoa
½ cup confectioners' sugar
3 tablespoons light rum
5 tablespoons melted butter

Combine all ingredients in a large bowl and beat with hand-held electric beater at medium speed for 3 minutes. Store in refrigerator.

Note: A thick, silky chocolate sauce for ice cream, puddings, or cake.

GRAMMY RING'S SUET PUDDING
Serves 6 to 8

2 eggs
1/2 cup molasses
1/2 cup finely chopped suet
3 cups all-purpose flour
2 teaspoons baking powder
1 teaspoon salt
1 cup candied fruit, raisins, and nuts
1/2 teaspoon cinnamon
1/2 teaspoon nutmeg
1/2 teaspoon ground cloves

HARD SAUCE
1 pound confectioners' sugar
1 cup (2 sticks) butter at room temperature
2 tablespoons brandy

Beat the eggs in a large bowl until frothy. Continue beating and add the molasses and chopped suet. Fold in the flour, baking powder, salt, candied fruit, raisins, and nuts, and spices.

Pour into individual greased pudding molds, filling each a little over half full, and cover tightly with aluminum foil. Place in a large kettle with about 2 inches of boiling water. Cover kettle and steam for 2 hours, keeping the water just to the boiling point, not above it. Remove puddings from molds and serve warm with hard sauce.

For the hard sauce, blend the confectioners' sugar into the softened butter until smooth, and flavor with brandy.

The innkeeper says: "Thanksgiving and Christmas dinner would not be complete without this recipe from my grandmother and passed on through the years."

The
EAST WIND
INN

GRAN'S UPPER CLYDE CARROT PUDDING
Serves 8

1 egg
1 cup sugar
1 teaspoon lemon extract
3 tablespoons melted butter
1 cup grated carrot
1 cup grated potato, mixed with 1 teaspoon baking soda
1 cup plus 2 tablespoons all-purpose flour
1 teaspoon cinnamon
1/4 teaspoon ground cloves
1/2 cup dried currants
1 cup raisins
1/2 cup chopped walnuts

SAUCE
1 cup sugar
2 eggs
1 cup (2 sticks) butter, melted
1/2 teaspoon salt
1 teaspoon vanilla extract

Beat together the eggs and sugar, and mix in the lemon extract. When well blended, add the melted butter and the grated vegetables and mix well. Combine flour with cinnamon and cloves and stir in. Add currants, raisins, and nuts. Pour into a buttered 2-quart pudding mold, cover tightly, and place on a rack over boiling water in a kettle. Cover the kettle and steam for 3 hours, adding water as needed. Unmold the pudding and serve topped with the chilled sauce.

To prepare the sauce, beat together the sugar and eggs until light and fluffy. Mix in the remaining ingredients and blend well. Chill before serving.

Gateways Inn
ICED PEARS CHARLIE CHAPLIN
Serves 6

6 perfect ripe pears, peeled and halved

SYRUP
2 cups sugar
2¹/₃ cups water
1 teaspoon vanilla extract
1 whole clove

2 cups raspberries, fresh or frozen
¹/₄ cup Strega liqueur
12 small scoops vanilla ice cream
Cold zabaglione**
1 tablespoon chopped toasted almonds

With a melon-ball cutter, scoop out the core of each pear half, leaving a small hollow.

In a large saucepan, combine the sugar, water, vanilla extract, and clove. Bring to a boil, reduce heat, add the pears, and poach them until they are just tender. Remove them with a slotted spoon and place in the refrigerator to chill.

Increase the heat under the saucepan containing the syrup and boil vigorously until it is reduced by half. Cool the syrup and pour over the raspberries, using enough to cover. Add the Strega and chill.

Prepare the zabaglione and chill.

To serve, place 2 pear halves in a large champagne or sherbet glass. Fill the hollows of the pears with raspberries and place a scoop of ice cream on each pear half. Coat with zabaglione and sprinkle with toasted almonds.

**Zabaglione (Italian Wine Custard) (supplied by the editors)*

4 egg yolks
¹/₄ cup granulated sugar
¹/₂ cup Marsala wine*

Combine egg yolks and sugar in the top of a double boiler, over hot but not boiling water. The water must not touch the top pan. Whisk the egg yolks and sugar until they are pale and foamy. Add wine gradually, beating constantly, until the custard has doubled and begins to thicken. It is ready when it forms soft mounds.

*Marsala is the classic wine, but you may use Madeira or sweet sherry.

MAPLE MOUSSE
Serves 6 to 8

1 tablespoon plus 2 teaspoons unflavored gelatin
½ cup cold water
4 eggs, separated
1 cup maple syrup
½ cup light brown sugar
2 cups heavy cream, whipped

Sprinkle the gelatin over cold water and let stand for 3 or 4 minutes until it softens. Place in the top of a double boiler with 4 egg yolks and maple syrup. Over medium heat, cook and stir with a wire whisk until smooth. Add brown sugar and continue to stir and cook until thickened.

Remove from heat and allow to cool slightly. While it is cooling, beat the egg whites until stiff but not dry. Beat the cream until it mounds softly. Fold the beaten egg whites into the gelatin mixture; then fold in the whipped cream. Transfer to a 2-quart bowl or soufflé dish and chill until ready to serve.

The chef says: "Very nicely presented in champagne glasses with a dot of freshly whipped cream. We use local maple syrup, which gives the mousse such a lovely flavor."

MOCHA FLAN
Serves 6

3 tablespoons sugar
3 eggs
¼ cup sugar
¼ teaspoon salt
1 teaspoon vanilla
3 cups milk, scalded
2 teaspoons instant coffee
1 tablespoon rum or brandy

Put the 3 tablespoons of sugar into a small iron skillet or a heavy-bottomed saucepan and place over low heat. Cook until a foamy golden caramel is obtained. Immediately pour into 6 custard cups and coat the bottoms evenly, tilting the cups. Preheat oven to 350°.

Beat the eggs lightly, just to blend. Beat in sugar, salt, and vanilla.

Heat the milk to the scalding point, when small bubbles begin to appear around the outside edge. Stir in the instant coffee and mix until dissolved. Pour slowly over the egg mixture, beating with a fork to keep smooth. Add the rum or brandy.

Pour into the custard cups and place them in a shallow baking pan lined with paper toweling. Pour 1 inch of hot (not boiling) water into the baking pan and bake for about 45 minutes. Make sure that the water does not come to a boil. The flan is done when a slim knife inserted in the center comes out clean.

Chill when cool. Unmold on individual dessert bowls or plates.

PEARS À LA VIGNERONNE
Serves 6

6 fine fresh, ripe pears
2 cups dry white wine
$\frac{1}{2}$ cup sugar
Rind of 1 lemon in thin julienne strips
1 2-inch length of cinnamon stick, or $\frac{1}{4}$ teaspoon ground
    cinnamon
1 teaspoon vanilla extract
$\frac{1}{4}$ cup orange marmalade
$\frac{1}{4}$ cup apricot preserves

Peel and core the pears and cut into eighths. Place pears in a saucepan
with wine, sugar, and julienne strips of lemon. Simmer for 10 minutes,
or until pears are tender but still hold their shape.

    Transfer pears and lemon peel to a serving bowl, using a slotted
spoon. Bring the liquid in which they were cooked to a boil and add
the cinnamon, vanilla extract, orange marmalade, and apricot preserves. Cook briskly for about 10 minutes, stirring well until sauce is
reduced. Discard cinnamon stick. Pour sauce over pears, mixing well.
Cool and chill.

RHUBARB CREAM
Serves 6

1 pound rhubarb, cut in 1-inch pieces
$1\frac{1}{2}$ cups orange juice
1 cup sugar
1 teaspoon grated lemon rind
$1\frac{1}{2}$ teaspoons unflavored gelatin ($\frac{1}{2}$ package)
$\frac{1}{2}$ cup heavy cream

Combine the rhubarb, 1 cup of orange juice, sugar, and lemon rind
in a medium-sized saucepan. Cover and bring to a boil. Lower heat

and simmer until rhubarb is tender, about 10 minutes.

Sprinkle gelatin over remaining ½ cup orange juice and let stand for a few minutes to soften. Stir into the hot rhubarb and cook, stirring, until the gelatin is dissolved. Remove from heat.

Mash the rhubarb mixture with a potato masher. Pour into a bowl and chill until slightly jelled.

Beat the cream until stiff and fold into the rhubarb mixture, blending until white streaks disappear. Spoon into a 5-cup serving dish or individual sherbet dishes. Chill for 2 hours or until soft-set.

SIX-MINUTE CHOCOLATE MOUSSE
Serves 4

1 6-ounce package semisweet chocolate chips
2 eggs
2 egg yolks
¼ cup sugar
1 tablespoon orange juice
2 tablespoons coffee liqueur (optional)
1 teaspoon vanilla
1 cup heavy cream
Topping: sweetened whipped cream

Melt the chocolate chips in the top of a double boiler over hot water. While they are melting, place all the ingredients except the cup of heavy cream in a blender and blend at highest speed for 3 minutes. Stop blender and add the cream. Blend for half a minute. Stop blender again and add the melted chocolate, carefully scraping all of it from the inside of the pan. Blend for 2½ minutes longer.

Pour into parfait glasses or large brandy snifters. Chill in the refrigerator for 4 hours or longer. Serve with a dollop of sweetened whipped cream flavored with a bit of vanilla and topped with a sprig of mint leaf or a sprinkle of shaved chocolate.

Gateways Inn

SNOW DUMPLINGS WITH PISTACHIO SAUCE
(Latte Alla Grotta)
Makes about 20 large dumplings

4 eggs, separated
4 tablespoons confectioners' sugar
1 teaspoon vanilla extract
5 cups milk
2 tablespoons granulated sugar
2½ tablespoons finely ground pistachio nuts
5 tablespoons all-purpose flour
Ground cinnamon

Have the egg whites at room temperature. Place in a large bowl and beat until soft peaks form. Slowly add the confectioners' sugar and vanilla, beating constantly until the egg whites become glossy and shiny and stand in stiff peaks.

Reserve ¾ cup of milk. Bring the remainder to a boil in a large, wide, shallow pan such as a skillet or sauté pan. Fill 1 tablespoon with the egg-white meringue and use another to shape it into a large, round dumpling. Drop gently into the simmering milk. Repeat this until the skillet is full. Poach the dumplings for about 2 minutes on each side, or until they are firm, turning them gently. Remove with a slotted spoon and drain them on cheesecloth set over a cake rack. Remove the milk from the heat and stir in the granulated sugar.

In a large bowl, stir together the reserved cold milk and ground pistachio nuts. In another bowl, beat the flour with the egg yolks and half the boiled milk used for poaching the dumplings. Stir this into the cold milk-nut mixture. Transfer to a heavy-bottomed saucepan and heat, stirring, until thick and smooth, with the consistency of a light cream sauce. Do not let it boil or it will curdle. Cool to room temperature, stirring from time to time to keep a skin from forming. Chill before using.

Arrange the dumplings in a deep serving dish. Pour the sauce carefully over them and sprinkle lightly with cinnamon.

STRAWBERRIES IN SHERRY CREAM
Serves 6 to 8

5 egg yolks
1 cup sugar
2 tablespoons brandy
³/₄ cup dry sherry
3 pints fresh strawberries, washed, hulled, and dried
1 cup heavy cream

In a medium-sized bowl, beat the egg yolks until thick and pale lemon colored. Add the sugar and continue beating until velvety. Mix in the brandy and sherry. Transfer to the top of a double boiler and cook over hot — not boiling — water, stirring constantly until thick. The upper pan must not touch the hot water in the pan below, and the water must never reach above a quiet simmer. When thick, place in bowl and cool.

Wash, hull, and dry the strawberries, setting aside 8 large berries to use as garnish. Just before serving time, beat the cream until very stiff and fold into the custard, blending well. Add the strawberries and blend gently until well covered.

Place in a large bowl or individual bowls and decorate with reserved berries. Serve very cold.

TIPSY TRIFLE
Serves 6 to 8

4–6 slices pound cake, cut ¹/₂ inch thick
¹/₃–¹/₂ cup sweet sherry
¹/₂ cup currant jelly
2 cups fresh peach slices (or raspberries, strawberries, or
    combination), sweetened to taste
Stirred custard**
Garnish: sweetened whipped cream and chocolate curls

continued

Line the bottom of a glass serving bowl with slices of pound cake. Sprinkle sherry over the cake. (This is the Tipsy portion, so don't be bashful.)

Spread currant jelly in a thin layer over the cake. Cover with peach slices. Fill the bowl to within 1 inch of the top with stirred custard. Refrigerate, covered, until well chilled. Garnish with whipped cream and chocolate curls and serve.

**Stirred Custard (Crème Anglais) (supplied by the editors)*
Makes 2¹/₂ cups

   6 egg yolks
   ¹/₂ cup sugar
   ¹/₄ teaspoon salt
   2 cups milk or light cream, or 1 cup of each, scalded
   1¹/₂ teaspoons vanilla extract
   2 tablespoons Grand Marnier, Cointreau, or Kirsch (optional)

In a heavy-bottomed saucepan, mix the egg yolks, sugar, and salt, and whisk briefly, only until well blended. Add the hot milk slowly, stirring well. Cook over medium heat, stirring constantly with a wooden spoon, until the mixture coats the spoon. Don't let it boil or the eggs will curdle.

Strain the sauce into a bowl and add the vanilla extract and liqueur, if using, and mix. Let cool to room temperature and stir from time to time to prevent a film from forming on the custard's surface.

INNS

Connecticut

AVON
Old Farms Inn

Auon

The Old Farms Inn has a long and noble history. John North, the first of the family to arrive in America from England, settled in 1635 in the vicinity of the town of Farmington, Connecticut, an area that later became Northington, a contraction for North Farmington. Still later it was called Nod, an abbreviation for "north district" of the Church of Farmington.

Thomas North, the son of John, settled the present site of the inn in 1678. After fighting with the British Colonial Army in King Philip's War, he became a "freeman" and for his services received from the King of England a grant of land on the east side of the Farmington River, "under the mountain and north of the Hartford-Albany Turnpike." His son, Nathaniel, built his home on a parcel of the grant in 1757; this building is now part of the Old Farms Inn, containing the foyer, lobby, private dining room, and second-floor bedrooms.

The estimated worth at the time was:

one house & barn & land adjoining & 6 acres $600.00
one shop $30.00
land north and adjacent to the turnpike (30 acres) $600.00
land and north piece (in the meadow) (11 acres) $176.00

In 1832, Joseph North, a blacksmith of the Nod area, remodeled his shop, erecting a fine stone building that is now the part of the inn known as the Forge Room.

The North Homestead gradually grew as an inn to its present size, and in 1923 became the Old Farms Inn. It now consists of the warm, barnwood-paneled Tavern Bar and Lounge; Tavern Dining Room; the delightful Private Dining Room with its unusual hanging lanterns and pottery; the Coach Room; and the Forge Room and Bar.

The heart of the inn is the gracious Coach Room, where you can enjoy many specialties, from steak to Veal Sentino. The cuisine is American with a Continental flair.

The Forge Room is an inviting spot for lunch or dinner. Its giant fireplace, antique tools, and booths that were formerly horse stalls are all reminders of its days as a blacksmith shop.

The comfortable sleeping rooms are tastefully and individually furnished, largely with antiques.

The surrounding area provides a full range of activities for all. Golf and tennis are close, as well as scenic drives, walks, and bike trails, unusual shops, museums, and craft centers.

In the fall the glorious coloring of New England draws one to the area for leisurely exploration of charming nearby towns and villages. With the arrival of snow, the Ski Sundown is but six miles away.

Christmas at the inn is a very special time, with holiday decorations everywhere and each public room festively adorned. A growing collection of antique and other unusual toys is on display.

INNKEEPERS:	Louis and Anne Panos
SEASON:	Year round
MEALS:	Lunch, dinner, and Sunday champagne brunch
TELEPHONE:	203-677-2818
ACCOMMODATIONS:	10 rooms, some with private bath; motel across the road with 85 rooms, all with private bath
ADDRESS:	P.O. Box 535 Avon, Connecticut 06001
DIRECTIONS:	*From New York:* Route 684 North to Route 84 East to Exit 39. At the second traffic light make a right onto Route 10. Drive 5 miles to the inn (see more details below). *From Boston:* I-90 (Massachusetts Turnpike) to Route 86 West to Route 84 West to Exit 39, which is Farmington. North on Route 4 to the center of Farmington. At the center take a right onto Route 10, which eventually intersects with Route 44. The inn is at the intersection of Routes 10 and 44.

ESSEX
The Griswold Inn

In historic Essex on the banks of the tranquil Connecticut River, where time seems to have stopped, stands a remarkable 205-year-old inn, which has been under the ownership of only five families — an extraordinary continuity.

From 1972 to the present, William and Victoria Winterer have been innkeepers and operators of one of Connecticut's most distinguished restaurants, featuring fresh seafood and a random variety of other favorites, ranging from their famous sausages to a nest of Canadian quail. The wine cellar presents labels from Germany, Italy, France, Portugal, and California. Although the Griswold once operated as a first-class temperance hotel, it now serves king-sized cocktails.

A Sunday event is the traditional Hunt Breakfast, served between noon and 2:30. Help yourself to unlimited quantities of scrambled eggs, ham, bacon, sausage, grits, fried potatoes, herring, fried chicken, lamb kidneys, and creamed chipped beef. In addition, there are specialties such as Maine smelts or seasonal favorites. (The British started this tradition when they occupied the inn during the War of 1812.)

In addition to the buildings, which in themselves are exquisite examples of eighteenth-century architecture, there are four major collections owned by the Griswold and exhibited in various rooms of the inn: steamboat prints by Currier & Ives and other important lithographers; the Jacobsen collection of sixteen canvases of marine oils dating from the turn of the century; a library of firearms housed appropriately in the Gun Room and comprising some fifty-five pieces, which trace guns from the fifteenth century; and a large collection of steamboat memorabilia.

The main building of the Griswold was constructed in 1776 and was the first three-story frame structure built in Connecticut. With the exception of the removal of the second-floor gallery, the building has remained structurally unchanged for two centuries.

Immediately behind but attached to the main building is the Tap Room. This room, possibly the most handsome barroom in America, was built in 1738 as the first schoolhouse in Essex. After its abandonment in the late eighteenth century, the building was moved to its present location by a team of oxen pulling it literally inch by inch as it rolled on logs down Main Street. The room is dominated by a potbellied stove purchased at the turn of the century from the Goodspeed Opera House at East Haddam. In autumn, winter, and early spring, a fire crackles in a wood-burning fireplace. An antique popcorn machine produces marvelous hot, buttered corn. Affable bartenders dispense products of their trade from behind a steamboat-gothic bar.

The original parlor of the inn is now part of the Library, a book-lined room with a wood-burning fireplace. The area between the main building and the annex houses the Steamboat Room. This dining room simulates the dining salon of a luxurious riverboat. With its steamboat-gothic decor, one can imagine a trip down the river from Hartford to perhaps New York. Aft of the room is a historically accurate mural of Essex as it appeared at the turn of the century. Indeed, the authenticity of the surroundings creates an illusion of rocking gently with the ship's movement and even seeing the wake from the steamboat's paddle.

The Covered Bridge is a dining room constructed from an abandoned New Hampshire covered bridge that was moved to Essex. It contains a large wood-burning fireplace and houses an important art collection and a curious collection of temperance banners.

The Captain Timothy Starkey House, built in 1793, is across the street, and the Amasa Hayden House, built in 1790, is next door. All are part of the Griswold community, providing additional dining facilities and other accommodations.

On Main Street and the lanes running down to the river — a very short walk — are many fine examples of Colonial and Federal architecture and restored interiors.

Within a short drive of the "Gris," as it is called by the natives, there are approximately twenty-five fine antique shops.

The New England Steamboat Line operates all-day excursions to Long Island as well as river trips. The steam train provides a scenic trip on turn-of-the-century rolling stock and is met by a riverboat for the next leg of the adventure. Passengers return to Essex via train. The combined excursion is great fun, recapturing the lively but relaxed style of nineteenth-century travel.

Goodspeed Opera House, a lovingly restored Victorian opera house, is just north in East Haddam. It features great musicals, which are frequently headed for Broadway. The famous Ivoryton Playhouse is but a five-minute drive away.

INNKEEPERS:	William and Victoria Winterer
SEASON:	Year round except Christmas Day
MEALS:	Breakfast, lunch, and dinner daily except Christmas Day; on Sundays, a New England Hunt Breakfast is a popular feature; reservations a must
TELEPHONE:	203-767-0991
ACCOMMODATIONS:	19 rooms and 3 suites, most with private bath
ADDRESS:	Essex, Connecticut 06426
DIRECTIONS:	I-95 (Connecticut Turnpike) to Exit 69. Route 9 North to Exit 3. Turn left at bottom of ramp, right at traffic light; proceed to river.

MIDDLETOWN
Town Farms Inn

Built as a country home in 1839 by Thomas Griswold Mather and sold in 1853 to the town of Middletown, which added the Victorian wing, the property was used as the town almshouse until 1946. That date marked the beginning of a thirty-year career as the Commodore MacDonough Inn. In 1977, the inn was bought by the owners of the historic Griswold Inn at Essex and renamed Town Farms, the name it had carried for nearly a century. Now operated as a gracious country inn on the banks of the Connecticut River, Town Farms Inn is considered one of the most beautiful country inns in America.

It is open daily for luncheon and dinner, and on Sunday features its famous Hunt Breakfast — abundant enough to be the main meal of the day for many guests.

The menu offers New England specialties such as Boston scrod, bluefish, sole, and scallops, in addition to chicken Cordon Bleu, beef Stroganoff, Canadian quail, and many Continental favorites. A special children's menu is available. Also featured is a complete wine cellar with over forty different vintages from which to select.

Three distinctive dining rooms offer a variety of settings: the formal

River Room, with crystal chandeliers and panoramic views of the Connecticut River; the informal American Indian Room, with a more casual air; and the cozy Study, with its hangings of old Middletown prints and engravings. On warm days luncheon or cocktails may be served outside on the Riverfront Terrace. In autumn and winter three wood-burning fireplaces blaze. On some nights live chamber music fills the air; on others, dancing under the stars is popular.

As of this writing, no sleeping accommodations are available at the inn, but the area, situated midway between New Haven and Hartford, provides a variety of good housing.

The inn has ideal recreational facilities nearby. The beaches of Long Island Sound are only a short drive away, as are the Shakespeare Festival at Stratford (forty-five minutes away), the Long Wharf Theater in New Haven (forty minutes away), and a good repertory theater in Hartford (a half hour's drive). Also nearby is the Goodspeed Opera House, presenting the best of musical theater. Many musicals first seen here have gone on to Broadway to become long-running hits; *Annie* is a recent example.

The rolling hills and quiet lakes of the area also beckon the traveler. A special delight is the State Recreation Area of Gillette Castle in East Haddam, which, along with the usual state park facilities, provides the very unusual medieval Rhine Gillette Castle built by actor William Gillette. Wesleyan University, founded in 1831, welcomes visitors to its grounds and certain buildings as well.

A Connecticut River trip via steam train and riverboat starts in Essex. For further information on this and other attractions, see listing for the Griswold Inn in Essex.

INNKEEPER:	Raymond Terrill
SEASON:	Year round
MEALS:	Lunch and dinner daily; Hunt Breakfast every Sunday; reservations suggested
TELEPHONE:	203-347-7438
ACCOMMODATIONS:	No sleeping rooms at present
ADDRESS:	River Road Middletown, Connecticut 06457
DIRECTIONS:	I-91 to Route 9 South. Take Exit 12 and follow signs to the inn.

NORWALK
Silvermine Tavern

The Silvermine Tavern crossroads have been the center of the little community of Silvermine since its pre-Revolutionary beginnings. Farmers settled along the winding edges of the river, whose name derived from the early belief that one of the settlers had discovered silver there. Today Silvermine is no longer a separate town but a loosely defined area lying partly in Norwalk, partly in New Canaan, and partly in Wilton.

Four buildings make up the tavern group. The Country Store now sells old-fashioned candy, old New England food specialties, and gifts that appeal to those who love the early American heritage. The back room of the store houses a museum of antique tools and gadgets and a fine collection of Currier & Ives prints. The Coach House has been remodeled for the accommodation of additional guests. The Old Mill— the oldest building in the group — was operated for many years as a wood-turning mill, producing quantities of wooden knobs and spindles. Now used as a guest house, it contains bedrooms and an unusually charming apartment, overlooking the waterfall and furnished with antiques. The Gatehouse, at one time a separate home, now serves as the entrance to the tavern itself, which was built in stagecoach days and has been at various times a country inn, part of the old mill next door, a gentleman's country seat, and a town meeting place. The tavern is famous for its unusual displays of primitive paintings, prints, early inn and store signs, and an extensive collection of rare early American tools, implements, and utensils. Another popular feature is Abigail, the life-size mannequin of an early Connecticut lady, who is the only woman in the state permitted by law to stand at a bar.

One of Connecticut's most famous restaurants is located in the tavern, specializing in time-tested New England fare and featuring an unforgettable view of the wooded banks of the Silvermine River and the peaceful Mill Pond, where pure-white swans drift gracefully along.

Special treats are the popular Sunday Champagne Brunch, with some twenty delectable offerings, and the famous Thursday Night Buffet Supper featuring roast beef and fried chicken and an unusual selection of salads.

Silvermine Tavern is a place for quiet reflection and tranquil pastimes, with each season bringing its own pleasures: feeding the swans and wild ducks in summer, walking along wooded trails, exploring colorful old villages and treasure-hunting for antiques, relaxing before a roaring fireplace in winter. The Stratford Shakespeare Festival and Westport Summer Theatre are both nearby, and the Silvermine Guild College of Art features art exhibits, workshops, and concerts.

INNKEEPER:	Francis C. Whitman
SEASON:	Year round
MEALS:	Breakfast, lunch, and dinner; Sunday brunch
TELEPHONE:	203-847-4558
ACCOMMODATIONS:	10 rooms, each with private bath
ADDRESS:	Silvermine and Perry Avenues Norwalk, Connecticut 06850
DIRECTIONS:	I-95 (Connecticut Turnpike) to Exit 15. Route 7 to Exit 2 to Silvermine Avenue; turn right and go 2 blocks to corner of Silvermine and Perry avenues.

TORRINGTON
Yankee Pedlar Inn

On July 28, 1891, Frank Conley delivered a speech at the grand opening of the Conley Inn, now the Yankee Pedlar.

Today marks an event that would have been undreamed of a half dozen years ago — the opening of a hotel in this town [Torrington] equal to any in the state.

Every room has a steam radiator and a 22-light chandelier. A 225-light Springfield gas machine and 30-horse power boiler light and heat the house. In summer hot water is furnished by a stove. There are modern closets on three floors and wash rooms on four. A hose bibb in the attic, which also has steam and gas, furnishes protection in case of fire. Every floor in the house is Alabama pine, finished; the doors are 1½ inch.

Taking up the furnishings, the parlor is a model of taste. Mrs. Conley has given her best thought to this. It has a beautiful Axminster carpet, Irish pointlace curtains with light silk drapery, hung with white enamel and gold curtain poles. Wilton rug couches, rocker and arm chairs, a cane conversation chair, pretty table, elegant Circassian walnut Fischner piano, and fine engravings make it a veritable boudoir.

The bed rooms throughout the hotel are models of comfort. They are largely alcove rooms, or in suites of twos and threes. No two are furnished just alike. All have the best Bigelow 5-frame body, Brussels carpets, of varying patterns; very pretty suites, mostly in oak — antique, 16th Century, and English, and with marble-top dresser and washstand. The red oak and red marble make a fine combination. The oak carving is in massive scroll work. Some of the sets are black walnut, which will be a rare wood in a few years.

Today, the interior of an old-fashioned inn welcomes the traveler weary of the chrome-and-glass cheerlessness of the modern motel. The Yankee Pedlar Inn is reminiscent of Colonial taverns, with each of the rooms decorated distinctively in early American manner, but with modern baths, year-round air conditioning, TV, and FM-radio reception.

Since it first opened, the inn has invited "Travelers, Wayfarers and Refined Persons" to partake of "Solid Food and Drink," and the tradition continues today. For lunch, seven specialties of the house are offered, as well as seven cold platters, and a variety of egg dishes and sandwiches.

Dinner provides a choice of twenty or more entrées, featuring such dishes as chicken à la Kiev, sauerbraten, and Shish Kabob Mashwi, as well as more traditional fare. Desserts are homemade and served from the pastry cart.

Torrington is situated in the heart of vacation country. Different seasons provide a wide range of activities and attractions: beautiful spring flower displays; Lakeridge and Woodridge recreational areas; Christmas Village; the restored opera house; exhibitions of Seth Thomas clocks and the famous Hitchcock furniture; golf and pool facilities. For the winter sports enthusiast, seven fine ski slopes are within a short drive.

INNKEEPER: Arthur J. Rubens, President

SEASON: Year round

MEALS:	Breakfast, lunch, and dinner
TELEPHONE:	203-489-9226
ACCOMMODATIONS:	75 rooms, all with private bath
ADDRESS:	93 Main Street Torrington, Connecticut 06790
DIRECTIONS:	*From New York:* I-84 East, to Route 8 North to Torrington.
	From Boston: Proceed to Hartford. Route 44 to Route 202 to Torrington.

Maine

BATH
Grane's Fairhaven Inn

Nestled into the hillside overlooking the wide Kennebec River in North Bath, Maine, sits this charming old country inn, a peaceful home surrounded by lush green lawns, luxuriant woods, and meadows. The Fairhaven welcomes guests to pause for a night or to vacation for a week or more, but always to enjoy the charming atmosphere of old Maine.

This beautiful home was built around 1790 by Pembleton Edgecomb for his new bride. For the next 125 years, the home was occupied by the children and grandchildren of the Edgecomb family.

In 1926, the home was sold to a family who named it Fairhaven. In the 1940s they added rooms to the west side, but the east facade of the long, low house remained practically the same as the original building.

The house was resold in 1969 to still another family, who, for the next nine years, devoted their time to refurbishing the estate.

In September 1978, Jane Wyllie and Gretchen Williams bought the Fairhaven and converted it to a country inn. A full range of outdoor and indoor seasonal activities is nearby, including duck and deer hunting in season.

While Grane's does not offer lunch or dinner, it serves a showstopping breakfast that includes some of the following: homemade muffins and breads, honey, jams and jellies, juices, and fruits in season; pancakes, cereals, hash browns, cheese and ham soufflés, mixed grills, Scotch eggs, scrapple, eggs Benedict, omelets, and finnan haddie.

For dinner you will find an excellent variety of restaurants just down the road in Bath, Brunswick, and Wiscasset.

Last year, for the first time, the "Ladies Grane" invited their guests to return for festive Thanksgiving and Christmas five-course dinners. The events, predictably, were hits.

INNKEEPERS:	Jane Wyllie and Gretchen Williams
SEASON:	Year round
MEALS:	Breakfast; lunch and dinner by special arrangement only
TELEPHONE:	207-443-4391
ACCOMMODATIONS:	8 rooms, 4 baths
ADDRESS:	Bath, Maine 04530
DIRECTIONS:	I-95 North to Route 1 to Bath-Brunswick. Continue on Route 1 to New Meadow Road. At golf club turn right to North Bath Road. Turn left, and go $1/2$ mile to the inn.

BRIDGTON
Tarry-a-While Resort
Switzer Stübli

It's like going to Switzerland without crossing the ocean. . . .

On beautiful, crystal-clear Highland Lake near Bridgton, Maine, sits a Swiss chalet — formerly a working farm — known as Tarry-a-While.

The original structure, now called the Gasthaus, was built over one hundred years ago; it now houses the Switzer Stübli Dining Room. Swiss-born co-innkeeper and chef Hans Jenni built the dining room and the tables from native pine trees. The walls are sparkling white plaster and old, weathered barnboards, and the room is charmingly decorated with Swiss cowbells, bittersweet, and an Alphorn, with fresh flowers on the scrubbed tables.

The guest rooms in the Gasthaus are furnished with antiques, while those in the chalets have desks, chairs, headboards, bureaus, and lamps also made by Hans. The main house and smaller buildings are decorated with hand-painted shutters and colorful flower boxes — all the fine work of Barbara Jenni.

Authentic Swiss and Continental specialties grace the daily menu, with such appetizing entrées as Cordon Bleu Monte Rosa, Kaninchen Bundnerat (rabbit in red wine sauce), Regenbogen Forella (boneless rainbow trout), Wiener Schnitzel, and a choice of delicious fondues. There is also a limited children's menu. All pastries, cheesecakes, rolls, and breads are prepared by French pastry chef Lorraine Laverdiere.

On the grounds and available to guests at the resort are tennis, canoeing, pedal boats, a putting green, Ping-Pong, shuffleboard, badminton, horseshoes, fishing, and, of course, comfortable spots for just sitting and rocking. There are two large sandy beaches at the Highland lakefront; motors, sailboats, and waterskiing are available at a nominal charge, and a golf course is just across the road.

For day trips, many attractions are an hour or less away by car — the Mt. Washington Cog Railway, Conway Scenic Railway, historic old Portland, the beautiful Maine coast. For a complete change of pace, check out the fabulous L. L. Bean store in Freeport, open twenty-four hours a day.

INNKEEPERS:	Hans and Barbara Jenni
SEASON:	June to early September
MEALS:	Breakfast, lunch, and dinner
TELEPHONE:	207-647-2522
ACCOMMODATIONS:	22 rooms with private bath, 14 rooms with shared bath
ADDRESS:	Bridgton, Maine 04009
DIRECTIONS:	I-95 North to Portland, Route 302 North to Bridgton.

CAMDEN
Aubergine

Aubergine is a charming French restaurant and a small, romantic inn — all that and more.

It is the product of the imagination of David and Kerlin Grant, who fell in love with the oldest inn in Camden, Maine, while looking for a new restaurant site. Built in 1890, the silver-gray Victorian building has been restored to its original charm. With antique furnishings and distinctive floral papers, each room is different, yet all share a special quality of serene hospitality.

The restaurant is light and airy yet intimate, with bouquets of fresh flowers and working fireplaces for chilly evenings. Aubergine is known for its new-style French menu, which combines classical dishes with the new lighter cuisine. The menu changes monthly and may include a pâté of fresh and smoked trout, medallions of lobster with mussels, and duck with fresh peaches. The wine list has been carefully chosen to represent the finest varietals and vintages while offering the best values. Dinner is by reservation only.

A very popular part of the Aubergine kitchen is Le Pic Nic, which offers elegant foods packed to travel — on a day trip, for a light supper, to take with you when you leave. A day's notice will provide you with the most interesting selection.

David Grant was graduated from the Restaurant School of Philadelphia and served an apprenticeship in the Armagnac district of France. Before coming to Maine, he gained practical experience working in a restaurant in Philadelphia, and he learned his trade well. His talent for combining the classical kitchen with innovative techniques delights both the eye and the palate.

The results of Kerlin's exquisite taste are to be seen in the restaurant as elsewhere — in the painted chairs in a setting of antiques, the tablecloths, the flower arrangements, the Laura Ashley wallpaper, and other fine touches.

Guests will find many activities in and near Camden, including biking, swimming, tennis, and golf. Sailing charters and day trips to nearby islands are easily arranged. In the evening there are Shakespearean theater and the Bay Chamber Concert series.

Kerlin Grant writes, "As the name of our establishment is a bit different, I thought I should mention that it is 'Aubergine' (without 'L' or 'the' preceding it). It is named for the color aubergine and is also a play on words for auberge and small inn."

INNKEEPERS:	David and Kerlin Grant
SEASON:	May through October
MEALS:	Breakfast, Le Pic Nic, and dinner; reservations required
TELEPHONE:	207-236-8053
ACCOMMODATIONS:	7 rooms, 3 private baths
ADDRESS:	6 Belmont Avenue Camden, Maine 04843
DIRECTIONS:	I-95 to Brunswick, then Route 1 North to Camden. Proceed on Route 1 just past the Route 90 interchange to the first street on the right at the first blinking light. Turn right onto Belmont Avenue. The inn is in the middle of the block on the right.

CAMDEN
Camden Harbour Inn

Built in the late nineteenth century, when Camden was bustling with cargo and fishing schooners, this charming Victorian inn sits on a hill overlooking the harbor and bay and the nearby mountains. In the early days, summer passengers disembarking from the Boston-to-Bangor steamship were picked up by the inn's horse-drawn carriage and driven around the harbor and up the hill to their rooms.

Today Camden Harbour Inn is open the year round, and guests still enjoy gathering on the now glass-enclosed wraparound porch or the front lawn to watch the schooner fleet that travels around Penobscot Bay and the islands.

The inn is comfortably furnished in nineteenth-century style, and some of the guest rooms even have baths with Victorian eagle-claw-footed tubs. Everywhere the emphasis is on old-fashioned warmth and hospitality.

Camden Harbour Restaurant was chosen by *Yankee* magazine as one of the six best restaurants on the Maine coast serving fresh seafood. Dinner is served on the porch during the long days of summer, and in the cozy Red Dining Room when the fireplace and candlelight beckon. While beef and other entrées are available, dishes featuring seafood — picked up locally each day — reign supreme. A typical menu might include seafood chowder and Maine shrimp or lobster stew, and such main courses as broiled haddock, halibut, or swordfish; seafood Newburg; Crab Dijon Casserole; and, of course, fresh-caught broiled Maine lobster. Smaller and simpler meals are also available, served each evening in the Thirsty Whale Tavern, which features live folk music, both traditional and contemporary. The tavern has become known throughout the state as a center for folk music, and local singers often drop in to join the regular performers.

A popular event is Sunday brunch, served year round on the porch and enthusiastically attended by local residents as well as by guests of the inn.

In addition to the spectacular views of the bay and islands from nearby Mt. Battie, and especially the autumn colors in the mountains, the area provides a wide variety of things to see and do throughout the year. In the warm months, boating, including sightseeing cruises on Penobscot Bay, hiking, and fishing are among the most popular activities, and the countless antique and specialty shops nearby entice visitors to shop or just browse.

In winter a prime attraction is cross-country and downhill skiing at Ragged Mountain, just five miles away, happily followed by relaxation by the living room fireplace with hot buttered rum or Irish coffee.

INNKEEPERS:	Jim and Laureen Gilbert
SEASON:	Year round
MEALS:	Breakfast and dinner; Sunday brunch
TELEPHONE:	207-236-4200
ACCOMMODATIONS:	18 rooms, 12 with private bath
ADDRESS:	Bay View Street, Camden, Maine 04843
DIRECTIONS:	I-95 to Brunswick, then Route 1 to Camden. Right at Camden National Bank, then 200 yards to inn.

CENTER LOVELL
Center Lovell Inn

CENTER LOVELL

This quiet country inn is located in a restored home that dates from 1805. Nestled in an area acclaimed as one of the most beautiful spots in the world, it offers spacious and comfortable rooms for vacationers.

Year round there is a wide variety of attractions: outdoor sports; antiquing; exhibitions of arts and crafts; and, in particular, spectacular fall foliage and the popular Fryeburg Fair — an old-fashioned week-long country fair.

For winter sports enthusiasts, nearby ski areas include Evergreen Valley, Pleasant Mountain, Sunday River in Maine, and Mt. Cranmore in New Hampshire. The closest is ten minutes away, the farthest is thirty minutes. Closer still is cross-country skiing from the back door, with miles of serene, unspoiled forest to explore.

The inn is the culmination of Bil and Sue Mosca's lifelong ambition to serve the fine Italian cuisine that has always been a part of their home. Meals represent the cooking of many Italian cities, including Florence, Venice, Naples, Rome, and, especially, Senegalia, a small town on the Adriatic to which the family's lineage can be traced.

The cheerful dining room, with its red and white tablecloths, Chianti-bottle candleholders, and fresh-cut flowers, provides the perfect setting. Daily dinner menus feature such specialties as Bistecca Milanese, Pollo alla Nicolo Firenze, Salsiccia i Peperoni di Luigi, and Pesce Arrosto Senegalia. There are also many pasta favorites, including Spaghetti Salsiccia, Spaghetti con Salsa di Vongoli with imported Romano cheese, and Manicotti ala Guido.

All of the recipes have been passed down through generations and are made with the finest ingredients; each dinner is prepared to order and reflects the careful attention to detail that goes into its creation.

Holidays call for special gastronomic celebration, with dinners of from five to eight courses. For New Year's Eve the menu may include bouillabaisse and roast suckling pig. On the Fourth of July it may be lobster or Agnellino Alforno con Prosciutto — baby leg of lamb stuffed with prosciutto and basted with cream sherry.

Space is limited, so reservations are suggested.
Salute!

INNKEEPERS:	Bil and Sue Mosca
SEASON:	May to October 15; December 20 to March 15.
MEALS:	Breakfast, box lunches (if ordered the night before), and dinner.
TELEPHONE:	207-925-1575
ACCOMMODATIONS:	2 rooms, private bath; 2 rooms, share bath
ADDRESS:	Center Lovell, Maine 04016
DIRECTIONS:	I-93 to Route 104 toward Meredith, New Hampshire (Lakes Region). Then Route 25 to Route 16 to Route 302 to Route 5, Fryeburg. The inn is 14 miles on Route 5.

DENNYSVILLE
Lincoln House Country Inn

Lincoln
House

Built in 1787 by Judge Theodore Lincoln, an ancestor of President Lincoln, historic Lincoln House Country Inn has stood for nearly two centuries as the first and oldest house in Dennysville. (Theodore Lincoln's father, General Benjamin Lincoln, accepted the sword of surrender from General Cornwallis to end the Revolutionary War.) John James Audubon stayed at the Lincoln House Country Inn on his way to Labrador. He loved the house and the Lincoln family so much that he named the Lincoln Sparrow in their honor.

In September 1976, Mary Carol and Jerry Haggerty bought the old house — a noble, classically beautiful, foursquare Georgian Colonial. Their dream — to restore the house to its original simple elegance and open a country inn that recreated as closely as possible, through food and furnishings, the atmosphere of the eighteenth century— became a reality on January 1, 1977.

Lincoln House Country Inn today offers dining and lodging to those who seek quiet hospitality in a secluded setting. In the old tradition, the inn offers the wayfarer simple but hearty meals — one entrée each evening, with salad, hot homemade bread, and a choice of appetizer and dessert. For overnight lodgers, breakfast is also available.

The kitchen — the heart of any home — is, of course, always handy for coffee and conversation. Guests enjoy the use of the comfortable living room with its Steinway grand piano, the handsome library, and unique "back hall." Once again, the latchstring is out at the summer-kitchen door, just as it was years ago for the weary Indians who spread their blankets before the huge brick fireplace.

The ninety-five wooded acres around the inn provide a great diversity of wildlife. Bald eagles are frequently sighted, as are ospreys; families of seal swim in the river, along with the famous North Atlantic salmon. Deer abound on the old logging roads and nature trails, as do birds of every description.

At Christmas, Lincoln House Country Inn celebrates in typical New England style. Wreaths with red bows and candles appear in every window; live indoor trees sparkle with homemade decorations, and the trimmings of the season are everywhere. Then, as in all seasons, the inn's warm hospitality recalls the rich tradition of the past.

INNKEEPERS:	Mary Carol and Jerry Haggerty
SEASON:	Main season is May 15 to November 15; lodging available year round by advance arrangement
MEALS:	In season, breakfast for guests only, family-style dinner; in winter, Fridays and Saturdays only; reservations required
TELEPHONE:	207-726-3953
ACCOMMODATIONS:	6 bedrooms, 4 baths — all semiprivate
ADDRESS:	Dennysville, Maine 04628
DIRECTIONS:	I-95 to Bangor, then Route 1A to Ellsworth. Pick up Route 1 in Ellsworth and continue to Dennysville and Route 86. Go left on Route 86; the inn is the first building on the right.

KENNEBUNKPORT
Village Cove Inn

In the midst of an artists' and writers' colony in Kennebunkport stands a contemporary inn. Less than five years old, the Village Cove Inn offers all the modern facilities and amenities one could wish in a small, well-run hotel: cheerfully appointed rooms with color television, two double beds, and individual heat controls; comfortable lounges; a large game room; a fully stocked bar. The comfortable dining room, decorated in reds, natural woods, and exposed beams, offers a breathtaking panoramic view of the surrounding beauty.

Chef Clair Epting, trained at the famous Brennan's of New Orleans, takes particular pride in his own spice box — a small garden of fresh herbs that are picked and immediately used in the kitchen.

The menus are large and varied, featuring Maine fare and Continental favorites with a touch of Creole; unusual fresh seafood, fowl, and veal dominate the dinner menu. The chef invites guests to request special dishes not listed.

Sunday brunch presents an ample selection of appetizing standards and savory, creative dishes, such as Russian omelet with caviar and sour cream, and Mediterranean omelet with seafood and spiced tomato sauce. In season, cocktails and lunch may be taken on the Patio on the Cove.

The inn provides year-round swimming in its indoor and outdoor pools as well as at three nearby beaches in season. Fishing abounds from rocks, bridges, and wharves, and boat rentals can be arranged.

Historic Kennebunkport, former home of author Kenneth Roberts, was used as background for some of Roberts's novels. It is also the home of the Mountain and Seashore Art Workshop, where classes in watercolor, oil, and pastel are conducted from May through early November by prominent artists such as Martin Ahearn, Miyo and Linda Onishi, David Millard, Charles Movalli, Bernard Gerstner, and others.

When winter comes to southern Maine, activities shift to beach-combing for sea treasures, shopping at the Dock Square specialty shops, or simply relaxing by the fireplace with a book.

INNKEEPERS:	Jacques and Carol Gagnon; Phil Colligan, General Manager
SEASON:	Year round
MEALS:	Breakfast, lunch, and dinner; Sunday brunch
TELEPHONE:	207-967-3993
ACCOMMODATIONS:	32 rooms, each with private bath
ADDRESS:	Chick's Cove Kennebunkport, Maine 04046
DIRECTIONS:	From I-95 (the Maine Turnpike), take Exit 3 and follow Route 35 to Kennebunk. Continue to Kennebunkport. Drive over the bridge and follow the yellow directional signs to the inn.

KINGFIELD
Winter's Inn

Kingfield, near Sugarloaf and Saddleback mountains, is the home of the Winter's Inn, a classic inn on the National Register of Historic Places.

Built by A. G. Winter, Jr., at the turn of the century, the Winter's Inn was designed by the ingenious twin brothers, F. E. and F. O. Stanley, who invented the Stanley Dry Plate Photographic Process, which they later sold to George Eastman, founder of the Eastman Kodak Company. The brothers also designed the Stanley Steamer automobile.

The inn provides old-world charm and elegance combined with a mood of warm informality. Its fine French restaurant, Le Papillon, serves sumptuous meals in the classic style. The fifty-seat Papillon dining room offers candlelight dining, rich oil paintings, and a panoramic view of streams, meadows, and majestic mountains. The Music Room boasts a box grand Chickering piano and a handsomely appointed cocktail bar. The Grand Hall with flowing formal staircase completes the main floor.

In season, guests enjoy tennis, swimming, biking, hiking, pool parties, and white-water canoe racing on the Carrabassett River. Local streams and ponds have been favorites with anglers for over a hundred years.

Kingfield is in the heart of western Maine's hunting country — prime territory for deer and upland birds. Vacationers may also be surprised from time to time by the appearance of moose, fox, beaver, and even bear.

The nearby mountains include Sugarloaf, Mt. Abram, and the Bigelow Range. There are over eighty miles of cross-country ski trails that start just north of town. Another network of snowmobile trails connects to surrounding towns and leads through the beautiful Maine wilderness.

INNKEEPER:	Michael Thom
SEASON:	Year round
MEALS:	Breakfast, dinner by reservation only
TELEPHONE:	207-265-5421
ACCOMMODATIONS:	11 rooms, 4 with private bath
ADDRESS:	Kingfield, Maine 04947
DIRECTIONS:	I-95 (Maine Turnpike) to Route 27 at Augusta, to Kingfield.

SOUTH BROOKSVILLE
Breezemere Farm Inn

Breezemere is a sixty-acre farm beautifully situated at the head of Orcutt Harbor on East Penobscot Bay. It runs from the easterly coastline — active with marine life — westward and upward to quiet, moss-covered rock ledges, through spruce and pine and open blueberry fields along the way.

The main house was built in 1850 and began taking in guests in 1917. (During the 1920s and '30s, milk and eggs were shipped from the farm to such places as Portland and Boston by packet boats, which in return brought guests from those towns to the inn.)

Joan and Jim Lippke bought Breezemere in 1977 and have put much time and effort into restoring and redecorating the main house, large barn, lodge, and cottages. The atmosphere at Breezemere is friendly, informal, and unhurried, whether in the old farmhouse with its antique furnishings, the pleasant cottages, or the rustic lodge with its huge fieldstone fireplace — a perfect place for conversation, games, and listening to local musicians.

The inn's country kitchen features local, organically grown vegetables, farm-fresh eggs, pure butter, and freshly baked breads and pastries. The day begins with a hearty farm breakfast and ends with a five-course gourmet dinner, which includes delicious appetizers, soups and chowders, and a choice of entrées. A specialty is the fish catch of the day — perhaps lobster, lemony stuffed cod, or Canadian salmon— and other favorite dishes are Honey Glazed Broiled Chicken and Black Skillet Pepper Steak Supreme. Mouth-watering homemade desserts round out the menu. Breezemere is not licensed to serve alcoholic beverages, but ice and mixes are available for guests who wish to bring their own liquor.

Many vacationers choose to spend most of their time right at the farm, exploring the coast, fields, and woods on foot, taking out a small boat for clamming at low tide, picking blueberries, cycling, sailing, or just enjoying the unspoiled rural surroundings.

Others use Breezemere as their home base for active days of touring picturesque Deer Isle, or taking the mail boat to Isle au Haut or a sightseeing cruise aboard a charter boat to watch the seals at play. Of special interest also are Acadia National Park to the east and the charming seacoast town of Castine and many quaint fishing villages to the west. Golf and tennis facilities are available at the nearby Blue Hill Country Club.

INNKEEPER:	Joan and Jim Lippke
SEASON:	May 30 to October 15
MEALS:	Breakfast and dinner
TELEPHONE:	207-326-8628
ACCOMMODATIONS:	7 rooms, 4 baths in farmhouse; cottages with private baths
ADDRESS:	Box 290
	South Brooksville, Maine 04617
DIRECTIONS:	I-95 to Augusta, the Route 3 to Bucksport and Route 175 to Brooksville.

SPRUCE HEAD
Craignair Inn
THE CRAIGNAIR

Craignair Inn is situated on four acres of shorefront within the 3500-odd miles of bays, peninsulas, inlets, and headlands that form a coastline unmatched anywhere for its beauty.

Built in 1928 on a granite ledge rising from the sea and surrounded by flower gardens, Craignair originally housed workers from the nearby quarry and has only recently been converted into a quaint and charming inn.

Downstairs is an exceedingly warm and cheery parlor-library, a sunny rustic dining room that looks out onto the sea, and an old-fashioned kitchen dominated by an antique cast-iron working stove. Upstairs, the bedrooms are furnished simply but comfortably, with quilt-covered beds, colorful wall hangings, and hooked rugs on the floors. The three shared baths on each floor are conveniently located.

Life tends to be uncomplicated at the shore and so does the dinner menu at Craignair Inn — usually a choice of two ample homemade entrées with all the fixin's. Sunday's offering may be a hot buffet with sweet and sour pork, pepper steak, and barbecued rice; another day may see shish kabob of tender beef and seasoned chicken. Homemade breads, soup du jour, and open salad and dessert bars round out the menu, which changes from week to week.

Craignair is especially attractive to visitors seeking serenity, simplicity, privacy, and natural beauty. Its location and atmosphere make it ideal for writers, artists, and naturalists, as well as for anyone looking for a slower pace.

Many guests enjoy just sitting in the garden, relaxing and watching the activities of shorebirds, clammers, and lobstermen. Others prefer to explore the coast along the many miles of paths adjacent to the inn, the spruce forests, clam flats, offshore islands, tidal pools, and meadows — all with their abundance of wild flowers and birds, and even seals in season. Bicycles are available for trips to Port Clyde, where the ferry leaves for Monhegan, or to Owls Head Lighthouse and State Park.

Spruce Head and neighboring towns and villages offer an almost endless variety of recreational facilities: deep-sea charters, windjammer trips, horseback riding, hiking and camping, as well as galleries and antique shows, summer festivals, museums, and the Rockport Summer Theatre.

In nearby Rockland and Camden are found shops, concerts, tennis courts and golf courses, riding facilities, and sailing; numerous country fairs and festivals celebrate the glories of seafood, blueberries, and other bounties of nature.

On warm afternoons, most guests head for the old granite quarry near the inn, a deep saltwater pool surrounded by spruce and birch, for a refreshing swim before dinner. During the colder months, one may hike, snowshoe, cross-country ski, or ice-skate in the immediate area, and downhill ski at the Camden Snow Bowl, just a short drive away. And, when the fog rolls in, the comfortable sitting room, with its large library and crackling fire, provides a cozy and pleasant refuge.

INNKEEPERS:	Norman and Terry Smith
SEASON:	Year round
MEALS:	Breakfast and dinner (included in room rate)
TELEPHONE:	207-594-7644
ACCOMMODATIONS:	20 rooms, most facing the Atlantic Ocean and Long Cove, some with private baths
ADDRESS:	Clark Island Spruce Head, Maine 04859
DIRECTIONS:	From I-95 take Route 1 in Brunswick, and follow it approximately one hour to Thomaston. South on Route 131 for 5½ miles; east on Route 73, 1 mile to Clark Island Road. Turn right and continue for 1½ miles. The inn is at the water's edge.

TENANTS HARBOR
The East Wind

Tenants Harbor is a peaceful village on the St. George peninsula, halfway up the coast of Maine, on beautiful Penobscot Bay.

Life slows to a comfortable pace in this tiny, seaside village still recognizable from the pages of Sarah Orne Jewett's account of a century ago as *The Country of the Pointed Firs.* No traffic jams, pollution, neon signs, or fast-food franchises upset the natural harmony here.

The East Wind, built in the 1800s and restored in 1974–1975 after being closed for nearly twenty-five years, sits on the edge of the water, overlooking the working harbor. The fishing boats, lobster traps, boat-yard, and docks that provide livelihoods for the residents of the town are also among its most picturesque attributes, as are the islands that mark the entrance to the harbor. An unobstructed view of all this scenic beauty — transformed by each tide, sunset, and change of weather — is provided from all of the East Wind's sixteen rooms and from the comfortable veranda that extends along three sides of the building.

The inn's property includes 350 feet of deep-water shore frontage and a small wharf, and the harbor offers an abundance of deep-water anchorage for large boats. The Cod End Fish Market, adjacent to the East Wind, has rental moorings, water, ice, gasoline, diesel fuel, charts, and other supplies for visiting yachtsmen. You'll find the folks at Cod End willing to pack lobster and your favorite fish for your trip home.

Open to the public and serving three times a day, the restaurant at the East Wind offers a truly enjoyable dining experience. Its charming atmosphere is enhanced by the varied flavors of authentic New England home-cooked meals, featuring fresh fish and tender lobster caught daily. The fine service and memorable dishes have been hailed by the critics of such publications as Chapin and Squire's *Guide to Recommended Country Inns,* the *Boston Globe, Down East* magazine, and *The New York Times.*

The inn is within walking distance of the village library, stores, post office, and weekend public suppers; in Tenants Harbor walking is still a safe and usual mode of transportation. No car is needed to tour the peninsula; all of its attractions — beaches, rock cliffs, tidal pools, and old cemeteries — can be reached in easy day trips by bicycle.

Activities for visitors include doing absolutely nothing; watching fishermen unload their daily catch; visiting nearby islands, shops, and museums; playing tennis or golf; swimming or hiking; or dining at one of the area's fine restaurants.

Winter sports enthusiasts will find this area perfectly suited to the peaceful pursuit of cross-country skiing, snowshoeing, or skating, and downhill skiers may commute easily to the uncrowded Camden Snow Bowl. All will find warmth, comfort, and good food at the East Wind, the area's only inn to remain open throughout the winter.

INNKEEPERS:	Tim Watts and Ginnie "Mama" Wheeler
SEASON:	Year round
MEALS:	Breakfast, lunch, and dinner
TELEPHONE:	207-372-8800/8908
ACCOMMODATIONS:	16 rooms, 2 with private bath; 14 rooms share baths. New planned expansion in adjacent building will have 4 rooms, each with private bath.
ADDRESS:	Tenants Harbor, Maine 04860
DIRECTIONS:	I-95 (Maine Turnpike) to Route 1 at Brunswick. Follow Route 1 for about 45 miles to Thomaston, then turn right onto Route 131 just outside the village. Continue 9½ miles on Route 131; at the Tenants Harbor Post Office bear left down the hill to the inn.

Massachusetts

ANDOVER
Andover Inn

ANDOVER INN

This fifty-year-old structure is located in the midst of Andover's academic community and offers a relaxed atmosphere in a peaceful and undisturbed setting.

The inn's thirty-three guest rooms artistically blend the charm of days gone by with completely modern service, convenience, and comfort. Every room has color television, radio, direct-dial telephone service, air conditioning, and a bright, modern bathroom; all rooms have a view of the garden, pond, or campus of Phillips Academy.

The genial innkeepers/chefs, Henry Broekhoff and John Oudheusden, grew up a block apart in Amsterdam, although they never knew each other then. Oudheusden, who was executive chef at Marriott Hotels in Washington, D.C., Houston, and at the Essex House in New York City, handles the cooking at the inn, assisted by other chefs. He also makes all the desserts, soups, and breads.

Before coming to New England, Broekhoff worked in restaurants in Holland, France, Belgium, and Germany. From 1965 on, he gained further experience at such distinguished establishments as the Brasserie and the Four Seasons in New York, Yard of Ale in Harvard Square, various Holiday Inns, and the Hotel Sonesta, also in Cambridge. Then, in partnership with Oudheusden, came Maxwell's, a fine small restaurant in Lawrence, Massachusetts.

An inviting dining room, with a beamed ceiling and wood-trimmed pillars, oriental carpet, crystal chandelier, crisp white table linen, and fresh flowers, provides the setting for a gourmet adventure at Andover Inn.

As an appetizer, one may have smoked trout or steak tartare or pâté of duckling, among many other choices. There is an abundance of fish and meat dishes, and no fewer than ten unusual specialties of the house; and, to top off the meal, a number of staple desserts as well as a selection from the pastry cart. The inn offers a wide variety of imported teas and coffees, including flaming Dutch coffee. On Sunday evenings, an authentic Rijsttafel (which consists of a main dish of rice and twenty to thirty different side dishes) is served. This Indonesian extravaganza, which is unique for the area, is very popular with guests.

An extensive selection of fine imported and domestic beverages is also available. Reservations for dinner are suggested.

On the grounds of Phillips Academy, the oldest incorporated academy in the country, are the Addison Gallery of American Art and the Robert S. Peabody Foundation for Archaeology, which, along with some other buildings, are open to the public.

For ski enthusiasts, the Boston Hills Ski Area is just off Massachusetts 114, less than ten miles from the inn.

INNKEEPERS:	Henry Broekhoff and John Oudheusden
SEASON:	Year round
MEALS:	Breakfast, lunch, and dinner; reservations for dinner a must; no meals Christmas Day
TELEPHONE:	617-475-5903
ACCOMMODATIONS:	33 rooms, 23 with private bath, 10 semiprivate
ADDRESS:	Chapel Avenue Andover, Massachusetts 01810
DIRECTIONS:	*From New York:* I-495 to Route 28, just past interchange with I-93. Follow Route 28 to Andover. *From Boston:* I-93 to Exit 15 to Route 125 East to Route 28 to Andover.

BREWSTER, CAPE COD
The Bramble Inn

In the heart of the historic district of the Cape you will find the Bramble Inn, located in an old Cape Cod house dating from Civil War days.

The Bramble Inn offers country charm and cozy accommodations in a friendly atmosphere — the choice for those who seek the ambience of an intimate inn. All rooms have either twin beds or a double bed, television, and shared bath. A complimentary breakfast is served to guests.

The same old Cape Cod house is also the site of the unique Bramble Inn Gallery and Café. Open for lunch and dinner, the café serves gourmet soups, Cape Cod clam chowder, quiche, crêpes, elegant cheese plates, fine wines, and imported beers. This fascinating café is also an art gallery, showing the works of local as well as off-Cape artists.

The inn is within walking distance of the ocean, adjacent to tennis courts, and close to Sealand of Cape Cod. Also close at hand are golf, fishing, hiking trails, boating, state parks, museums, and summer theaters.

Brewster, the home of the Bramble Inn, is a perfect jumping-off place for exploring the Cape, being almost equidistant from Buzzards Bay, where the island begins, and Provincetown, where it ends. Visitors will find countless sightseeing options, from Sandwich, with its famous Glass Museum, to Provincetown itself, where the Mayflower first dropped anchor in the New World, and which is today the home of hundreds of shops, galleries, restaurants, historic houses, and museums. Along the way are all the many attractions for which Cape Cod is famous, including the Salt Marsh Visitors Center in Eastham, Monomoy National Wildlife Refuge in Chatham, Aqua Circus, day boat trips from Hyannis to Nantucket and Martha's Vineyard, and, of course, miles and miles of some of the most spectacular of Atlantic Ocean beaches.

INNKEEPERS:	Elaine Brennan and Karen Etsell
SEASON:	June to September
MEALS:	Complimentary breakfast for guests; lunch and dinner at the Café

TELEPHONE:	617-896-7644
ACCOMMODATIONS:	3 rooms, all share bath
ADDRESS:	Route 6A, P.O. Box 159
	Brewster, Cape Cod, Massachusetts 02631
DIRECTIONS:	Cross the Cape Cod Canal at the Sagamore Bridge, to Route 6. Get off Route 6 at Exit 10, and go right on Route 124 to Route 6A, and right on Route 6A to the inn.

CHATHAM, CAPE COD
The Queen Anne Inn

The Queen Anne Inn has enjoyed a long and colorful history. The center portion of the structure was built in 1840 by sea captain Solomon Howes as a wedding present for his daughter; it remained a private home for many years. In 1930 a new owner christened the residence the Queen Anne Inn and opened its doors to the public. Since its opening day, without interruption, the inn has welcomed guests in season.

Over the years several wings have been added. During the winter of 1978–1979, the old Queen was completely restored by the present owners with great love and effort, which are apparent everywhere one looks.

The genial Continental innkeepers — "The Two Gentlemen from Vienna" — are justifiably proud of their painstakingly restored public rooms. The gracious lounge is spacious and impressive in its elegant simplicity; soft gray velvet, complemented by warm salmon and burgundy tones, highlights the beauty of the genuine Victorian loveseats and sofas. The restored sofa in the reception lobby is said to have a current value in the thousands of dollars. In fact, virtually all of the appointments are authentic Victoriana.

The inn offers thirty large guest rooms and suites, all also furnished with beautiful antiques. Each room is different and all feature a modern bathroom and private telephone.

Dining at the inn's Earl of Chatham Restaurant is truly a magnificent adventure. During a recent stay at the Queen we counted no fewer than thirty-five Continental and New England entrées. The Continental Sunday Brunch is a traffic-stopper; the serving tables overflow with hot and cold dishes, roasts, salads, quiches, fruits, and freshly baked breads and pastries.

A sociable starter or an encore of coffee and brandy are always a delight in the Salon Champlain.

Located at the very tip of the elbow of Cape Cod, the inn is central to all the sightseeing and recreational activities the island has to offer.

For an unusual luncheon experience, one cannot do better than a visit to the Impudent Oyster just two blocks from the inn.

INNKEEPERS:	Gunther and Nicole Weinkopf, Siegfried and Trudy Kiesewetter
SEASON:	Early spring to late fall
MEALS:	Breakfast, lunch, and dinner; full Continental brunch on Sunday
TELEPHONE:	617-945-0394
ACCOMMODATIONS:	30 rooms and suites, each with private bath
ADDRESS:	70 Queen Anne Road Chatham, Cape Cod, Massachusetts 02633
DIRECTIONS:	Cross the Cape Cod Canal on the Sagamore Bridge, getting onto Route 6. At Exit 11 go south on Route 137 (straight through two intersections) to its end, where it joins Route 28. Turn left on Route 28 toward Chatham center. At first traffic light (about 3 miles), turn right onto Queen Anne Road. The inn is immediately to the right.

LENOX
Gateways Inn

Gateways Inn

The historic village of Lenox is nestled in the foothills of the rolling Berkshires. Near the center of town stands a magnificent two-story mansion, built in 1912 as a summer residence by Harley Procter (of Procter and Gamble) and now known as Gateways Inn. Gateways was rated in 1981 as the only Mobil four-star inn and restaurant in the country.

Reminders of the Old World, with its quiet traditional elegance, are everywhere, and guests relax in the comfort of Colonial-style rooms with antique furnishings. In the formal, handsomely decorated Gateways restaurant, dining is a memorable experience. The culinary expertise of chef-owner Gerhard Schmid is evident in every dish to reach the table — a fine selection representing the best of both Continental and classical American cuisine.

Winner of both a gold and silver medal in the 1968 International Culinary Competition, which is held every four years in Frankfurt, West Germany, Chef Gerhard also received three Olympic gold medals in 1976. He had the further honor of preparing Boston's royal luncheon for Queen Elizabeth during our Bicentennial celebration.

During the spring and summer months the outdoor terrace and gardens invite relaxation. Gateways guests are offered free guest privileges for the use of the pool, bicycles, and tennis court at the sister inn, Haus Andreas, located just five minutes away. In summer, the area is alive with cultural activities of all kinds; the most famous are Tanglewood, Berkshire Theater, and Jacob's Pillow. There are also boutiques, antique shops, galleries, museums, theaters, dance companies, and historical sites of interest.

The Hancock Shaker Museum Village, which was an active community between 1781 and 1960, is certainly worth a visit. Among the most interesting exhibits are the remarkable furniture, the Round Stone Barn, Meeting House, Tea House, Laundry, and Machine Shop. Located three miles west of Pittsfield on Route 20, it is an easy and pleasant drive.

Autumn brings brilliant foliage, which can be enjoyed along miles of country roads with breathtaking views of the Berkshire hills. And for winter fun, there are seven major ski areas nearby as well as almost limitless cross-country skiing.

INNKEEPERS:	Lillian and Gerhard Schmid
SEASON:	Year round, except two weeks at end of November and two weeks at end of March
MEALS:	Continental breakfast and dinner; reservations suggested
TELEPHONE:	413-637-2532
ACCOMMODATIONS:	8 rooms, most with private bath
ADDRESS:	71 Walker Street Lenox, Massachusetts 01240
DIRECTIONS:	*From New York:* Taconic State Parkway to Route 23, Hillsdale exit. Follow Route 23 to Great Barrington, then Route 7 North to Stockbridge and on to Lenox. Turn left onto 7A (Kemble Street) and go to the top of the hill. The inn is diagonally left across the intersection of 7A and Route 183.
	From Boston: Take Exit 2 off I-90 (Massachusetts Turnpike). After toll, bear right toward town of Lee (Route 20). Drive through Lee and continue on Route 20 to first set of lights at intersection of Route 183. Turn left onto Route 183 (Walker Street) and go for about 1 mile. The inn is on the right, just before the center of town.

LENOX
Wheatleigh Inn

In the heart of the beautiful Berkshires, overlooking a lake, amidst lawns and gardens, on twenty-two self-contained acres, stands the estate of Wheatleigh. Its centerpiece is a grand, cream-colored manse fashioned after a sixteenth-century Florentine palazzo, which combines the beauty of a European "hotel" with the comfort of an Edwardian American home.

The thirty-two-room palazzo was built in 1893 by American industrialist H. H. Cook, who, in order to ensure accuracy of design and detail, imported 150 Italian craftsmen to carve its ceilings, mantels, and walls. When his daughter married the Count de Heredia of Italy in the 1920s, Cook gave her the house and its surrounding acres of rolling Berkshire hillside as a wedding present. Crowning a rise south of Lenox, the magnificent residence, with its sprawling grounds, manicured gardens, and panoramic views of the surrounding countryside, became the showplace of the Berkshires.

It was sold by the Countess's heirs in 1949, and had grown somewhat shabby before David Weisgal and Florence Brooks-Dunay discovered it in 1976, refurbished the mansion, and reopened it as Wheatleigh, perhaps the most imposing country inn in America.

The house is filled with old-world, nineteenth-century flourishes, which, with David and Florence's good taste and sense of style, seem timeless and equally well suited to modern life. The public rooms include a Great Hall with magnificent stained-glass windows, gleaming wood floors, grand staircase, and fireplace with mantel of sculptured cupids and flowers. In the bar, formerly the library, one may enjoy cocktails before dinner, and coffee and dessert after, amidst music and volumes of the classics.

The Victorian-inspired dining room has claret walls hung with paintings of the impressionist and post-impressionist periods. One dines by candlelight in an atmosphere of quiet grandeur. A full menu of Continental and American fare is available nightly; entrées are usually standards of the French and Italian repertoires. In season, cocktails and luncheon are served on the terrace.

Each bedroom has a flavor of its own, which reflects and adds to the unique character of the house. Many have fireplaces; some have balconies.

Wheatleigh boasts easy access to the whole panorama of cultural activities and sports to be found in the Berkshires. Swimming, tennis, and cross-country skiing may be enjoyed on the premises. Nearby are golf, horseback riding, trout fishing, and alpine skiing. The inn is within ten minutes' walking distance of the Berkshire Music Center and Festival at Tanglewood, world-famous summer home of the Boston Symphony Orchestra. (Morning rehearsals are open to the public.) Chamber music is presented at the South Mountain Concerts in Pittsfield, and jazz and folk concerts are at the Music Inn, five minutes' walking distance from Wheatleigh.

There is summer theater showing Broadway and off-Broadway productions at the Berkshire Theater in Stockbridge and at the Williamstown Playhouse in Williamstown.

For collectors and browsers, Wheatleigh is surrounded by a wide variety of fine antique galleries and shops.

HOST:	A. David Weisgal
SEASON:	Year round
MEALS:	Breakfast and dinner; lunch in summer
TELEPHONE:	413-637-0610
ACCOMMODATIONS:	18 rooms, all with private bath
ADDRESS:	Lenox, Massachusetts 01240
DIRECTIONS:	*From New York:* Taconic State Parkway to Route 23, Hillsdale exit. Continue on Route 23 to Great Barrington and intersection with Route 7. Turn left on Route 7 to Stockbridge. At Red Lion Inn where Route 7 turns right, go straight on Prospect Hill Road, bearing left, for about 5 miles. The inn is on the right, past the Stockbridge Bowl and Music Inn.
	From Boston: I-90 (Massachusetts Turnpike) to Lee exit. Follow signs into Lenox. In center of Lenox, at Curtis Hotel corner, take Route 183 to fork. Bear left at fork, go one-tenth of a mile, and turn left on West Hawthorne Road; go 1 mile to inn entrance.

NANTUCKET
Jared Coffin House

Located in the heart of Nantucket's Historic District — only two blocks from Main Street and from the head of Steamboat Wharf — this gracious inn recaptures the spirit of the glorious days of Nantucket's reign as queen of the whaling ports.

The main house was built in 1845 by Jared Coffin, one of the island's most successful ship owners. Only two years later the family moved to Boston and the house was bought by the Nantucket Steamboat Company for use as a hotel, and named the Ocean House. Eben W. Allen was the owner from 1857 to 1872, during which time he built an addition on the north side of the house. After Allen sold the property, the Ocean House passed through many hands until 1961, when the Nantucket Historical Trust bought it and renamed it the Jared Coffin House. In 1976 the Trust sold it to Philip and Margaret Read, who had leased and managed the inn since 1966.

The inn now consists of five buildings, all restored to their original style in both architecture and furnishings. The original Jared Coffin House includes a living room and library beautifully furnished in Chippendale, Sheraton, and American Federal, as well as sleeping rooms with Continental and Nantucket furniture, period antiques, and fabrics woven on the island. The Eben Allen Wing offers simply decorated yet attractive rooms, and the eighteenth-century "Old House" directly behind it has three special rooms decorated with crewel embroidery. The Daniel Webster House combines contemporary and Colonial style, and an 1821 Federal-style house directly across the street has six charming period rooms.

The Patio provides a perfect spot for enjoying lunch or a beverage during the summer months.

From April through December, dining is in the quiet, elegant Jared Coffin Dining Room, enhanced by authentic period wallpaper, handsome paintings, decorated tole chandeliers, and fine American china and silverware. The menu features classical American cuisine, an innovative yet traditional presentation of the region's finest food products. Among the specialties are Nantucket pheasant and quail; such seafoods as bay scallops, striped bass, and bluefish, mussels, clams, oysters, and lobsters — all freshly caught and deliciously prepared — and local cranberry and beach plum jellies and sauces.

During the winter months an informal pub-style menu is offered in the Tap Room, which also serves lunch all year round. This rustic, inviting rendezvous has old-pine walls and hand-hewn beams, scrubbed-oak-topped tables, oak captain's chairs, and interesting wall decorations, and is a truly charming place for sharing good food, good conversation, and good times with old and new friends.

Thanksgiving is traditional at the Jared Coffin House, and the inn's Twelve Days of Christmas celebration blends new and old customs from around the world, including festive decorations with holly, garlands, and a special cranberry wreath on the front door.

While Nantucket Island is a year-round retreat, it really starts to blossom in the spring. There are excellent public beaches within walking distance of the inn and challenging surf swimming at Madaket and Cisco. All manner of warm-weather activities are but a short walk or drive away: tennis, cycling, waterskiing, sailing, fishing, and, for browsing and just looking, historic houses, museums, and quaint shops everywhere.

INNKEEPERS:	Philip and Margaret Read
SEASON:	Year round
MEALS:	Breakfast, lunch, and dinner
TELEPHONE:	617-228-2405
ACCOMMODATIONS:	46 rooms, all with private bath
ADDRESS:	Nantucket, Massachusetts 02554
DIRECTIONS:	Ferry from Woods Hole or Hyannis. (Check first for months of service.) Reservations required.

STOCKBRIDGE
The Red Lion Inn

SINCE 1773

On Main Street in the center of historic Stockbridge stands the Red Lion Inn, one of the largest and most popular in New England and among the few remaining inns in the area to have been in continuous use since before 1800. Although a red lion has appeared on the inn's signboard since it opened, it has been known by its present name only since the turn of the century.

In 1773, Silas Pepoon built a small tavern that served as a stop for stagecoaches traveling between Albany, Hartford, and Boston. One year later it was the site at which delegates from various Berkshire County towns protested the use of articles imported from England.

The building was greatly enlarged in 1848. In 1862, following a succession of owners, the inn was purchased by Mr. and Mrs. Charles H. Plumb, the great-uncle and -aunt of Congressman Allen T. Treadway, and it remained in the Treadway family for over ninety years. During the early years, Mrs. Plumb added to her outstanding collection of antique furniture, china, and pewter, most of which is on display in the inn today.

The inn had been further enlarged several times before it was destroyed by fire in 1896. Rebuilt in the following year, it remained virtually unchanged until 1961, when the southern end of the building was converted into a motor lodge, and a swimming pool–recreation area complex was added.

In 1968, Mr. and Mrs. John H. Fitzpatrick, owners of Country Curtains, bought the inn. Following extensive improvements to the kitchen and the dining room, as well as the addition of a new tavern, the inn opened in May 1969 for a four-season year.

Among the guests who have stayed at the inn over the years are five presidents — Cleveland, McKinley, Theodore Roosevelt, Coolidge, and Franklin D. Roosevelt — and such other notables as Nathaniel Hawthorne, William Cullen Bryant, and Henry Wadsworth Longfellow.

The elegant dining room and the more intimate Widow Bingham Tavern, with its dark paneling, offer a classic menu of Continental and American specialties. As many as twenty entrées are offered daily, ranging from roast prime ribs of beef to Shrimp Scampi alla Livornese.

In warm weather the flower-laden courtyard with its Back-of-the-Bank Bar is a delightful place for meals and drinks.

In summer the area around Stockbridge throbs with activity as the Berkshire Music Festival opens its season, Broadway comes to the Berkshire Theater Festival, and the Jacob's Pillow Dance Festival is in town. The inn's heated pool is popular, and golf and tennis are near at hand.

The beautiful fall foliage attracts thousands of visitors, as does the Harvest Festival held in early October. A popular activity is just to wander along Main Street looking at the many historic buildings and interesting shops with such inviting names as the Pink Kitty, Woffin's Corner, the Hodge Podge, and Collectible Media. Among the many other places of interest are the Norman Rockwell Museum, the Children's Chimes, and Indian Monument.

The snow-covered hills of the Berkshires make skiing and skating the major sports in winter.

The quiet unfolding of a Berkshire spring is not to be missed. This is a time for woodland walks on clearly marked trails or perhaps a side trip to Pleasant Valley Bird Sanctuary in neighboring Lenox.

INNKEEPER:	Betsy Holtzinger
SEASON:	Year round
MEALS:	Breakfast, lunch, and dinner
TELEPHONE:	413-298-5545
ACCOMMODATIONS:	Can accommodate 175 guests; many rooms with private baths
ADDRESS:	Stockbridge, Massachusetts 01262
DIRECTIONS:	*From New York:* Taconic State Parkway to Route 23, Hillsdale exit. Follow Route 23 to Great Barrington, then Route 7 North to Stockbridge. The inn is at the corner of Route 7 and Main Street.
	From Boston: I-90 (Massachusetts Turnpike) to Route 7. Proceed as above.

SUDBURY
Longfellow's Wayside Inn

"Food, drink, lodging for man and beast" announces a sign in front of historic Longfellow's Wayside Inn in South Sudbury, Massachusetts. The oldest operating inn in the country, it was built on the original Boston Post Road in pre-stagecoach days by the Howes of Sudbury, and has offered hospitality to eight generations of wayfarers. First licensed at the end of the seventeenth century, it was originally called Howes Tavern, then the Red Horse, and in 1863 changed its name to Wayside Inn after the publication of Longfellow's *Tales of a Wayside Inn.*

The village on the grounds consists of several buildings: the old inn itself, of Colonial architecture; the Redstone School (also known as the Little Red School House of *Mary and Her Little Lamb* fame), which was moved in 1926 by Henry Ford from its former location in Sterling, Massachusetts, where it had stood since 1798; Wayside Grist Mill, added in 1929 by Mr. Ford, which operates today in eighteenth-century style, grinding flour and meal for the inn's use; and Wayside's Martha-Mary Chapel, built in 1939 by Mr. Ford to honor his mother and mother-in-law.

The inn was restored by a grant from the Ford Foundation in 1958 to preserve it as a historical and literary landmark.

A number of exhibition rooms at the inn — preserved in their original state — include the oldest, the Old Barroom; the Longfellow bedroom; and the Drovers' and Drivers' Room commemorating the days when cattle raised in Massachusetts were driven over the road to the Boston seaport.

Traditional hearty American fare and drinks are served daily in the historic dining room. Guests with a spirit of adventure may wish to partake of a cocktail called The Coow Woow — America's first mixed drink, made with rum — or, perhaps, a Stonewall — a Revolutionary War favorite, made with gin. For large parties, Meeting House Punch may be ordered in advance; its original formula called for 4 barrels of beer, 24 gallons of West Indian rum, 35 gallons of New England rum, 25 pounds of brown sugar, 25 pounds of loaf sugar, and 465 lemons.

Longfellow's words aptly sum up the spirit and atmosphere of Wayside Inn to this day:

> *As ancient is this hostelry*
> *As any in the land may be,*
> *Built in the old Colonial Day,*
> *When men lived in a grander way,*
> *With ampler hospitality.*

INNKEEPER:	Francis Koppeis
SEASON:	Year round, except Christmas Day
MEALS:	Breakfast, lunch, and dinner
TELEPHONE:	617-443-8846
ACCOMMODATIONS:	10 rooms, each with private bath
ADDRESS:	Sudbury, Massachusetts 01776
DIRECTIONS:	*From New York:* I-90 (Massachusetts Turnpike) to I-495 North to Route 20. East on Route 20, 7 miles to the inn.
	From Boston: I-90 to Route 128. North on Route 128 to Exit 49, Route 20. West on Route 20 (follow Weston-Marlboro signs in rotary), 11 miles to the inn.

WARE
Wildwood Inn
The
Wildwood

In the quiet town of Ware, Massachusetts, just where the sidewalk ends, stands the impressive 101-year-old Victorian mansion called the Wildwood Inn, one of a growing breed of bed-and-breakfast places.

Built by a contractor in a race with his brother, who built the inn's "twin" across the way, the inn still retains many of its fine features: the beautiful beveled glass in the front door, the signed tile Victorian fireplace, the splendid carriage house out back. The house is informally known as the Lincoln House for the family that occupied it for many years in the early part of this century. (It was the Lincoln brothers who entered the Quabbin Reservoir area late one night right before it was flooded and brought back the magnificent stand of firs that can be seen from the breakfast room.) Lovely watercolors of New England scenes by Elizabeth Howe Lincoln presently decorate the walls of the inn.

While the building is Victorian and is graced by the bay windows and high ceilings of that period, it is furnished with American-primitive antiques and heirloom quilts. Many of these pieces came from the Clinton, Connecticut, homestead that has been in the Lobenstine-Elliot family ever since it was built by John Elliot in 1763.

The Lobenstines acquired the Lincoln House in 1979 and opened it to the public as the Wildwood Inn that fall. Since then it has served as a home away from home for travelers from all over the country and from many foreign lands as well.

Margaret Lobenstine writes: "If you've ever wanted to live in a big old New England house with a wide wraparound porch, you'll know why this hundred-year-old Victorian home with its two acres of lovely grounds nestled against a deep woods and a river [is] so appealing."

As the New England seasons change, so do the activities enjoyed by visitors. In the spring, there is the incredibly beautiful blossoming of old apple trees and dogwoods. Tennis is just a short walk away, or you may opt for canoeing on the river or a visit to Old Sturbridge Village, while the lambs are young and the crowds small.

Summer brings antique shows, auctions, country fairs, and summer theater. Glorious Quabbin with its famous fishing and boating is only minutes away.

The explosion of color that is New England foliage takes center stage in the fall. Old Deerfield and other colonial villages are uncrowded at that time of year.

Winter is the time for celebrating an old-fashioned Christmas, for skating on the river, and sledding on the grounds.

Cross-country skiing can be enjoyed throughout the area, and Mt. Tom is nearby for downhill skiing.

While the inn serves a hearty breakfast only, many restaurants in the area offer a variety of dining pleasures.

INNKEEPERS:	Margaret and Geoff Lobenstine
SEASON:	Year round
MEALS:	Full breakfast only
TELEPHONE:	413-967-7798
ACCOMMODATIONS:	5 rooms, most share bath
ADDRESS:	121 Church Street Ware, Massachusetts 01082
DIRECTIONS:	I-90 (Massachusetts Turnpike) to Exit 8 (between I-91 and I-86). North on Route 32 toward Ware. The inn is located at intersection of Route 32 and Route 9.

New Hampshire

BRADFORD
Bradford Inn

The town of Bradford celebrated its two-hundredth anniversary in 1976. Situated at the end of the railroad line, it served as a summer resort community during the nineteenth century, and many of its stately homes today stand as reminders of that bygone era. Like so many New England inns, the Bradford Inn, which is located within the Dartmouth–Lake Sunapee region of New Hampshire, combines modern comfort with the elegance of the past.

While the present structure has stood watch over the surrounding lakes and valleys since 1890, there has been a lodging facility on the grounds for approximately two centuries.

Accommodations are scrupulously clean, comfortable, and replete with old-world charm. The wide old staircase recalls the building's beginnings in the era of hoopskirts.

All of the food is prepared and cooked on the premises under the watchful eye of Tom Best, the master chef and co-owner. A full menu of traditional New England favorites is available for dinner and breakfast, and lunch may be had by prearrangement. All of the preserves and relishes, plus breads, buns, cakes, pies, and soups, are fresh and homemade.

Woody Best, the co-innkeeper, runs the front office and oversees many other activities.

The guest book of this inn reads like an international gazetteer, with visitors coming from practically every state in the union, as well as countries in Europe and South America, Australia, Japan, and the Islands. We are told that about 75 percent of the guests return again and again.

The Bradford Inn is open throughout the year. Holidays are always very special at the inn. The interior and grounds are festively decorated in the Christmas season, and a traditional turkey-and-all-the-trimmings buffet is offered. Other holidays see the dining room and lounge graced with rabbits, hearts, shamrocks, pumpkins, or witches.

Nearby facilities for seasonal sports abound. Three major ski areas are located within an eight-mile radius of the inn: Pat's Peak, King Ridge, and Mt. Sunapee. Rent a skimobile or iceboat at the harbor in Sunapee or Newbury. Enjoy ice-skating, ice-fishing, cross-country skiing, and sleigh riding.

Summertime activities are plentiful: swimming, canoeing, sailing, waterskiing at three nearby lakes (Todd, Massasecum, and Sunapee), boat rentals at Sunapee. Trails for bicyclists and hikers, hayrides, professional summer theater, concerts, country fairs, tennis courts, golf courses, picnic areas, soaring and gliding clubs, places to fish and hunt — are all within a comfortable distance of the inn. Seekers of antiques and yard sales need look no farther than the Bradford area.

Champ's auction barn is just around a country corner from the front door.

Also, a short distance away is Dartmouth College, established in 1769, where visitors may explore the historic grounds and open buildings.

INNKEEPERS:	Tom and Woody Best
SEASON:	Year round
MEALS:	Breakfast and dinner
TELEPHONE:	603-938-5309
ACCOMMODATIONS:	12 rooms and 3 suites, some with private bath
ADDRESS:	Main Street Bradford, New Hampshire 03221
DIRECTIONS:	*From New York:* I-91 North to Brattleboro, Vermont, to Route 9 to Keene, New Hampshire. Then Route 114 to Route 103, which becomes Main Street in Bradford. *From Boston:* I-93 to I-89, to Route 103 (Main Street in Bradford).

BRIDGEWATER
The Pasquaney Inn

The Pasquaney Inn, on lovely Newfound Lake near Lake Winnipesaukee in central New Hampshire, is a family vacation resort. The historic country inn is now in its second century of offering comfortable rooms, excellent meals, and beautiful sandy beaches to New England vacationers.

The "Main House," built in the late 1800s, is furnished in a charming blend of periods, from a Hepplewhite sideboard in the lobby to an overstuffed leather sofa in the living room. There is also the "Summer House," or "Annex," which stands close to the Main House.

Dinner is a casual, informal affair served family style. There are two or three main choices daily, with selections changed frequently. Typical dishes are baked trout with seafood stuffing and baked chicken with shallots and artichoke hearts. All soups are homemade, and breads and pastries come from the inn's own bakery. There are special menus for children and for guests on restricted diets.

The inn is truly a resort for all seasons. In the spring, when the forsythia begins to open and the trees to bud, lake and stream fishing are favorite pastimes. The maple trees have been tapped and this year's syrup is on the table.

Summer is the king of the seasons in the Newfound Lake area. Bathing is superb from the inn's private sandy beach, and Pasquaney has skiffs for guests who wish to take a row around the cove. Sailboats may be rented at nearby marinas. Golf is available on eight courses within a half hour's drive. Weekly dances are held at the local church hall.

On the Pasquaney grounds there are also shuffleboard, croquet, lawn bowling, and horseshoe pitching. The Recreation Barn offers a square-dance floor and other forms of indoor entertainment. Summer theaters, the New Hampshire Music Festival, auctions, and antique shops are all close by.

In the fall there is no lovelier place than New England, as the maples begin to change from summer green to gleaming reds and golds. Drive along the Kancamagus Highway and through the mountain notches. Pasquaney will prepare a box lunch for a picnic along the way.

In winter, with the White Mountains as a backdrop, downhill skiing takes over. Also within range are cross-country skiing, skating, and alpine slides.

Several miles south on I-93 in the Laconia area, visitors will find many additional summer and winter recreational activities, such as lake cruises from Weirs Beach on Lake Winnipesaukee, a children's amusement park and Aquaboggan, and a winery open to the public. The Laconia Winter Carnival with competitive events is held toward the end of February.

INNKEEPERS:	Mary Jo and Jim Shipe, along with their four teenage children, John, Jennifer, Andy, and Caroline
SEASON:	From mid May through late October, and during the winter as ski conditions permit
MEALS:	Breakfast and dinner family style; box lunches available; dinner reservations requested by 3:00 P.M.

TELEPHONE:	603-744-2712
ACCOMMODATIONS:	28 rooms, 10 with private bath
ADDRESS:	Bridgewater, New Hampshire 03222
DIRECTIONS:	I-93 to Exit 23 (Bristol). From Bristol follow Route 3A North 5½ miles to Newfound Lake and the inn.

EATON CENTER
Palmer House Inn
Palmer House

Back in 1884, Nathaniel G. Palmer built a home with spacious rooms and airy balconies at Crystal Lake in Eaton, New Hampshire. A practical Yankee entrepreneur, Nathaniel manufactured ladies' dresses by buying wholesale material, cutting it to fashion patterns, and then distributing the pieces to the ladies of Eaton to sew at home.

His house design was an equally enterprising use of its steep hillside site; he built a Victorian split-level, unique for the times. Those were the days when trains brought trunk-laden city-dwellers to the country for the summer. Soon Nathaniel was in the summer lodging business as well, and the place became known as the Palmer House Inn.

During the 1950s and '60s the building was used as a small private school: Palmer House School for Children. The attic loft became the dormitory, the bedrooms were classrooms, and the kitchen was converted to a science lab. When the Palmer House changed hands again in 1975, the kitchen consisted of one long wooden bench with a few burner jets and a single-spigot lab sink.

The new owners restored the old house to its original glory, and it became a perfect setting for their personal collection of antique Victorian furniture.

While Palmer House does not provide a printed menu, the daily choice may be beef Stroganoff, roast turkey with oyster-pecan stuffing, smoked fresh bluefish, or poulet à la Crème d'Estragon. There are no steam tables, microwave ovens, or friolaters. Guests frequently wander through the kitchen to see what's cooking, and how.

All ingredients are fresh, with vegetables coming from the garden in season. All baking and desserts are done in-house.

Visitors will find that each season brings its special pleasures in recreational activities. In spring, enjoy the greening of New Hampshire and the beauty of mountain streams along the scenic Kancamagus Highway seven miles away. Angle for brookies or lake trout and bass, or, if you're a white-water enthusiast, take on the challenges of the Swift and Saco rivers.

In the summer, swim in the cool, clear waters of Crystal Lake or bask in the sun on the sloping sandy beach. The Palmer House provides a sailboat for guests' use, and tennis on clay courts and trail riding are available nearby. The inn is close to the hundreds of National Forest hiking trails that crisscross the mountains. Summer theater, alpine slides, gondola lifts, and a variety of good entertainment in Conway and North Conway offer a change of pace as do special events such as bicycle races, tennis tournaments, antique auctions, and country fairs.

When autumn comes, the foliage is spectacular in Eaton Center, as are the vistas of the Presidential Range just minutes away. As the leaves fade and fall, deer and other game abound.

In winter, Palmer House is convenient and comfortable for cross-country and downhill skiers, both expert and novice. Miles of un-plowed dirt roads and abandoned rights-of-way crisscross the woods and fields of Eaton. Foss Mountain Ski Touring, just across Crystal Lake, maintains groomed trails and offers instruction and rentals. King Pine, an ideal family downhill-ski area, is only three miles away. The Mt. Washington Valley ski areas (Wildcat, Attitash, Black Mountain, and Cranmore), Mt. Whittier, Sunday River and Pleasant Mountain in Maine are all within easy driving range. Ice-skating on Crystal Lake is also a popular winter sport.

INNKEEPERS:	Frank and Mary Gospodarek
SEASON:	Year round
MEALS:	Hearty breakfast included in room rates; dinner is country style. Non-guests are requested to make reservations as early as possible. Special requests with advance notice. No liquor license at this writing.
TELEPHONE:	603-447-2120
ACCOMMODATIONS:	4 rooms, share 2 baths, in main house. Family room is a spacious pine-paneled apartment for large families or small groups; sleeps 5 to 8 in 3 double beds and 2

twins. The bunkroom is a dormitory providing bunk beds with hot showers.

ADDRESS:
Box 12
Eaton Center, New Hampshire 03832

DIRECTIONS:
I-95 North to Portsmouth and Spaulding Turnpike, to Route 16 North to Route 25 East to Route 153 North to Eaton Center. The inn is located on Route 153 at the very sharp curve where the road turns at Crystal Lake.

FRANCONIA
Sugar Hill Inn

Sugar Hill Inn

Hospitality begins at the sign of the pineapple at Sugar Hill Inn, located in the heart of the White Mountains.

Built as a farmhouse in 1748 and converted to its present use in 1929, the inn has been run by Lois and Karl Taylor since 1977. Lois has done all of the decorating, in early American style, and her decorative art is featured throughout the rooms, with stenciled walls, colorful theorems on velvet, and beautiful gold leaf trays.

The cozy living room invites conversation, reading, or just relaxing, and the guest rooms — individually and tastefully decorated — provide the same sense of warmth and comfort.

The dining room is papered in a delicate Laura Ashley print, complemented by stenciled Hitchcock chairs and country tin accent pieces. The inn has an outstanding reputation for fine country cooking, with the dinner menu usually offering a choice of two entrées, along with appetizer, soup, salad, home-baked rolls and breads and desserts. Among the favorites are such classic dishes as roast fresh turkey with herb dressing and baked ham with raisin sauce.

The Pewter Pub provides a convivial atmosphere where guests can get acquainted and even enjoy an old-fashioned player piano.

The pace at Sugar Hill is relaxed and unhurried, with as much or as little activity as one prefers. Horseback riding, canoeing, tennis, and golf are all available nearby, and hiking is one of the most popular sports in the area, with special, quiet places just waiting to be discovered. For winter sports enthusiasts, of course, both cross-country and downhill skiing facilities are near at hand.

Scores of antique shops as well as country flea markets are scattered throughout this corner of New Hampshire, and there is even a small gift shop right in the inn, where Lois sells her theorem paintings and other handmade folk-art items.

INNKEEPERS:	Lois and Karl Taylor
SEASON:	December 26 to late March or early April; mid May to late October
MEALS:	Breakfast and dinner
TELEPHONE:	603-823-5621
ACCOMMODATIONS:	9 rooms in inn, 3 with private bath; 6 motel units, all with private bath (spring to fall only)
ADDRESS:	Route 117 Franconia, New Hampshire 03580
DIRECTIONS:	*From New York:* I-91 to Exit 17. East on Route 302, then right on Route 117 (2 miles east of Lisbon). The inn is on the left ½ mile before bottom of hill. *From Boston:* I-93 to Exit 38. Right on Route 18 through Franconia, then left on Route 117. The inn is ½ mile up hill on the right.

GLEN
The Bernerhof

New England is the home of a number of unusual inns and restaurants whose roots extend across the Atlantic to western Europe. One such inn is the Bernerhof — a touch of old Switzerland in Glen, New Hampshire.

"Pleasant Valley Hall" was its first name, back in the early 1890s, and in almost a century the inn has changed owners and names several times. In 1956, Claire and Charlie Zumstein became the new restaurateurs/innkeepers (they were part of a musical troupe from Switzerland who made their mark at Harvey Gibson's Eastern Slope Inn), and it was then that the most dramatic changes began to occur, with the advent of fine Swiss cuisine and meticulous attention to guests' comfort. The Bernerhof, meaning the House of Bern, after the Swiss canton, was to be the inn's last change of name.

Hermann Pfeuti, Claire's nephew, took over the inn in 1971 and operated it until 1977, when its new and current owners, Ted and Sharon Wroblewski, began to carry on the fine tradition. Today the Bernerhof Inn and Restaurant continues to feature "Fine European Cuisine in the Old-World Tradition."

On entering the inn, which is cheerfully lighted and decorated with charming Swiss touches, one seems instantly transported to a chalet. Under the watchful eyes of the innkeepers, the Bernerhof presents an outstanding menu featuring authentic Swiss and Continental favorites. For starters you may consider Gougère au Frommage, Tarte aux Champignon, Escargots Bourguignonne, or a choice of three or four homemade soups. For the main course you may choose from Schnitzel Cordon Bleu, Beef Wellington, Frog Legs Provençales, and as many as a dozen other entrées. As a finishing touch, delight your palate with Cherries Jubilee or Chocolate Fondue in the elegant Zumstein Room, with a choice of Jamaican, Dutch, or Irish coffee.

The inn is located near North Conway and Attitash and Wildcat mountains, where all the winter sports reign supreme. In the summer, scenic rides and walks, lake and river swimming, golf, tennis, and antique hunting take over.

As the Swiss say, "May each of your visits be full of pleasant and satisfying experiences."

INNKEEPERS:	Ted and Sharon Wroblewski
SEASON:	Christmas to mid April; Memorial Day through Columbus Day
MEALS:	Breakfast, lunch, and dinner (reservations, please)
TELEPHONE:	603-383-4414
ACCOMMODATIONS:	8 rooms with private bath; others share bath
ADDRESS:	Route 302 Glen, New Hampshire 03838
DIRECTIONS:	I-95 to Portsmouth. Spaulding Turnpike to Route 16, then North on Route 16 to Glen. Bear left at fork onto Route 302.

INTERVALE
Holiday Inn

In Intervale, New Hampshire, stands Holiday Inn (not connected with the chain bearing the same name). The building was erected in the early nineteenth century, and it first housed a general store. In the latter part of the century it was joined with the house next door, and upper floors were added to the combined structure. Operation as an inn began about 1890 and has continued since that time. After undergoing several changes of name, it has been known as Holiday Inn since the late 1940s.

The inn is a member of Authentic Country Inns of New Hampshire, Inc., whose endorsement assures the traveler of high standards in accommodations, food, service, and hospitality.

Dinner is served family style. The inn offers one or two entrées each night, such as roast beef, ham, chicken, fillet of sole, beef Stroganoff, pork chops, seafood Stroganoff, turkey, and other favorites — all full-course meals. While Holiday Inn does not have a liquor license, guests may bring wine to the table.

For summer and fall recreation, there is a heated pool and, of course, swimming in the sparkling rivers and lakes of the area. Indoor and outdoor tennis courts are available nearby, as well as three public golf courses. There are on-property hiking trails in addition to the miles of mountain trails in the region of Intervale. Canoes, boats, and kayaks may be rented.

Guests who prefer less strenuous activities enjoy visiting the many art galleries and craft shops near the inn as well as local summer theater and concerts. And, in every season, the surrounding area offers scenic drives to delight the eye — with the lush greenery of spring and summer, the brilliant foliage of autumn, the snow-covered mountains in winter.

When winter comes, skiing begins at the doorstep. In cooperation with the N.E.I. Cross-Country Learning Center, the inn now offers complete ski-touring facilities. The trail system is mapped and groomed to accommodate skiers at every level of experience, from beginner to expert. In addition, there are some lighted trails in the woodlands for night skiing — a first in the area.

Other attractions include the Cog Railway, Conway Scenic Railroad and Museum, Storyland, Attitash Alpine Slide, and downhill skiing at nearby White Mountain ski areas.

INNKEEPERS:	Bob and Lois Gregory
SEASON:	Late May to mid October; December 26 to late March
MEALS:	Breakfast and dinner by reservation only
TELEPHONE:	603-356-9772
ACCOMMODATIONS:	10 units, each with private bath
ADDRESS:	Intervale, New Hampshire 03845
DIRECTIONS:	I-95 North to Portsmouth. Spaulding Turnpike to Route 16 North to North Conway. Three miles from the center of town, turn right on Route 16A. The inn is 1½ miles on the right.

INTERVALE
New England Inn

There is a new breed of innkeeper in New England: successful professional and business people looking for a different life-style. Such a couple is Joe and Linda Johnston, who, four years ago, abandoned busy careers in selling and real estate to buy the New England Inn and Anna Martin's Restaurant, which had been landmarks for travelers for well over a century.

The eastern slope of the White Mountains was still a vast, untamed wilderness when the original farmhouse was built on the site by Samuel Bloodgood in 1809, on the banks of the east branch of the Saco River. For decades the Bloodgood farm was famous for its hospitality, and in the late 1830s it became an inn, with a roadside sign inviting the traveling public to its hearth and table as they ventured north to the Great Notches of the White Mountains.

The earliest man-made attraction was the Mt. Washington Cog Railway, erected in 1866 as the first railroad in the world to reach the summit of a mountain.

During the next sixty years inns multiplied rapidly, and large and splendid summer hotels were built as railroad developers made remote sections accessible for the first time. From 1907 to 1910, no fewer than twenty-eight trains daily brought vacationers from Boston to North Conway throughout the season.

The '20s brought increased prosperity and leisure time, and "country" inns such as the New England Inn were quick to adapt to changing conditions without losing their reputation for personal attention — usually provided by a husband and wife who combined the functions of managers and friendly hosts.

Skiing began its rapid rise as a popular sport in the 1930s, and the small inns responded by remaining open longer. Black Mountain and Cranmore installed tow facilities in the late 1930s, which changed skiing from a walk-up to a ride-up sport. The "ski trains" of the 1930s and 1940s brought thousands to North Conway in winter to learn the newly popular sport.

Once again the inns kept pace with the times, retaining their traditional charm and hospitality while constantly improving their facilities and accommodations. At the New England Inn, small duplex Colonial cottages were built on the grounds only a few steps from the main building. Here guests could enjoy privacy yet retain the opportunity to join the social activities of the inn if they wished.

Cordiality is the feeling you encounter from the moment you step through the front door at the New England Inn, its heritage polished bright by the passing years. Anna Martin's Restaurant, which first opened its doors in 1809, continues to offer hearty traditional fare. Its full menu ranges from chicken apricot to Down East lobster pie and fisherman's bounty. Hot popovers and a selection of homemade breads and rolls are baked daily. The service is warm and pleasant.

From earliest times the Intervale Tavern at the inn was really a club for locals and travelers alike. It retains this conviviality today, offering a blazing fire in winter, fully stocked bar, dancing, and live entertainment. After a brisk day in the North Country, the tavern is a popular place for guests to take their cocktails, make lasting friendships, and meet neighborhood patrons. The tavern's cheerful atmosphere is enhanced with antique tools, old skis, and early New England "gimcracks" that make interesting conversation pieces.

Among the recreational facilities available at the inn are three tennis courts, shuffleboard and volleyball courts, swimming and wading pool, a cross-country learning center, and touring and hiking trails.

INNKEEPERS:	Joe and Linda Johnston
SEASON:	Year round except April and November
MEALS:	Full breakfast and dinner included in room rates
TELEPHONE:	603-356-5541
ACCOMMODATIONS:	45 rooms and suites, all but 3 with private bath
ADDRESS:	Route 16 Resort Loop Intervale, New Hampshire 03845
DIRECTIONS:	I-91 or I-93 North to Route 302 East to Route 16 South to North Conway. The inn is 3¼ miles from Intervale village on Route 16A, which is a 2-mile loop off Route 16.

JACKSON
Whitneys' Village Inn

Jackson, New Hampshire, year round population 300, has long been well known as the skiingest town in the East. Beautifully situated at the foot of Mt. Washington and surrounded by the White Mountain National Forest, it is a typical unspoiled New England village.

The property on which Whitneys' stands was part of a King's Grant in 1771 to David Gilman and was used for farming. The house itself dates from the early 1800s and was originally a characteristic 1½-story Cape with attached shed and barn. It is believed that sometime around 1910 the Cape was raised and a first story built beneath it.

Improvement and expansion of the inn's facilities since the Second World War have included the installation of private baths, addition of more sleeping rooms and the present dining room, refurbishing of the cottages, the construction of all-season tennis courts, and the transformation of the barn into the Shovel Handle Pub, adjacent to the main building, which offers panoramic views of Black Mountain from its multilevel interior. Before- or after-dinner beverages are served in front of the two fireplaces, and there is frequent live entertainment, as well as first-run motion pictures.

The Garden Spot, the inn's restaurant, was named in 1981 as "one of the outstanding restaurants of the world" by *Travel/Holiday* magazine — one of only three restaurants in New Hampshire to have been so honored.

In addition to traditional New England fare, the restaurant offers such gourmet dishes as quiche of the day, French onion soup, and Escargot Bourguignonne to begin the meal, followed by Sautéed Provini, calves liver, Poultry Pleasure, Sole Meunière, Chef's Whim of the day, and other choices. Weekly favorites include Sunday Evening New England Festival and Wednesday Evening Barbecue Bash. Guests will find this a country dining experience with a touch of class.

The Jackson and Glen areas, surrounded by eighty-six mountains, provide every year-round activity one may seek. There are scenic golf courses, tennis, swimming, hiking, biking, and fishing — and breathtaking views for the sightseer or photographer, especially with the changing colors of early autumn. From Mt. Washington, the highest peak in the Northeast, on a clear day one can see four states and even a Canadian province. The area abounds in scenic drives.

In winter the region, which receives some of the heaviest snowfall in the East, becomes an attraction for all snow and ice sports.

INNKEEPERS:	Darrell Trapp and Bob DePaolo
SEASON:	Year round
MEALS:	Breakfast, lunch, and dinner
TELEPHONE:	603-383-6886
	For reservations from Massachusetts: 800-272-2550
	from other states: 800-225-2550
ACCOMMODATIONS:	In main inn 36 rooms, 30 with private bath; the Chalet, Cottages, and Brookside, all with private baths
ADDRESS:	Route 16B
	Jackson, New Hampshire 03846
DIRECTIONS:	I-95 to Portsmouth. Spaulding Turnpike to Route 16 North to Jackson. The inn is 1½ miles north of the village on Route 16B.

LYME
The Lyme Inn

Lyme is a picturesque New England town located on the Connecticut River. Chartered in 1761 and named after Lyme Regis, England, it was during the mid 1800s the most productive sheep-raising center in New England. It is now a peaceful town with most of its residents engaged in activities relating to the operation of Dartmouth College and the Mary Hitchcock Regional Hospital in nearby Hanover.

The Lyme Inn, built in 1809, offers quiet and comfortable accommodations, with all bedrooms distinctively furnished in antiques. Fires blaze throughout the winter months in the tavern and two sitting rooms. The unhurried pace of the past is expressed in poster beds, hooked rugs, hand-stitched quilts, wide pine floorboards, and a picket to close up the tavern. Stenciled wallpaper, wing chairs, wicker furniture on the huge screened porch, Currier & Ives samplers, and fireplaces in many of the guest rooms further distinguish the Lyme Inn as a place for an extended visit, not just an overnight stop.

The dining room offers a continually changing menu featuring unusual recipes from many countries, as well as traditional New England fare. Although fresh seafood is the specialty, veal, lamb, beef, and pork are all prepared to perfection and served in an informal country setting.

The tavern, small and intimate, features a number of hot spirits in the winter and very tall, very cool spirits in the summer. It is a quiet place — the entertainment is limited to the gregariousness of the guests.

The Lyme area offers outstanding recreational facilities during all four seasons. Some fifty days a year, Dartmouth College offers Ivy League competition: in football, basketball, hockey, track, and gymnastics. In addition to these spectator sports, facilities are available to the public for bowling, squash, tennis, and handball. There is a local golf course, and canoeing on the Connecticut River is a relaxing way to spend a summer afternoon. Of course, one of the most popular pastimes is that great New England solitary sport, "watching": the tourists, the birds, the passing cars, each other, the trees swaying in the breeze, the grass growing.

Night ice-skating on a lighted pond, alpine skiing at the Dartmouth

Skiway (three miles from the inn) and at five other ski areas within an hour's drive from Lyme, cross-country skiing on many informal trails throughout the area, snowshoeing in virgin timber — these are the pleasures of a winter in Lyme.

A historical gem is St. Gaudens' Gardens in nearby Plainfield, a national museum dedicated to the home and works of Gaudens. It is a perfect place to spend a summer Sunday afternoon with a picnic, listening to the weekly concert presented by local artists.

Colorful country stores filled with home-smoked meats and other delicacies, and antique shops piled high with treasures abound throughout the small towns bordering the Connecticut River and in the adjacent Vermont and New Hampshire hills.

The beauty of the countryside is striking in the winter, peaceful in the summer, and overwhelming in the fall, when the color of the foliage and the crisp, clean air hold special appeal for visitors escaping from the city. Many of northern New England's attractions may be visited easily from the inn's central location.

INNKEEPERS:	Fred and Judy Siemons
SEASON:	Open year round except for 3 weeks following Thanksgiving and 2 weeks in the spring
MEALS:	Breakfast, dinner, light supper; early reservations suggested for dinner
TELEPHONE:	603-695-2222
ACCOMMODATIONS:	18 rooms, many with private bath
ADDRESS:	On the Common Lyme, New Hampshire 03768
DIRECTIONS:	I-91 to Exit 14 toward Lyme. The inn is on the Common on Route 10.

NORTH SUTTON
Follansbee Inn

A restaurant review of the Follansbee Inn appearing in the *New Hampshire Times* headlined the article "Like Visiting Friends for Dinner."

The innkeepers, Larry and Joan Wadman, obviously like people and do everything possible to accommodate and please their guests, who soon become their friends.

The Follansbee Inn is a stately white structure with fresh green trim. Wrapped around the building is a veranda decorated with hanging plants, which sway gently in the breeze.

The sitting room is tastefully furnished with the Wadmans' own living room furniture. Antique pewterware and candles decorate the tables and walls of the dining room, and charming old clocks — each showing a different time — are everywhere.

The inn, on the shores of tranquil Kezar Lake, was originally built in 1835 and enlarged in 1928. The Wadmans became innkeepers there in 1978.

The master chef prepares everything from scratch. Be it hot breads, soups, salad dressings, desserts, an appetizing variety of entrées, you may be certain that all of the ingredients are fresh and of the highest quality obtainable.

Dinner, served by reservation only, may feature such delicacies as baked stuffed mushrooms with crabmeat and shrimp, French leek soup au gratin, sautéed rainbow trout almandine, escargots à la Bourguignonne, or drunken bird with cheddar cheese and a sauce of honey, sherry, and walnuts.

The area provides activities for all seasons, including hiking trails, golf courses, horseback riding, tennis, boating; the wintertime joys of cross-country and alpine skiing, snowmobiling, ice fishing; and cultural offerings such as theater, art galleries, exhibits, film festivals, concerts, and summer stock — all nearby.

For the more sedentary, there are the scenic New Hampshire countryside, state parks, historic villages, covered bridges, quiet lakes, or the pleasure of just settin' and bird watching.

INNKEEPERS:	Larry and Joan Wadman
SEASON:	Year round except part of April and November
MEALS:	Breakfast and dinner
TELEPHONE:	603-927-4221
ACCOMMODATIONS:	23 rooms, about half with private baths (others to share)
ADDRESS:	North Sutton, New Hampshire 03260
DIRECTIONS:	*From New York:* I-91 North to Ascutney, Vermont. Then Route 103 East to Route 11 East to Route 114 South. Follow Route 114 to North Sutton. *From Boston:* I-89 to Exit 12 (Route 11). Proceed as above.

NORTHWOOD
Lake Shore Farm

Receive Ye Welcome

Let the guest sojourning here know that in this home our life is simple. What we cannot afford, we do not offer, but what good cheer we can give . . . we give gladly.

We make no strife for appearance sake. Know also, friend, that we live a life of labour. Therefor, if at times we separate ourselves from you, do ye occupy thyself according to thine heart's desire.

We will not defer to thee in opinion or ask thee to defer to us. What thou thinkest, ye shall say, if ye wish, without giving offense. What we think we also say, believing that truth has many aspects . . . and that love is large enough to encompass them all.

So, while ye tarry here with us we would have thee enjoy the blessings of a home, health, love and freedom, and we pray that thou mayst find the final blessing of life. . . .

These words of greeting, taken from an anonymous writing from Colonial days, welcome guests to Eloise and Ellis Ring's Lake Shore Farm.

The inn's history goes back to 1848, when Reuben Watson started to build a farmhouse for his family; summer guests were first welcomed in 1926. The original structure still stands, on 150 peaceful acres of land, and over the years tasteful additions have accommodated the ever-growing number of guests.

All of the guest rooms, the original ones and the newer ones, which blend gracefully with the old, are light, airy, and cheerful. All afford a view of the lake, and some have their own screened-in balconies.

The menu at Lake Shore Farm includes many delicious, time-tested New England recipes as well as favorite dishes from other regions of the country. The informal family-style atmosphere makes every meal an eagerly anticipated and enjoyable experience. There are also weekly cookouts, and box lunches are provided for day trips or for the drive home.

The once actively farmed fields around the inn are now all lawns, and slope down to a private beach of natural fine sand and a lake that is spring-fed and crystal clear. The beach is a safe haven for children, but the lake becomes deep enough to challenge those who enjoy snorkeling.

If you like fishing, boats are available at no charge, and there are also canoes for quietly exploring the shoreline, islands, coves, and rock formations. The lake is stocked with bass and pickerel, and the chef is always happy to cook your catch.

For those who prefer more strenuous activity, the inn provides cushioned acrylic-finished tennis courts, designed to professional standards. Instruction is available for beginners as well as for more advanced players wishing to improve their techniques.

The area provides many scenic drives throughout the year, and winter brings a complete range of snow and ice sports.

INNKEEPERS:	Ellis and Eloise Ring
SEASON:	Year round
MEALS:	Breakfast, lunch, and dinner — family style
TELEPHONE:	603-942-5921/5521
ACCOMMODATIONS:	28 rooms, some with private bath
ADDRESS:	Jenness Pond Road Northwood, New Hampshire 03261
DIRECTIONS:	I-93 North to Concord. Right at Exit 15, left at Route 4, turning east after about 20 minutes, to 107 North. Go 1 mile; bear right onto Jenness Pond Road for about 1½ miles to the inn.

SNOWVILLE
Snowvillage Inn
𝕾𝖓𝖔𝖜𝖇𝖎𝖑𝖑

Innkeeping at the Snowvillage Inn is truly a family affair. Patrick and Ginger Blymyer run the inn with the help of their two daughters, Tanya and Xochi. The family sheepdog, Louise, and her shaggy side-kick, Flump, are self-appointed greeters as they welcome guests at the front door, and Gracie, the handsome Hampshire pig, is the overseer of outdoor activities.

Patrick does his magic in the kitchen — where there is one entrée daily — producing such delights as veal piccata, roast lamb, coq au vin, beef Stroganoff, or whatever strikes his fancy that evening. Tanya is the baker and also creates superb desserts of fantastic design: grasshopper pies, Brandy Alexanders, or apricot and chocolate mousses.

Ginger, when not tending bar, and the teenaged Xochi seem to be everywhere doing whatever needs to be done.

(Life was not always so bucolic for the Blymyers, who come from long and highly successful careers in Hollywood — Ginger as hairdresser to such stars as Natalie Wood, Jane Fonda, Tuesday Weld, Hal Holbrook, James Mason, and Laurence Olivier, and Pat as chief lighting engineer for *Day of the Dolphin, Close Encounters, Jaws,* and other noteworthy films. From time to time Hollywood still beckons one or the other Blymyer, who flies off for a picture assignment while the other remains to manage the inn.)

Snowvillage Inn clings to the side of a mountain with a vista of Crystal Lake, mountains, and forests — the best of the scenic wonder that is New Hampshire. The cheery, comfortably furnished sleeping rooms and the big, inviting living room, with oversize fireplace, encourage a sense of relaxation and ease; the wide porches are perfect for viewing the magnificent sunsets and the appearance of the first stars.

Spring and summer in the White Mountains are nature's gift — with long, lazy days of clear skies and warm, gentle breezes. Tennis is available on the grounds, as are swimming in nearby Crystal Lake and trout fishing in miles of mountain streams. There are many interesting shops in North Conway only five miles away, and the summer attractions and special events of Mt. Washington Valley are all close to the inn.

Fall is breathtaking in this area, with the trees bursting into glorious color as far as one can see.

New Hampshire is a winter place, too. Clear sunlight reflecting off the crisp, fresh snow invites cross-country skiing or a short trip to any of the five alpine ski areas of Mt. Washington, or skating on Crystal Lake.

INNKEEPERS:	Pat and Ginger Blymyer
SEASON:	Year round
MEALS:	Breakfast and dinner
TELEPHONE:	603-447-2818
ACCOMMODATIONS:	14 rooms, 12 with private bath
ADDRESS:	Snowville, New Hampshire 03849
DIRECTIONS:	I-95 to Portsmouth. Spaulding Turnpike to Route 16 North to Snowville (just south of Conway).

TAMWORTH
Tamworth Inn

Located in the center of the picturesque village of Tamworth — between the Lakes Region and the White Mountains — the Tamworth Inn has been serving the public since 1888. Innkeepers Larry and Kelly Hubbell took it over early in 1981 and have brought an atmosphere of relaxation and warm hospitality, not only to their guests but to the entire community, for which they sponsor such events as Easter egg hunts and Christmas open houses.

The inn's sleeping rooms and public rooms (two dining rooms, a living room, and library) are simply but tastefully decorated. For before- or after-dinner drinks, there is also an inviting pub, which, like the living room, has a working fireplace and interesting antique appointments.

The dinner menu at Tamworth offers a choice of excellently prepared entrées ranging from hearty steaks to Veal Provençal to such delicate seafood dishes as shrimp Rockefeller and trout with walnut stuffing.

Recreational activities begin right on the premises. The inn has a swimming pool available to guests during the summer months, and the backyard offers croquet, softball, badminton, and trout fishing in the stream that borders the property.

Tamworth is near just about every kind of leisure-time activity New England has to offer throughout the year. The village itself is home to a small theater group that performs during the summer months, and the area is filled with fascinating shops for antiquers and browsers, scattered through many charming hamlets and towns.

Chocorua and Ossipee lakes are nearby, and Lake Winnipesaukee to the south offers fine beaches and a variety of water sports, as well as boating facilities of all kinds and delightful sightseeing cruises. The Appalachian Trail is within easy driving distance of the inn, and other hiking and horseback-riding trails crisscross the entire region.

Of special interest to children are Fantasy Farm in Lincoln — with rides as well as animals — and Six Gun City in Jefferson — a replica of a small western town. (Both are open during the summer months only.)

In winter, cross-country skiing is popular, and for downhill skiers the White Mountain National Forest to the north includes Mt. Washington, White Lake, Crawford Notch, and Pinkham Notch, among other ski centers.

During the foliage season, when the maples and birch trees take on their fall colors, the drive along the Kancamagus Highway is one of the most spectacular in all New England, with many inviting spots along the way for picnicking and camping.

INNKEEPERS:	Larry and Kelly Hubbell
SEASON:	Year round, except 4 weeks in the fall and 4 weeks in the spring
MEALS:	Breakfast, lunch in spring and summer, dinner
TELEPHONE:	603-323-7721
ACCOMMODATIONS:	21 rooms, 10 with private bath (11 shared)
ADDRESS:	Tamworth, New Hampshire 03886
DIRECTIONS:	I-93 to Route 104 East (Exit 23), to Route 25 East to Route 113 to Tamworth. The inn is in the center of town.

WHITEFIELD
Playhouse Motor Inn

In the center of Whitefield, a sleepy New Hampshire hamlet, stands a historic old house now known as the Playhouse Motor Inn.

This charming inn offers the finest in comfortable, traditional accommodations and warm European–New England hospitality. Chef-innkeeper Noel Lacan, the recipient of numerous culinary awards, supervises the activities in the kitchen, while his wife, Lucienne, guides the service staff to excellence.

The Weatherhaven Theatre, located just across the square, provides the theme for the menu of the inn's renowned French restaurant. The bill of fare is arranged like a theater program. The Prelude is a selection of cold appetizers such as mousse of duck liver, followed by the Overture, an offering of four or five hot appetizers; and then, the Curtain Raiser — three or four fresh soups. Diners are now ready for the Play. Act I consists of seafood entrées; Act II, fowl; and Critic's Choice, special cuts of beef and chops. The Grand Finale, of course, consists of the tempting homemade desserts, and Curtain Calls are such beverages as Flaming Spanish Coffee or Espresso.

In its peaceful setting, with the White Mountains as backdrop and lush forests, cool lakes, and streams all around, the inn suggests a feeling of tranquillity. For those with energy to expend, there is the new swimming pool on the grounds, and golf and tennis courts a five-minute walk away.

The Mt. Washington area offers a seemingly endless array of attractions for visitors of all ages — state parks for picnicking, hiking, swimming, and bird-watching; superb scenery from the Franconia and Kingsman ranges and the spectacular Flume gorge. On Moore Reservoir there is fishing, boat launching, and waterskiing. To please yet another taste, the League of New Hampshire Craftsmen operates nearby with working demonstrations, and a museum and shop offering samples of the best work of local artists.

| INNKEEPERS: | Lucienne and Noel Lacan |
| SEASON: | Mid May to mid October |

MEALS:	Breakfast, lunch, and dinner
TELEPHONE:	603-837-2527
ACCOMMODATIONS:	12 rooms, 8 with private bath
ADDRESS:	Whitefield, New Hampshire 03598
DIRECTIONS:	*From New York:* I-91 North to Route 302 East to Route 3 North. The inn is 1½ miles north of Whitefield on Route 3.
	From Boston: I-93 North to Route 3 North. Proceed as above.

Vermont

BROWNSVILLE
The Inn at Mt. Ascutney

The Inn at Mt. Ascutney

Occupying a commanding position on a hill overlooking rich mead-owlands to the east and Mt. Ascutney to the immediate south, this intimate country inn is housed in a converted 180-year-old farmhouse.

The original house was expanded in the mid-nineteenth century to include a parlor, sun room, and additional bedrooms; then, about fifteen years ago, the stable was combined with the old carriage house to make a single, L-shaped dining room, cocktail lounge, and open kitchen. When Eric and Margaret Rothchild took over the operation of the inn three years ago, they completely refurbished and improved the main house and outbuildings with loving care.

The inn's comfortable bedrooms and public rooms, which also include a large and bright living room with fireplace and a sunny breakfast room, are handsomely decorated with English and American antiques and enhanced by panoramic views of the mountain, countryside, and Mill Brook valley.

The carriage house with its open kitchen offers guests the opportunity of watching Margaret — a Cordon Bleu chef — prepare meals, which feature wholesome country cooking with a Continental flair. A typical menu may include a choice of soups and other appetizers; entrées ranging from steak and onion pie to roast duck with orange wine sauce to shrimp Florentine; and a fresh selection daily from the dessert trolley. A special treat is Margaret's Chocolate Ascutney dessert. Eric is responsible for the carefully selected and balanced wine list.

Recreation activities range from total rest and relaxation to just about anything you can think of. You can hike or ski Mt. Ascutney, or cross-country ski right outside the front door. A horse paddock is attached to the inn's renovated barn, with miles of trails nearby, and bicycles and croquet are yours for the asking. The pond provides refreshing swimming in the summer and ice-skating in the winter, and there are tennis courts right on Mt. Ascutney as well as others nearby, and an excellent choice of golf courses in adjacent towns in both Vermont and New Hampshire.

Among the many things to see and do within easy range of the inn are the world's longest covered bridge; Vermont's Constitution House; Vermont State Craft Center; theater, dance, concerts, and art galleries at Hopkins Center for the Creative and Performing Arts; historic Woodstock; Marlboro Music Festival; country fairs of all kinds; and day trips to the White and Green mountains.

INNKEEPERS:	Eric and Margaret Rothchild
SEASON:	Year round, except April and November
MEALS:	Breakfast and dinner; dinner reservations suggested
TELEPHONE:	802-484-7725
ADDRESS:	Brownsville, Vermont 05037
ACCOMMODATIONS:	8 rooms, 4 with private bath, 4 sharing 2 baths
DIRECTIONS:	I-91 to Exit 8 in Vermont, then north on Route 5 toward Windsor for about 1 mile. Take the left fork onto Back Mountain Road (the signs will point to the Ascutney State Park) and proceed about 3½ miles to the end. Then proceed left for about 2 miles to sign for Brownsville. Turn right at the sign and go ½ mile to a fork; take left fork up the hill to the inn.

CHITTENDEN
Mountain Top Inn

Mountain Top Inn

In 1940, the original inn was framed in on the beams of a hundred-year-old barn. The next year an additional wing was built, with large rooms facing the magnificent view of pristine lakes and the majestic Green Mountains.

In 1946, when Mr. and Mrs. William P. Wolfe purchased the

Mountain Top Inn, the main section of the building was reconstructed in a post-and-beam style. In 1979 all the preexisting rooms were completely refurbished to bring the inn up to luxury level.

And so, the inn has grown into a complete resort facility on a 500-acre estate near Rutland, Vermont. Antique appointments, inviting sitting rooms, and up-to-date amenities in the guest rooms combine to assure the comfort and relaxation of visitors, and a wide assortment of activities provides recreation. Tennis, badminton, shuffleboard, chip 'n' putt golf; a heated pool; sandy-beached lakefront with Sunfish sailboats, canoes, and rowboats; fishing equipment; and pony cart are right on the premises. Nearby are fifty-five miles of cross-country ski trails; tobogganning, sledding, and ice-skating. And for the less energetic, there are sleigh rides through the countryside.

A charmingly appointed cocktail lounge, with convivial bartenders, is a happy gathering place for guests and local residents.

Mealtimes are a gracious and enjoyable part of each day, with plentiful selections served by a friendly, courteous staff in a classic New England setting. The dinner fare changes daily and may include such gourmet delights as succulent Chicken Breast Barbados, Curry of Lamb Rajah, Scallops Delmonico, and Tournedos Royal. For the last act you might consider the English Trifle, Hot Mincemeat Pie, or a Kahlua Parfait. *Bon appétit.*

INNKEEPER:	Richard P. Clark, General Manager
SEASON:	Early June to late October; week before Christmas to end of skiing season
MEALS:	Breakfast, lunch, and dinner
TELEPHONE:	802-483-2311
ACCOMMODATIONS:	39 rooms, all with private bath
ADDRESS:	Chittenden, Vermont 05737
DIRECTIONS:	*From New York:* New York State Thruway to Exit 24, the Northway, to Exit 20 connecting to Route 4 into Rutland. In Rutland go north on Route 7, 3 miles to the Chittenden Road and follow signs to the inn.
	From Boston: I-93 to I-89 to White River Junction. Route 4 West toward Woodstock and Rutland. In Mendon, about 4 miles beyond Pico Ski Area, look for signs for turning right to the inn.

GRAFTON
Woodchuck Hill Farm

Two miles from the tiny town of Grafton (population under 500), high on a hill, is perched an old farm, circa 1780.

The charming old house was built for the first minister in Grafton. It was a working farm for many, many years, and at one time a blacksmith had his shop out back, and a cobbler plied his trade on the third floor.

The inn has been completely restored and redecorated within the past twenty years by the current innkeepers, who also operate an antique shop, Gabriel's Barn, on the grounds. The main house is decorated throughout with American antiques, as well as objects collected in Europe and the Far East while Mr. Gabriel was on tours of duty with the U.S. Army.

The cheerful dining room is appointed with fine china and silver in traditional formal style, but a relaxed atmosphere prevails. Before dinner, guests gather on the large porch, with its magnificent seventy-five-mile view, to enjoy Grafton cheese with crackers and refreshments (BYOB). In the fall everyone congregates in the lounge in front of a roaring fire.

There is no programmed menu, and a typical hearty dinner may be Vintage Soup, a salad of fresh greens, English grill, noisette potatoes, vegetables in season, herbed bread, and mocha flan. In the spring, grilled fresh trout from the pond is almost always offered.

For a change of pace, Grafton is within easy driving distance of many fine inns, well known for their cuisine and open to the public by reservation.

The beauty and tranquillity of the area encourage relaxation, bird-watching, rocking on the porch, and daydreaming. Leisurely walks in lanes and meadows and sunbathing are also popular occupations. For the more energetic, there is swimming in the pond and tennis in Grafton.

Miles of scenic drives show off New England at its spectacular best: all the natural splendor of the area as well as the villages with their church steeples, classic architecture, and marvelous country stores that dot the countryside.

Grafton itself, a village restored by the Windham Foundation, is considered one of the loveliest in Vermont. Country auctions are a popular event almost every weekend during summer and fall. The local cheese factory conducts public tours by appointment.

INNKEEPERS:	Anne and Frank Gabriel
SEASON:	May through mid November
MEALS:	Breakfast, afternoon tea, and dinner
TELEPHONE:	802-843-2398
ACCOMMODATIONS:	7 units, all shared baths
ADDRESS:	Middletown Road Grafton, Vermont 05146
DIRECTIONS:	I-91 North to Exit 5. West on Route 121 for 12 miles.

JAY
Le Jay Village Inn

Le Jay Village Inn and Restaurant was originally built as a three-story farmhouse around 1900. When neighboring Jay Peak grew from a local two-rope-tow ski area to a major resort community in the early '60s, the building was renovated, a main wing and swimming pool added, and the inn operation begun.

The inn is nestled at the base of magnificent Jay Peak at the edge of the forest, five minutes from the ski area, in the heart of little Jay Village.

Its rustic beamed ceilings and barnboard interior enhance the cozy ambience of the inn, which is famous throughout the "Northeast Kingdom" for its homey and friendly family atmosphere.

Lodgings include a variety of comfortable and attractive accommodations — suites and private rooms — handsomely appointed and individually heated.

Although its development as a fine restaurant was initiated by previous owners, the former Jay Barn Inn has progressed to a more elegant

French-influenced cuisine since the innkeeping was taken over by Pat and Bill Schug and family in 1978. With its paintings, antiques, and objets d'art, the dining room is quite appropriately named Galerie d'Art.

Pat's parents (Mama and Papa) and her brother and his wife have more recently come from Paris to join the inn, bringing to it their Continental charm. The entire family is involved in the successful operation of the inn, right down to the design of the menus. But it is the talents of chef Charlotte and her cooking partner, Papa, that make Le Jay Village Inn a really special treat. Papa's day starts early in the morning when he enters the kitchen to make his famous Parisian bread, and continues into the evening until the last guest leaves the dining room.

Charlotte Vincent is la Cook. Born a Connecticut Yankee, she moved to Vermont as a young woman in 1971. Her interest in cooking began at home at the age of nine, under the tutelage of her mother and great-grandmother. A skiing enthusiast, she began cooking commercially at a local ski dorm where she was living. She was first hired as a sous chef at Jay Village Inn in 1976 and, under the new ownership, rapidly rose to head chef. Since her takeover of the kitchen, guests' compliments have soared as Charlotte's creativeness flowers with each meal.

INNKEEPERS:	Patricia and Bill Schug
SEASON:	All year except mid April to late May, and open weekends only during peripheral season
MEALS:	Breakfast and dinner
TELEPHONE:	802-988-2643
ACCOMMODATIONS:	6 private rooms and 4 two-room suites, each with private bath
ADDRESS:	Route 242 Jay, Vermont 05859
DIRECTIONS:	*From New York:* I-91 to Exit 26 (Orleans), then Route 5 North to Coventry and Route 14 North (toward Jay), to Route 100 South to Troy. Then Route 101 North to Route 242, and Route 242 West 1 mile to Jay. *From Boston:* I-93 to I-91 at St. Johnsbury. Proceed as above.

KILLINGTON
The Vermont Inn

Running an inn is not always glamorous or even fun — frequently working until after midnight, then rising in time to get breakfast, tending to groaning plumbing and other daily repairs, keeping up the grounds, tending bar, and more. There are compensations as well — the joy of operating a successful and popular inn and restaurant, the pleasure of meeting new guests and welcoming returning travelers as friends.

Alan and Judy Carmasin, who have operated the Vermont Inn since 1977, have worked hard and enjoyed themselves, and their success is reflected in the charming and relaxed atmosphere that surrounds visitors to the inn. The inn was built in the nineteenth century as a farmhouse and became a stopping place for travelers early in its history. In more recent times a rope tow was installed on the hill in back of the inn by the parents of Olympic champion Andrea Mead before they opened Pico Peak Ski Area.

Today the Vermont Inn tastefully blends the old and the new. The public rooms, with their original beams, hardwood floors, a working wood-burning stove, and original fireplaces retain all the charm of times past. The lounge almost resembles a formal garden, with hanging and standing plants dominating the scene. Unusual wall hangings complete the setting, carrying out the combination of contemporary comfort and interesting antique furnishings. Each bedroom is individually decorated, with many personal touches.

The inn's restaurant offers an appetizing array of the conventional and the unconventional. On a typical evening one may find herb quiche and escargot en champignons, Entrecôte Bercy, Steak Diane, Fresh Boston Scrod Morray, Coulade of Sole Newburg, and Veal à la Crème, among other specialties. Sweets may include frozen cranberry pie, mousse au chocolat, and Amaretto cream puffs. A special children's menu is available.

Located near Rutland, the inn is surrounded by the highest peaks of the Green Mountains, displaying magnificent panoramic views. The Killington and Pico areas offer a wide variety of things to see and do throughout the year. Summer theater, the Rutland Farmers' Market, antiquing, touring, pool and stream swimming, golf, tennis, and riding are all near at hand.

Fall brings an explosion of color as the leaves turn, and winter presents a full range of snow and ice sports.

INNKEEPERS:	Judy and Alan Carmasin
SEASON:	Year round, except from the end of April to the first week in June
MEALS:	Breakfast and dinner
TELEPHONE:	802-773-9847
ACCOMMODATIONS:	14 rooms, 8 with private bath
ADDRESS:	Route 4 Killington, Vermont 05751
DIRECTIONS:	*From New York:* New York State Thruway to Exit 24, the Northway, for 50 miles to Exit 20, Fort Ann, Route 149. Route 149 for 12 miles to Route 4 North, then east to Rutland. East on Route 4 for 6 miles after the intersection of Routes 4 and 7 in Rutland. The inn is on the left side heading east.
	From Boston: I-91 to Route 4 West. The inn is 2 miles past the Pico Ski Area.

LOWER WATERFORD
The Rabbit Hill Inn

The inn has been part of the scene in Lower Waterford since 1795, when the small building now known as the Briar Patch was constructed by Samuel Hodby as a tavern and general store. The main house was built around 1827 by Jonathan Cummings as a one-room-deep, three-story home; he used the present living room as a shop, where he made sleighs, winnowing machines, wagons, and wheels.

The main structure first became an inn in 1834, and six years later its owners enlarged it to its present size so that it might service the very active trade route to Portland, Maine — with as many as one hundred teams a day plying the road by the inn on the fourteen-to-sixteen-day round trip.

During this time the two front piazzas with the alcove in the peak were constructed, supported by four solid Doric pillars made from pine trees dragged by oxen across the ice of the Connecticut River and worked into shape by hand.

Several owners and changes of name later, during the mid 1850s, a third building, housing the ballroom, was constructed, with woodsheds and carriage house below. Elegant chandeliers hung from an arched ceiling, and the hall was guarded by a huge eagle, painted by an impoverished guest in payment of his hotel bill. This eagle now graces the peak of the main building; one of the ceiling arches remains behind the columns in the inside dining room; and a chandelier hangs in the second floor hall.

The main building was used as a summer home by the widow of J. W. Davies, who owned the inn and all the houses on the street in front of it during the '20s and '30s; it was Mrs. Davies who named the place Rabbit Hill after the knob behind the property.

In the late '50s, the ballroom was reconstructed as motel units and the property became a summer hotel known as Rabbit Hill Motor Inn. Ten years later John and Ruth Carroll opened the inn as a year-round lodging and dining establishment under the name of Rabbit Hill Inn, running it until it was sold to the present innkeepers, Eric and Beryl Charlton.

The guest rooms range from the old-fashioned to the more contemporary. Charming antique furnishings grace the older guest rooms as well as the public rooms. Everywhere the atmosphere is one of relaxation and warm hospitality.

Chef Russell Carlson, a New Englander trained by the well-known Parisian chef, teacher, and writer Madeleine Kamman, has helped gain the inn the reputation for being one of the best eating places between Boston and Montreal. Among his many specialties are Sautéed Chicken Cointreau and lamb curry, prepared to perfection. The inn's bakery produces delicious oatmeal bread, Scotch shortbread, and blueberry muffins, as well as original and mouth-watering desserts.

A cross-country ski center is now part of the inn, complete with a ski instructor and equipment rentals. Thanks to the generosity of the inn's neighbors, there are extensive trails in the surrounding countryside for all levels of ability. These trails also offer a variety of nature walks at other times of the year.

INNKEEPERS:	Eric and Beryl Charlton
SEASON:	Year round except April, November, and early December
MEALS:	Breakfast and dinner
TELEPHONE:	802-748-5168
ACCOMMODATIONS:	20 rooms, each with private bath
ADDRESS:	State Route 18 Lower Waterford, Vermont 05848
DIRECTIONS:	*From New York:* I-91 to Exit 20, St. Johnsbury, then Route 18 South to the inn. *From Boston:* I-93 to Littleton, New Hampshire, then Route 18 North to the inn.

LUDLOW
The Combes Family Inn

**Combes
Family Inn**

As the name indicates, this is truly a family inn — situated on a quiet country back road in the heart of Vermont's mountain and lake region and surrounded by fifty acres of rolling meadows and woods. Sharing the grounds with the innkeepers and guests are several cats and dogs as well as Cupcake and Brownie, reported to be the friendliest goats around.

The inn itself is a century-old farmhouse. The dining room has exposed beams and a large bay window overlooking pastures and Okemo Mountain. The lounge is paneled in Vermont barnboards and is furnished with turn-of-the-century oak; cocktails (BYOB), cards, and conversation are the specialties around the fire.

Thanks to the tireless efforts of the Combes family, the venerable inn structure has kept pace with the times — with the addition of all new siding and a new porch, a recreation center for juniors, a swimming pool for all ages, and a colorful garden.

Meals at the inn are hearty Vermont-style feasts, consisting of fresh vegetables; cream soups; turkey, lamb, or pork roasts; and heaps of home-baked breads and desserts. During the summer, visitors are even invited to help in picking the vegetables from the inn's garden. The coffee pot is always on and guests are welcome, too, to help themselves to homemade cakes and cookies.

There is swimming on Lake Rescue and Echo Lake, tennis, bicycling on country roads, hiking, and picnicking. (The innkeepers, Ruth and Bill Combes, will be happy to see that you have a box lunch for day trips.) Golf and tennis facilities are nearby, and there is live theater in season every evening at both the Weston and Killington Playhouses. The area's many small towns abound with interesting shops for buying or just browsing; other nearby attractions include the Coolidge birthplace and museum, Steamtown U.S.A. in Bellows Falls, the Alpine Slide at Bromley (especially great for younger members of the family), and cheese and maple syrup factories. And, of course, there's always an old-time Vermont auction to test your bidding skills.

The inn is only minutes away from Okemo and Round Top ski areas, and within a half hour of Killington, Pico, Bromley, Magic, and Stratton mountains. If you're a ski-touring enthusiast, there are several centers in nearby towns, including Viking and Mountain Meadows.

INNKEEPERS:	Ruth and Bill Combes
SEASON:	Year round except April 15 through May 15
MEALS:	Breakfast and dinner; box lunch by request
TELEPHONE:	802-228-8799
ACCOMMODATIONS:	4 rooms, all share bath; attached motel units, 5 rooms, all with private baths
ADDRESS:	R.F.D. 1 Ludlow, Vermont 05149
DIRECTIONS:	I-91 to Exit 6 in Vermont, to Route 103 through Ludlow and Route 100 North past Ludlow. Follow state signs at this point.

MANCHESTER
The Inn at Manchester

The Inn at Manchester was built in 1904, probably as a summer residence; it was operated as an inn during the '40s and '50s and then reverted to use as a home. In 1978 Stan and Harriet Rosenberg moved into the old house, which had been vacant for four years. Stan had been a stockbroker and his wife a schoolteacher; they both yearned for a different kind of life and they found it running the Inn at Manchester.

Their first step was to renovate the house from top to bottom — scouring, painting, papering, and shining every inch. The inn is now furnished with antiques, interspersed with the Rosenbergs' extensive art collection. Each guest room is individually decorated with distinctive personal touches. There are three public rooms for relaxing, all with fireplace or wood-burning stove.

Meals are served family style in the cranberry-papered dining room; everything from soup to dessert is prepared from the finest fresh ingredients. The menu changes daily. Since there is no printed menu, guests, lured by the enticing aromas, come to the kitchen to inquire about dinner and to observe the preparation of the meal — perhaps English tomato soup, honey-curried chicken, potato pie, vegetables of the season, newly baked farm bread, and apricot meringue cake.

The inn's location on Route 7 in the village of Manchester makes all of the area's seasonal attractions readily available. Winter guests are only ten minutes from Bromley and twenty-five minutes from Stratton Mountain. Cross-country skiing is even closer, with the trails of the new Hildene Touring Center only five minutes away. Summertime guests have but a short trip to several of southern Vermont's summer playhouses and the classical concerts of the Southern Vermont Arts Center. Antique shops, boutiques, and specialty craft shops are close by. If golf or tennis is your warm-weather sport, the greens and courts are within walking distance of the front door. The pool is set in a secluded, sunny meadow between the inn's barn and the creek.

The leaves of autumn, of course, are always the dazzlers of the year, and with the shoulder of Equinox Mountain out the back door, you'll never be disappointed by the view. If you wish, you can climb that shoulder using the Burr and Burton Trail, which is also an easy walk from the front door.

INNKEEPERS:	Stan and Harriet Rosenberg
SEASON:	All year except April and November
MEALS:	Breakfast and dinner
TELEPHONE:	802-362-1793
ACCOMMODATIONS:	11 rooms, 3 with private bath; 8 rooms share bath
ADDRESS:	Route 7 Manchester, Vermont 05254 For mail: Box 452 Manchester, Vermont 05254
DIRECTIONS:	*From New York:* Taconic State Parkway to Route 295 East to Route 22. North to Route 313 (Cambridge), east to Arlington, then north on Route 7 to Manchester and the inn.
	From Boston: I-91 North to Brattleboro, Route 30 to Manchester, then south on Route 7 to the inn (about 1 mile from intersection).

MIDDLEBURY
The Middlebury Inn
ॐ The Middlebury Inn ॐ

The roots of the Middlebury Inn reach far back onto the history of the town. Its site was a natural one for a tavern, since it lay near the intersection of east-west and north-south roads that once were scarcely more than trails.

The original tavern house, built in 1794, continued under a series of owners until it was destroyed by fire in 1816. It was replaced by a brick "public house," which opened as the Vermont House in 1827 and twenty-five years later became the Addison House. Various improvements were made over the years, and in 1925 the Addison House was sold to the Middlebury Hotel Company, which sandblasted the old yellow paint from the exterior; installed a new heating plant, new plumbing, and modern conveniences; and made extensive repairs. In 1927 the tavern reopened as the Middlebury Inn and has continued as such to the present time.

Standing majestically on Court Square in the center of town, the inn gracefully blends past and present. The main house reflects the quiet ambience of a gentler era, yet does not conflict with the new and completely modern motel which now shares the grounds.

The large and airy dining room offers a wide range of traditional New England fare, presented with friendly and unobtrusive service. Chef Tom Phelps presides over the kitchen and supervises the preparation of such dishes as baked Boston scrod served with crabmeat stuffing, sautéed breast of chicken Marsala, and London broil with Béarnaise sauce. Homemade popovers and vegetables from an unusual casserole table are served daily. On the lighter side is a delicious chilled strawberry or blueberry soup.

Frank and Jane Emanuel have been innkeepers since the fall of 1977, Frank having gained experience in inn and hotel management at the Woodstock Inn, Delray Beach Hotel, and The Tyler Place in Highgate Springs, Vermont.

The historic Middlebury area provides a full range of recreational activities for all seasons, as well as interesting buildings, museums, and fine shops. Nearby Middlebury College, rich in tradition, houses the college bowl with chair lift, three jumps, cross-country trails, and a ski school. In season the campus is a center of athletic activity, with hockey, basketball, and do-it-yourself sports dominating the winter.

The campus and town also offer a variety of cultural events. Typical recent attractions include an exhibition of "Things Made by Hand for Christmas," performances by composer John Cage and choreographer Merce Cunningham in "Dialogue"; "Messiah" presented by the Middlebury College Choir and Community Chorus and the Vermont Symphony Orchestra; and performances by the Meredith Monk Dance Company.

Vermont State Craft Center at Frog Hollow is a restored mill as well as a museum and stage for crafts from some two hundred local craftsmen. The Morgan Horse Farm, open to the public, is just outside of town.

Guides and/or maps are available for the historic village walking tour, hikes on Long Trail in the Green Mountains, and the Morgan Horse Farm.

INNKEEPERS:	Frank and Jane Emanuel
SEASON:	Open all year
MEALS:	Breakfast, lunch, and dinner
TELEPHONE:	802-388-4961
ACCOMMODATIONS:	20 motel units (private bath) 5 guest rooms in Porter Annex (private bath) 9 two-room suites (shared bath) 23 guest rooms in Main House (private bath) 14 guest rooms in Main House (shared bath)
ADDRESS:	14 Courthouse Square Middlebury, Vermont 05751
DIRECTIONS:	*From New York:* New York State Thruway to the Northway. Exit 20 to Route 149 through Fort Ann and Whitehall, New York, crossing over to Vermont just above Fair Haven. North on Route 22A to Route 74 until it meets Route 30 leading into Middlebury. *From Boston:* I-93 to I-89 through White River Junction to Exit 3 near Royalton. Then Route 107 to Route 100 North to Route 125. Take Route 125 West (approximately 20 miles) until it meets Route 7 into Middlebury.

STOWE
Edson Hill Manor

Edson Hill
MANOR

The original owner of the Edson Hill Manor estate of 500 acres envisioned constructing a Georgian Colonial mansion designed by the famous architect Bottomley. To complete the work, architects Samuel Van Allen of Newport and Wigham of Philadelphia traveled through Canada to study many French Provincial cottage-style roofs. The result of their labors was the Manor Building, finished in 1940 and used as a gentleman's estate for about ten years. It was enlarged to its present size in 1954.

The bricks of the building were mostly salvaged from the remains of the old Sherwood Hotel in Burlington, which burned in the '30s. The old fireplace tile came from Holland. Some of the hardware was made by Stowe's smithy, Edmund Wells, and the brass is from Williamsburg, Virginia, as were the original roof shingles.

The manor living room has beams hewn for Ira and Ethan Allen's barn, which stood in North Burlington for over a century. Enhancing the charm of this large room, you'll find a beautiful oriental rug, a spacious fireplace flanked by comfortable divans, and pine-paneled walls hung with paintings. There are floor-to-ceiling windows with elegant draperies, and bookshelves filled with volumes rich in New England history.

A sense of casual luxury, with all the privacy and quiet pace of times gone by, extends throughout the property.

Located in the heart of ski country, Edson Hill offers a wide range of sports activities. In addition to unparalleled skiing conditions, which begin right outside the door, there are an award-winning swimming pool, fishing in stocked ponds, a putting green, and riding stables offering English and Western instruction on the premises; tennis courts nearby, and golf at the picturesque Stowe Country Club.

The manor dining room offers a varied menu featuring New England and Continental specialties and fresh seafood. A typical dinner menu might include such inventive dishes as Crevette Dauphine, with sweet and sour sauce or hot mustard; Coquilles St. Jacques Parisienne (bay scallops); Eggplant Sydney; rissole potatoes; and a Praline Delight. The wine cellar is well stocked with labels from some of the finest vineyards of California and Europe.

INNKEEPERS:	Laurence Heath; Elizabeth Turner, General Manager
SEASON:	Open year round
MEALS:	Modified American Plan. Cost of breakfast and dinner included in price of lodging. When ski-touring center is open, a fireside lunch is available in the lounge at modest prices.
TELEPHONE:	802-253-7371
ACCOMMODATIONS:	Variety of accommodation in four structures houses from 25 to 35 guests; some private baths
ADDRESS:	Stowe, Vermont 05672
DIRECTIONS:	*From New York*: I-91 to I-89 to Waterbury, then Route 100 North to Stowe, north on Route 108 for 4.9 miles. Turn right on Edson Hill Road and follow signs.
	From Boston: I-93 to I-89. Proceed as above.

WESTON
The Inn at Weston

Since Stu and Sue Douglas left the frantic pace of New York City to become innkeepers in Vermont, some good things have happened.

In less than ten years, the Inn at Weston has gained an impressive national reputation. Recent feature articles in *Gourmet* magazine, the *Los Angeles Times*, and other periodicals have praised its high culinary standards and comfortable accommodations, and the special spirit of warm hospitality embodied in the inn's theme "Where Friendships Begin."

The tiny hill town of Weston nestles by the slopes of Mount Terrible and Maskham Mountain — a classic nineteenth-century New England village offering tranquillity, natural beauty, and activity aplenty for those who seek it.

The inn itself is a rambling clapboard farmhouse built in 1848 and first converted into a guest house in 1951. Charming traces of the past remain, as in the lovely pub with fieldstone fireplace — formerly the hayloft — and the original, unspoiled barnboards paneling the dining room. The kitchen is a passageway between the dining room and sitting room, where guests stop to chat, watch the preparation of meals, or even join in the chores. Upstairs the guest rooms are charmingly furnished with antiques, and everywhere the results of the Douglases' continuing work of renovation and improvement are evident.

The dining room, with its comfortable captain's chairs, homespun tablecloths, dried flower arrangements, and hand-thrown pottery tableware, provides the perfect setting for the creative meals the inn presents. The menu changes daily, offering — in addition to delicious appetizers, homemade soups and chowders, garden-fresh vegetables, and home-baked whole-grain breads — a choice of four entrées. A typical menu may include country roast tenderloin of pork, Lamb en Croûte, Turkey Scallopine, and Veal Loaf with watercress hollandaise. One of the most popular dishes is chicken Kiev, kept on the menu because returning guests ask for it so often. Dessert brings such tempting creations as spiced apple mousse and blueberry torte with nuts.

The inn also serves a hearty country breakfast with contributions from both Sue and Stu, and a special Sunday brunch in the summer and fall. A lovely dining porch is used in warm weather.

Winter brings a flock of sports enthusiasts to the inn, since Weston is in the heart of ski country, both downhill and cross-country. A cross-country trail starts right across the street, in fact, and leads to Viking Ski Touring Center, and Bromley, Magic, and Stratton are all nearby. Sledding and snowshoeing are also popular winter activities.

The village of Weston itself offers many attractions to visitors, starting with one of the prettiest town greens in all of New England, complete with bandstand and lovely old buildings, including the famous Weston Playhouse, the oldest professional summer theater in Vermont. Flowing through Weston is the West River, which once powered the gristmill in the heart of town. The Grist Mill is now a working museum housing antique tools and implements, where craftsmen work and sell their wares. The adjacent Vermont Craftsman Building features rug braiding and woodworking, and the Farrar-Mansur House, built in 1797 as a tavern, is now a historical museum showing Vermont life of the period. There are also many country stores and craft and antique shops to tempt browsers — all within a short stroll of the inn.

In season, fishing, swimming, picnicking, and camping are available in nearby Green Mountain Forest areas.

INNKEEPERS:	Stuart and Susan Douglas
SEASON:	Year round, except November and mid April to mid May
MEALS:	Breakfast and dinner
TELEPHONE:	802-824-5804
ACCOMMODATIONS:	13 rooms, 10 with bath
ADDRESS:	P.O. Box 56 Weston, Vermont 05161
DIRECTIONS:	I-91 to Exit 6 (just above Bellows Falls). Then Route 103 to Chester to Route 11 to Londonderry. Turn right on Route 100 to Weston. The inn is in the village.

Index to Recipes

Corn (*cont.*)
  Bread, 179–80
  Bread-Apple-Pecan Stuffing, 148–49
  Bread, Bundt Pan, 179
  Bread for Stuffing, 149
  Chowder, Grane's, 34
  Pone (Yankee Corn Sticks), 185–86
Crab (Crabmeat):
  and Cheddar Soup, 31
  Chicken Breast, Stuffed with, 135
  Dijon, 63
  au Gratin, 64
  Pasta with Saffron Aubergine, 195–96
  Sauce, 71
  Spread, 6
Crackers, Spread for, 8–9
Cranberry:
  Chiffon Pie, 202
  -Raisin Pie with Walnut Crust, 202–3
  Soup, Cold, 22
Cream Cheese Dip, Herbed, 10–11
Crème Anglais, 242
Crêpe(s):
  Batter, 65–66
  Chicken Élégante, 125
  St. Jacques, 65–66
Cucumber Salad with Yogurt, Dilled, 46–47
Cucumber Soup, Cold, 23
Curry Sauce, 82–83

Délices de Gruyère, 7
Desserts, 230–42:
  Apples, Baked, 230
  Blueberries with Dumplings, 230–31
  Carrot Pudding, Gran's Upper Clyde, 234
  Chocolate Ascutney, 231–32
  Chocolate Mousse, Six-minute, 239
  Chocolate Rum Sauce, 232
  Latte Alla Grotta, 240
  Maple Mousse, 236
  Mocha Flan, 237
  Pears à la Vigneronne, 238
  Pears Charlie Chaplin, Iced, 235–36
  Rhubarb Cream, 238–39
  Snow Dumplings with Pistachio Sauce, 240
  Strawberries in Sherry Cream, 241
  Suet Pudding, Grammy Ring's, 233
  Trifle, Tipsy, 241–42
Dip, Herbed Cream Cheese, 10–11
Down East Anadama Bread, 187
Drunken Bird, 136
Duck(ling):
  Breast of, Supreme, 143
  à l'Orange, 144–46
  Pâté, 8

Easy Spread for Crackers, 8–9
Eaton Wild Blueberry Cheesecake, 217–18
Egg and Sausage Casserole with Herbs, 154–55

Eggs and Cheese, 152–61
Eggs Florentine, 155–56
Escargots à la Bourguignonne, 9

Fillet of Beef Wellington, 98–99
Fish:
  Best, Chowder Down East, 27–28
  Jane's Baked, with Crabmeat Sauce, 70–71
  Soup, Vermont-style, 42
  Stock, 62
  See also Seafood; specific fish
Flan, Mocha, 237
Florentine de Mer, 67–68
Fondue, Cheese (Switzer Käse), 160–61

Garbanzos (Ceci Romano), 29
Gazpacho, 24
Genoise, Fresh Peach Aubergine, 218–19
Goulash (Gulyás), Hungarian, 99–100
Gourmet Fried Cheese, 10
Grains, Pasta, and Legumes, 193–97:
  Baked Beans, 193
  Granola, Breezemere, 194
  Pasta with Saffron and Crab Aubergine, 195
  Polenta, 196
  Pudding, Norwegian Noodle, 194
  Rice (Swiss Risotto), 197
Grane's Dressing for Greens, 55
Granola, Breezemere, 194
Gravy, Pan, 112
Gravy for Pot Roast, 105–6
Green Bean Casserole, 164
Green Pea Soup, Puree of, 39
Green Onion Salad Dressing, 55–56
Gruyère, Délices de, 7

Haddock Pudding, Old Boston, 75–76
Halibut Parmesan, Baked, 59
Ham and Cheese Soufflé, Mock, 158
Hard Sauce, 233
Hasenpfeffer (Stewed Rabbit), 118–19
Herbed Cream Cheese Dip, 10–11
Hollandaise Sauce, 79–80
Hollandaise Sauce, Quick Blender, 93–94
Hot Fudge Pudding Cake, 221
Hungarian Goulash (Gulyás), 99–100

Icing, Chocolate, 228–29
Icing, Fluffy White, 216
Insalata di Fontina, 48
Irish Soda Bread, 180

Käseschnitten nach Switzer Stubli (grilled cheese sandwich), 156
Kuchen, German Plum (Zwetschkenkuchen), 220

Lamb, 113–17:
  Curry, 115–16

Index to Inns